Republicans and the Black Vote

Republicans and the Black Vote

Michael K. Fauntroy

LYNNE
RIENNER
PUBLISHERS

BOULDER
LONDON

Published in the United States of America in 2007 by
Lynne Rienner Publishers, Inc.
1800 30th Street, Boulder, Colorado 80301
www.rienner.com

and in the United Kingdom by
Lynne Rienner Publishers, Inc.
3 Henrietta Street, Covent Garden, London WC2E 8LU

Library of Congress Cataloging-in-Publication Data
Fauntroy, Michael K.
  Republicans and the Black vote / Michael K. Fauntroy.
      p. cm.
  Includes bibliographical references and index.
  ISBN-13: 978-1-58826-470-1 (hardcover : alk. paper)
  ISBN-10: 1-58826-470-X (hardcover : alk. paper)
1. Republican Party (U.S. : 1854–) 2. African Americans—Politics and government.
I. Title.
JK2356.F38 2006
324.2734'08996073—dc22

                                                         2006026504

British Cataloguing in Publication Data
A Cataloguing in Publication record for this book
is available from the British Library.

Printed and bound in the United States of America

      The paper used in this publication meets the requirements
 ∞   of the American National Standard for Permanence of
      Paper for Printed Library Materials Z39.48-1992.

  5   4   3   2

For love, for life, for Lisa

Contents

Preface   ix

1 Afros and Elephants: An Introduction to a Political Paradox   1

2 The GOP's Early Lock on Black Votes   13

3 The Republicans Fall Out of Favor   39

4 Efforts to Regain and Retain African American Support   61

5 Public Policies Speak Louder Than Words   95

6 GOP Political Symbolism Angers African Americans   127

7 An Ongoing Quest for Black Votes?   163

Selected Bibliography   169
Index   173
About the Book   181

Preface

THIS BOOK WAS CONCEIVED IN EVER GROWING SKEPTICISM THAT
began as I watched the television coverage of the November 1996 elections.
During much of the coverage I saw, I noticed that whenever Republican
elected officials, activists, and conservative commentators talked about the
newly elected members of the House of Representatives, they noted the
inroads the party was making in the South. "This is the first Republican
elected in this district since Reconstruction!" they kept saying. The mention
of Reconstruction struck me as more than just election night chitchat. To
those who are at least vaguely familiar with the history of US politics,
Reconstruction is a critical milepost, particularly as it relates to black people. Also notable is that it was during this period that the link between
African Americans and the Republican Party was strongest.

I saw these comments as attaching a misleading historical significance
to the wins, inasmuch as the Republican Party of 1996 (and since) and the
Republican Party during Reconstruction had little in common on racial politics, other than the name "Republican." The Republicans elected during the
last generation or so have been more likely to be ideologically conservative
and to oppose policy changes that would result in an enhanced position for
African Americans, a perceived diminution of status for whites, or both.
This is a far cry from the Republican Party of the Reconstruction era, which
was formed on racially liberal positions.

Indeed, political labels reversed themselves over time. By 1996, the
conservative southern Democrats of the Reconstruction era had been
replaced by conservative Republicans. But why would the conservatives
who now control the Republican Party use the Reconstruction era as a point
of pride? To ingratiate themselves to white racial moderates and make
inroads into the African American community? Perhaps.

My election night skepticism made me wonder why the GOP is in such
trouble with African American voters. This book is my attempt to assess the

Republican Party and its relationship with African Americans. I am particularly interested in how the GOP's public policy positions have developed, as
well as how their use of political symbolism has resulted in dismal levels of
black support for the party. On some level, this book is less about party than
ideology. Party is the vehicle for analysis, though, because the dominant parties have become so polarized in contemporary US politics. Republicans
have become synonymous with conservatism, while Democrats are universally seen as liberal. The intraparty ideological diversity that existed until the
1960s is largely gone, almost as much a relic of the past as movies filmed in
black and white, the Model T Ford, and the Lindy Hop. Where conservative
Democrats and liberal Republicans once dominated their respective parties,
they are now relegated to secondary status within their parties and their
views are often subjugated "for the good of the party." While party and ideology are not synonymous, they are increasingly similar, given the fact that
both parties have moved away from the ideological center and closer to their
respective poles. Hence, the use of party to analyze what is largely an ideological phenomenon.

*   *   *

The book you hold in your hands has been made possible by a number of
people who have helped me better understand the interaction of ideology,
race, and party politics. While they are responsible for supporting me in a
variety of ways both small and large, responsibility for the research and
writing of this book falls to me alone.

My family's pride in me has been a source of energy that has sustained
my work even on days when I would rather have done something else.
Writing is a long, arduous, and sometimes doubt-ridden process, but it is
much easier to deal with when family and friends continually offer encour-
agement. I'm lucky to have that support.

The School of Public Policy at George Mason University promotes an
environment that is more than conducive to scholarly production. Dean
Kingsley Haynes generously supported my research by providing the
resources that enabled me to conduct the interviews necessary to get a han-
dle on the issues I sought to address and to present some of my findings at
conferences. James Finkelstein, David Hart, Jeremy Mayer, John Peterson,
James Pfiffner, Ken Reinert, Mark Rozell, Catherine Rudder, Roger Stough,
and Susan Tolchin are among my many colleagues who have helped me to
think about the issues in this book. In addition, Brett Palat and Stephen
Wray provided valuable research assistance.

I am particularly grateful to the numerous people who allowed me to
interview them for this project. I want to single out former representative
from Oklahoma J. C. Watts; Maryland lieutenant governor Michael Steele;

Niger Innis of the Congress of Racial Equality; Faye Anderson; Alvin Williams of Black America's Political Action Committee; and Bill Calhoun of the Black Republican Council of Texas for their candor, sober analysis, and forthrightness. They and all the other interviewees provided me with important insights on the relationship between African Americans and the Republican Party that I would not have understood otherwise.

Linda Cashdan's editorial assistance was great. Joia Jefferson Nuri and Tracey Walker provided important conceptual assistance. Leanne Anderson at Lynne Rienner Publishers graciously helped me through the publishing process. I underestimated how long it would take to prepare the manuscript, and Leanne's patience was more than a little reassuring to me.

Thank you all very, very much.

1

Afros and Elephants: An Introduction to a Political Paradox

THE EXTENT OF THE HISTORICAL LINKAGE BETWEEN AFRICAN Americans and the Republican Party, while lost on many contemporary observers of US politics, is clear and unambiguous. The party once had deep roots and great popularity in the African American community; today, it is difficult to imagine the party being less popular among African Americans. However, the nation's changing demography and more closely contested national elections are among the factors that are forcing the Grand Old Party (GOP) to reach out for support from previously untapped voter reservoirs. Failing such outreach, the party risks losing its current position in US politics. The GOP's most untapped—and challenging—voter reservoir is the African American community. The challenge is particularly obvious when one considers that President Bush did better with gay voters in 2004 than African American voters, 25 percent to 11 percent, respectively.

The GOP's lack of black support should be an embarrassment to a party that, during Reconstruction, enjoyed more African American support than Democrats do now. Republicans contend that they have poured considerable resources over the years into being a more appealing party to African American voters. Their lack of success in this regard, however, stems from the fact that they have been uncomfortable talking about racial issues, leaving many to conclude that they simply "don't get it" on race.[1] J. C. Watts, an African American former member of the US House of Representatives, stated, "I think that disconnect comes with the race issue because we missed it, or the party has missed it, on the race issue."[2]

The relationship between African Americans and the Republican Party garners attention every national election cycle and raises a number of concerns. Many analysts wonder why the GOP has been unable to gain a significant foothold in the black community. Still others want to know how the GOP found itself in its current predicament with a formerly supportive constituency. Some even implicitly criticize black voters for not being more

1

open to supporting the GOP. Still others, given current political trends, suggest that the GOP should simply throw up its collective hands and spend no additional time or resources seeking black votes and focus more attention, instead, on Hispanic voters. And then there are the cynics who wonder, GOP pronouncements notwithstanding, if Republicans really want black votes or just want to *appear* to want black votes as a way of showing racial moderation to center and center-left voters.

Making the policy changes necessary to get large numbers of African American votes, after all, would alienate white conservatives, particularly those who fled the Democratic Party over its policy evolution. Such cynicism is heightened by the fact that GOP pronouncements wanting African American votes are not always aimed at black America. They are often offered for the consumption of white middle-class suburban voters who agree with Republican economics but don't feel comfortable voting for a party that has a reputation for apathy—or worse—toward African Americans and other minorities. The argument could be that the Republicans prefer to have issues on which to abuse Democrats as opposed to actually overturning controversial policies like affirmative action, gay marriage, abortion, and school prayer.

Throughout the twentieth century, a "bill of particulars" developed that helps explain why African Americans, without regard to geography or socioeconomic status, are so resistant to the GOP. The lengthy list of factors that have contributed to this heightened resistance can be better understood through the exploration of four areas: (1) the GOP's efforts to increase African American support; (2) Republican Party public policy that has repelled black voters; (3) Republican political strategy relative to issues of acute interest to African Americans; and (4) the potential implications for national electoral politics if the GOP does not reverse its inability to woo African American voters.

These issues are of general interest for three reasons. First, with the House, Senate, and White House so closely contested in recent years, the Democrats and the Republicans must find new sources of votes to win close elections. While Republicans control Congress and the presidency, their partisan margins in both chambers are too close to simply rely on the same universe of voters to continue winning elections. George W. Bush lost the 2000 popular vote while winning the presidency and generated more opposition votes in 2004 than when he first won the presidency. In many cases, new sources of votes mean African Americans–Democrats need to keep their historically high vote levels; Republicans need to improve their historically low levels of black support.

Second, Republican strategists appear to be unable to understand why African Americans have not responded favorably to the GOP. Many of these strategists seem to ignore the depth of suspicion and distrust that many

African Americans feel toward the GOP. The lack of Republican success with black voters is particularly vexing to the GOP when one considers African American conservatism on a number of social issues, such as abortion and gay marriage.[3]

Finally, now may be the time for African American voters to rethink their resistance to the GOP. With the national legislature so closely contested, African Americans may be positioned to secure policy concessions from Republicans that were previously unthinkable. A move by a critical mass of African Americans to the GOP would push the Republican Party over the top in its quest to put an electoral lock on US politics. If the GOP achieves this electoral lock without substantial black support, then African American policy interests are likely to continue to suffer, particularly given the tightening of federal budget purse strings. The Congressional Budget Office forecasts budget deficits for the next decade. With military and homeland defense spending increasing, domestic spending will decrease, rendering many policies favored by African Americans underfunded, unsupportable, and unlikely to meet the needs of their intended beneficiaries.

Many contemporary observers overlook the centrality of race in US political development, as if the end of de jure segregation removed all barriers to political, economic, and social empowerment. Some even attack scholars and others for even hinting that race is still a factor in politics today, dismissively charging that one is "playing the race card." Too often, this is a ploy to obfuscate an issue and avoid having a serious discussion on race in contemporary US politics.

A Relationship Born of Pragmatic Politics

African Americans, like all Americans, can be very pragmatic in pursuing their dreams and aspirations and will support candidates they believe will use public policy to achieve those ends. African American voters have chosen to support candidates and parties that will at least refrain from impeding their efforts and have consciously gravitated to candidates and parties that help them achieve their goals. Indeed, the historical shifts in African American support for the Republicans and Democrats are directly "tied to perceptions of which party best advanced Black interests."[4] African Americans were intensely loyal to the Republican Party during the Reconstruction era because the GOP actively advocated for black interests in the face of considerable and comprehensive opposition from a conservative Democratic Party. The tables have turned, and now the Republicans are the conservative party in US politics and the party is near its nadir in terms of the black support it receives.

There have been consistent headlines over the years reporting on renewed efforts by the Grand Old Party to woo African American voters.[5] Since becoming chair of the Republican National Committee, Ken Mehlman has made very public pronouncements to that end. Despite these and previous efforts, the GOP seems far from its goal of attracting a higher percentage of the African American vote. Texas governor George W. Bush received 9 percent of the African American vote in the 2000 presidential election and 11 percent in his 2004 reelection effort. Republicans constitute fewer than fifty of the more than 9,000 African American elected officials in the United States.[6]

As Table 1.1 indicates, African American party identification with or presidential voting for Republican presidential nominees has not exceeded 15 percent since 1960.[7] In five presidential election years—1972, 1976, 1980, 1984, and 2004—more African Americans registered as Independents than as Republicans. The most notable shift in black support for and identification with the Republican Party occurred in 1964, when 6 percent of African Americans supported party nominee Barry Goldwater—a 26 percentage point decline from 1960. That campaign is a landmark in US politics. States' rights was a major theme in Goldwater's campaign and was particularly resonant in the South, where he had his most significant success. *States' rights* is a politically charged term for African Americans because it has historically connoted racism and white supremacy. The Republican embrace and espousal of states' rights sent an important symbolic signal to African Americans that has yet to be forgotten or undone.

The disconnect between African Americans and the GOP is comprehensive and extends beyond elections. For example, African American participation in GOP national conventions is poor. According to the Joint Center for Political and Economic Studies, African Americans made up 4.1 percent of delegates to the 2000 Republican national convention, compared with 20.1 percent of the delegates to the Democratic national convention.[8] African American representation on convention committees was similarly skewed. Six African Americans served on committees at the 2000 Republican convention. The Democratic convention that year had 101 African American committee members, including the cochair of the Platform Committee.[9] African American participation at the 2004 Republican convention was better than in 2000, but still poor. African Americans constituted 6.7 percent of all GOP convention delegates; black participation at the Democratic National Convention remained the same as in 2000.[10] For the first time ever, the GOP was able to present high-level black governmental officials to the public to show more inclusiveness. The GOP hopes that this represents a developing momentum toward more success in the black community.

Republicans also have to contend with the well-established belief that the GOP doesn't work for black interests. The 1980s were particularly

Table 1.1   Presidential Vote and Party Identification of African Americans, 1936–2004

		Democratic	Republican	Other/Independent
1936	Presidential vote	71	28	1
	Party identification	44	37	19
1940	Presidential vote	67	32	
	Party identification	42	42	16
1944	Presidential vote	68	40	
	Party identification	40	32	21
1948	Presidential vote	77	23	
	Party identification	56	25	19
1952	Presidential vote	76	24	
	Party identification	66	18	16
1956	Presidential vote	61	39	
	Party identification	56	24	22
1960	Presidential vote	68	32	
	Party identification	58	22	20
1964	Presidential vote	94	6	
	Party identification	82	8	10
1968	Presidential vote	85	15	
	Party identification	92	3	5
1972	Presidential vote	87	13	
	Party identification	75	5	20
1976	Presidential vote	85	15	
	Party identification	84	5	11
1980	Presidential vote	86	12	2
	Party identification	81	8	10
1984	Presidential vote	89	9	2
	Party identification	77	5	18
1988	Presidential vote	88	10	2
	Party identification	83	9	8
1992	Presidential vote	82	11	7
	Party identification	86	9	5
1996	Presidential vote	84	12	4
	Party identification	81	9	6
2000	Presidential vote	90	8	2
	Party identification	88	7	5
2004	Presidential vote	88	11	1
	Party identification	75	8	17

Sources: David Bositis, *Blacks and the 2004 Republican National Convention* (Washington, DC: Joint Center for Political and Economic Studies, 2004), p. 9, citing 1936–1956 data from Everett Carll Ladd Jr. and Charles D. Hadley, *Transformations of the American Party System: Political Coalitions from the New Deal to the 1970s* (New York: Norton, 1975); 1960–1980 partisan identification from Paul R. Abramson, John H. Aldrich, and David W. Rohde, *Change and Continuity in the 1984 Elections* (Washington, DC: CQ Press, 1986); 1960–1980 presidential preference data from Gallup Opinion Index 1980; 1984 presidential preference data from CBS/*New York Times* exit poll, November 1986; 1988 presidential preference data from ABC News/Capital Cities; 1988 party identification data from JCPES Gallup Survey; 1992 party identification data from Home Box Office/Joint Center Survey; 1992 presidential preference data from Voter Research and Surveys; 1996 vote data from Voter News Service; 1996 party identification data from 1996 JCPES National Opinion Poll; 2000 vote data from Voter News Service; 2000 party identification data from 2000 JCPES National Opinion Poll; and 2004 vote party identification data from JCPES, *The Black Vote*, 2004.

notable in this regard. During the Reagan years, and since, there was an open hostility to the civil rights establishment, race-specific legislation and policy, and social programs designed to alleviate the economic hardship many Americans, not just blacks, felt. African Americans internalized that hostility and returned it to the Republican Party with decreasing favorability ratings. The 1984 National Black Election Panel Study revealed that 75 percent of African Americans surveyed reported believing that Republicans worked either "not hard at all" or "not too hard" on black issues; the 1988 survey figure was 67 percent.[11] Conversely, the Democrats were seen as particularly interested and committed to working on black issues. In 1984, 74 percent of African Americans surveyed believed that Democrats worked "fairly hard" or "very hard" on black issues; 72 percent agreed with that sentiment in 1988.[12]

Republican concerns about attracting African American votes have practical political implications. African Americans make up between 10 percent and 36 percent of the population in twenty-one states, representing 305 of 538 Electoral College votes.[13] Also, more than 130 congressional districts, the majority of which are in the South, have African American populations in excess of 10 percent. Consequently, African Americans can play a large role in a number of closely contested presidential and congressional elections. Republicans understand this and feel they must gain more African American votes to solidify their hold on the White House and Congress. Not doing so would leave the party vulnerable in the event that some part of its electoral coalition (e.g., economic conservatives worried about expanding deficit spending and the outsourcing of US jobs) were to become less supportive of the GOP.

This poor standing notwithstanding, there is much optimism among Republicans and their black supporters. President Bush is credited with leading the party toward more inclusion of African Americans, which has provided important emotional support to those within the party who understand the need to pursue black votes and want greater emphasis placed on this goal within the party. His historic appointments of Colin Powell, as secretary of state, and Condoleezza Rice, as national security adviser and, later, secretary of state, are universally seen as potential magnets for more black support for the GOP. One prominent black Republican touted Bush's upbringing in a racially tolerant family and his having long-standing black personal friends as being a prime contributor to his willingness to court black votes.[14] While notable, this raises through inference the possibility of a party problem going forward: A GOP president or presidential candidate without a personal history of substantial interaction with blacks may be less sensitive to their issues and, thus, less inclined to seek their support.

Further, African Americans ran credible races for prominent statewide positions around the nation in 2006. Ohio secretary of state J. Kenneth

Blackwell sought his state's governorship. Maryland lieutenant governor Michael Steele sought a seat in the US Senate. Lynn Swann sought to defeat an incumbent governor in Pennsylvania. All of these candidates won their respective state GOP nominations, and their candidacies represent a level of opportunity for the Republicans to make inroads into the black community. For much of the last half century, African American Republicans have been seen as weak candidates with no real chance of victory—the political equivalent of cannon fodder.

That the GOP has nowhere to go but up with regard to African American voters presents a great opportunity for Republicans. Small increases in black support can take on substantial significance, inasmuch as they could not only secure its electoral strength, but also devastate the Democratic Party by siphoning some of its loyal supporters. Some Republicans go so far as to contend that the Democratic Party can be sent into oblivion if the GOP can peel off a critical mass of black votes.[15] The test for the GOP, then, is to win more black votes without losing a portion of its base.

The Political Paradox

The GOP is in a difficult position. On the one hand, it wants to appear to be an inclusive party that is open and inviting to all—an important value to many Americans. On the other hand, its electoral success over the last three decades has been built largely on its ability to rally conservative white voters to its cause, often through the demonization of blacks and other minorities. Republicans' success with racial conservatives could actually be jeopardized if the GOP meets its stated goal of attracting more black voters, particularly if those voters turn out for black Republican candidates. Two points should be made in this regard. First, racially conservative white voters could take umbrage at GOP attempts to embrace African American voters; after all, that is what drove many of them away from the Democratic Party. Such an action could move many racially conservative Republicans to either stay home or vote for third-party candidates. Second, if many black voters turn out in an election featuring an attractive black Republican, they could vote Democratic on the rest of the ballot, thereby undermining the chances of winning for other Republicans.

Given this paradox, why should the GOP seek more black votes? Three reasons may be offered here. First, not doing so is divisive and corrosive to the US political system. By winning elections without earnestly seeking black votes, the GOP sends the message that a significant segment of the United States is irrelevant to its policy goals. The problem here may be less political than moral. The GOP also may be implicitly stating that policy positions that are particularly popular with African Americans will not find a home in the Republican Party. That message permeates the public at large and may help fuel the "us against them" mentality that is all too pervasive in US politics. By seeking to win this way, the GOP divides the nation racially, which is more harmful to the body politic than exploiting ideological distinctions. Of course, an alternative argument can be made here too: Democratic Party campaigning has positioned Republicans in such a way that the only way the GOP can meet with electoral success is by campaigning and governing as it currently does. Also, African Americans almost ask to be marginalized by voting so significantly for one party.

Second, political and electoral circumstances could change, and the GOP may find itself needing larger numbers of black votes to win close elections. The GOP's hold on suburbanites, white Protestants, conservatives, white men, or some combination thereof, could loosen sufficiently to compel the GOP to turn to black voters. Consider the concerns fiscal conservatives have about federal spending. Republicans campaigned for years that the Democrats were poor stewards of the people's money. Now, after twelve consecutive years of GOP House control and nearly as many consecutive years of Senate control, coupled with Republican control of the presidency for eighteen out of the last twenty-six years, some longtime Republicans are wondering if their party can control spending. From 2000, the last full year of the last Democratic presidential administration, to December 2004, the federal government has gone from an $86 billion budget surplus to a $567 billion budget deficit.[16] If fiscally conservative voters conclude that the GOP is not up to the task of responsible spending, perhaps the door would open for those voters to reconsider their allegiance to the party. After all, it was under a Democratic president that the federal budget was last balanced.

Social conservatives are also upset with the current state of the Republican Party. After a generation of movement from religious voters to the GOP, some of those voters have wondered when they would get legislation on some of their most important issues—outlawing abortion, funding education vouchers, and bringing religion more deeply into the public square. To date, social conservatives have yet to receive legislative action from the GOP commensurate with their contribution to Republican victories.

Conservatives of all varieties have become angry with the Republican Party at one level or another. One prominent Republican operative criticized the Bush administration for its "extensive intrusion into state and local education," its "budget-busting Medicare prescription drug benefit," its "refusal to enforce immigration laws," and Bush's signing of campaign finance laws that he had opposed during his 2000 presidential campaign.[17] These moves have come to be seen by some conservatives as a betrayal of their movement and could lead them to stay home on election day. If some of the various sects of the Republican Party were to stay home rather than support the party at the ballot box, the GOP would be forced to harvest black votes in large numbers just to maintain and expand its electoral strength in the wake of conservative defections.

The final and perhaps most significant reason for reaching out to black voters is America's changing demographics. The coalition of white conservative voters that elevated the GOP to control Congress and the White House for much of the last two decades is graying, while the minority population in the United States is growing. This is problematic for the GOP, as it has had very limited success with African Americans and fair to good success with Hispanic voters. While the success with Hispanic voters is notable, it will not be enough to continuously overcome its poor showing with African Americans. This changing demography places more pressure on the GOP to win minority voters who have traditionally been unsupportive or undersupportive of the party. An unfavorable response by the party to this new pressure is risky. Sooner or later, demographic shifts will leave the GOP without a winning voter coalition if it does not add new segments of the electorate.

The demographic changes have some Republicans worried about how the party will fare a decade from now. As Senator Lindsay Graham indicated in the wake of the 2004 election, "If we continue to lose 90 percent of the African American vote—and I got 7 percent—if we continue to lose 65 percent of the Hispanic vote, we're toast; just look at the electoral map."[18] Senator Graham's black support level is representative of what most white southern Republicans get from African American voters. The demographic change represents a double-edged sword for the GOP. It rose to prominence on racial conservatism that came under increasing pressure as the country became more racially diverse. As historian Louis Gould notes, "Balancing the racial views of a predominantly southern leadership with the changing demographics of a more ethnically and racially diverse nation did not prove easy as the twentieth century ended; a party that did not reach out to minorities could find itself at a permanent electoral disadvantage."[19]

For decades, the GOP built its platform for electoral success on appeals to southern white voters, which left the party with a very distinct support base. Democratic pollster Stanley Greenberg developed a seven-category typology to explain where the GOP's support comes from. Notable here is that none of the categories include substantial numbers of minorities, particularly African Americans:

1. *The faithful*: white Protestants who identify themselves as evangelical, fundamentalist, charismatic, or pentecostal.
2. *Deep South*: whites who live in Alabama, Arkansas, Florida,

Georgia, Louisiana, Mississippi, North Carolina, South Carolina, Texas, or Virginia.

3. *Country folk*: whites who live in counties located outside metropolitan areas.

4. *Exurbs*: high-growth counties in suburban and rural areas within 100 miles of cities with more than 100,000 residents, excluding those counties where growth is predominantly Hispanic, African American, or senior citizen.

5. *F-you boys*: white married men under fifty years of age who have not earned a college degree.

6. *F-you old men*: white senior men sixty-five years of age and older.

7. *Privileged men*: white married men with a college education (either a four-year or an advanced degree).[20]

The extent to which someone is more conservative, more Republican, or less likely to endorse policies supportive of African Americans can be linked to how many of these categories he or she belongs to. For example, a forty-five-year-old white male college graduate who lives in Smithfield County, Virginia, and attends a Pentecostal church at least once a week is far more likely to be a Republican than a Democrat. Some members of these groups—Deep South and f-you boys, for example—might be less supportive of the GOP if it did what is necessary to win African American support. This is in part because the overwhelming characteristic that links those who belong to at least one of the above groupings is race—they are more likely than not to be white.

Going forward, however, demographic trends pose a number of problems for the GOP in its quest to win future elections. The nation is becoming more diverse, as evidenced by the 2005 announcement that Texas now has a "majority-minority" population in which African Americans and Hispanics together account for the majority of the state's populace. Census Bureau projections indicate that the nation will be "majority-minority" at approximately the midpoint of this century.[21] The political implications for the GOP with regard to this increasing diversity are substantial. As authors John Judis and Ruy Teixera note, "Minority voters, including Blacks, Hispanics, and Asians, who had been variously committed to the Democratic Party, became overwhelmingly Democratic in the 1990s, while expanding from about a tenth of the voting electorate in 1972 to almost a fifth in 2000."[22] This trend works against Republican electoral interests and explains why the GOP *must* seek black votes and those of other minorities. It is a matter of political survival. The GOP will begin to lose elections if increases in minority voters as a percentage of the electorate continue their current trend—and all demographic trends suggest that they will—and the GOP maintains its current rate of minority support. If minorities tend to vote Democratic, then more minorities will mean more Democratic votes and wholesale electoral and political problems for the Republicans. A party that bases many of its policies on opposition to the interests of minorities—for example, immigration policy and affirmative action—can only expect those groups to respond accordingly at the ballot box.

This trend is further complicated by the fact that most new immigrants tend to settle in inner cities or close-in suburbs. This, then, makes metropolitan areas, not just cities, potentially fertile ground for the Democrats. So GOP-friendly states with large metropolitan areas—for example, Arizona (Phoenix), Florida (Tampa, Orlando, and Miami), Georgia (Atlanta), Nevada (Las Vegas), North Carolina (Research Triangle), and Virginia (Northern Virginia)—could become more competitive, if not Democratic, states. These new voters may be resistant to the GOP because of its immigration policies, which are seen by many as "anti-immigrant."

Book Overview

This book is organized into seven chapters. Chapter 2 follows this introduction and offers an analysis of the Republican Party, black politics, and the nearly unanimous support the party once enjoyed in the African American community. Chapter 3 explores when and why the GOP fell out of favor with African Americans. Chapter 4 examines GOP efforts during the last thirty-five years to win more black support. Chapter 5 addresses the various policy positions taken by the GOP that run counter to African American preferences. Chapter 6 analyzes the various ways in which Republican candidates and strategists have used racially tinged political symbolism to appeal to white conservatives. Chapter 7 considers the political implications for the party and for African Americans should the status quo continue.

Notes

1. J. C. Watts, interview by author, tape recorded, October 12, 2005.
2. Ibid.
3. An important study in this regard is Richard Seltzer and Robert C. Smith, "Race and Ideology: A Research Note Measuring Liberalism and Conservatism in Black America," *Phylon* 46 (Summer 1985).
4. Michael Dawson, *Behind the Mule: Race and Class in African-American Politics* (Princeton: Princeton University Press, 1994), p. 108.
5. Among the many articles in this regard during the past twenty-five years are Joe Davidson, "GOP Seeks Ways to Draw Blacks," *Wall Street Journal*, November 28, 1984, p. 64; Juan Williams, "White House Wooing Blacks," *Washington Post*, January 20, 1985, p. A17; Juan Williams, "Reagan Tries to Convert Middle-Class Blacks to GOP," *Washington Post*, February 5, 1985, p. A3;

Rhodes Cook, "GOP Planning to Woo Blacks to Widen Its Local Base," *CQ* 47, no. 9 (March 4, 1989): 474–477; Daniel Sneider, "Powell, Kemp Polish GOP Appeal to Blacks," *Christian Science Monitor*, August 13, 1996, p. 6; Rachel Van Dongen, "GOP Steps Up Minority Outreach Efforts," *Roll Call*, September 11, 1997, p. 1; Steve Miller, "GOP Plots Tactics to Lure Black Voters: Bush Netted Only 9% in 2000 Election," *Washington Times*, April 12, 2001, p. A6; Susan Crabtree, "Watts Plans Bus Trips, Reorganizes PAC to Attract Minorities, Money to GOP," *Roll Call*, November 12, 2001, p. 3; Darryl Fears, "GOP Makes 'Top Priority' of Converting Black Voters," *Washington Post*, December 25, 2003, p. A3; Chuck Raasch, "GOP Works to Overcome Skepticism Among Blacks," *USA Today*, March 30, 2005; and Michael Fletcher, "GOP Plans More Outreach to Blacks, Mehlman Says: Goal Is to Broaden Party Base, Help Swing Future Races," *Washington Post*, August 7, 2005, p. A5.

6. David Bositis, "Black Elected Officials: A Statistical Summary, 2000," Joint Center for Political and Economic Studies, Washington, DC, 2002; David Bositis, "African Americans and the Republican Party, 1996," Joint Center for Political and Economic Studies, Washington, DC, 1997. See also Fears, "GOP Makes 'Top Priority' of Converting Black Voters," p. A4. It should be noted that many public offices around the country are nonpartisan, so while it's likely that there are additional African American Republicans holding office, they were not elected as Republicans.

7. David Bositis, "Blacks and the 2000 Democratic National Convention," Joint Center for Political and Economic Studies, Washington, DC, 2000, p. 9.

8. Ibid., p. 8.

9. Ibid.

10. Ibid., p. 10.

11. Dawson, *Behind the Mule,* p. 109, citing the 1984–1988 National Black Election Study Panel.

12. Ibid., p. 109.

13. *Statistical Abstract of the United States: 2001*, 121st ed. (Washington, DC: US Census Bureau, 2002), table 24, p. 27. Additional calculations are derived from US Census Bureau data.

14. Armstrong Williams, interview by author, tape recorded, Washington, DC, July 22, 2005.

15. Peter Kirsanow, interview by author, tape recorded, Washington, DC, and Cleveland, OH, July 19, 2005.

16. See Congressional Budget Office, Table 1: Revenues, Outlays, Deficits, Surpluses, and Debt Held by the Public, 1962 to 2004, available online at www.cbo.gov/showdoc.cfm?index=1821&sequence=0 (accessed January 11, 2006).

17. Richard Viguerie, "Bush's Base Betrayal," *Washington Post*, May 21, 2006, p. B1.

18. Dan Balz and John F. Harris, "Some Republicans Predict Upheaval Within the Party: Concerns Include Changing Electorate, Lack of Heir Apparent," *Washington Post*, September 4, 2004, p. A8.

19. Louis Gould, *Grand Old Party: A History of the Republicans* (New York: Random House, 2003), p. 489.

20. Ibid., p. 96.

21. US Census Bureau, 2004, "U.S. Interim Projections by Age, Sex, Race, and Hispanic Origin," available online at www.census.gov/ipc/www/usinterimproj (accessed September 16, 2005).

22. John Judis and Ruy Teixera, *The Emerging Democratic Majority* (New York: Scribner, 2002), p. 4.

2

The GOP's Early Lock
on Black Votes

THE RELATIONSHIP BETWEEN AFRICAN AMERICANS AND THE
Republican Party must be seen in the larger context of political parties. The
formulation of political parties is a reflection of the factionalism that per-
vades US governance and politics. It was the subject of much concern by
the constitutional framers, and James Madison wrote about it in *Federalist
No. 10*. Madison and others worried that factions could have a corrupting
influence on the new government and should be resisted to the greatest
extent possible. There was additional concern that factional behavior would
lead groups to forsake the common good in pursuit of their own more narrowly defined interests. Madison argued that the proposed US Constitution
should and would make it difficult for parties to play a particularly strong
role in the nascent government. Thus the Constitution, as it pertained to factions, was based "on the conviction that the only good political party was
either none at all or one that disregarded the most disruptive political questions of the time."[1]

Some will no doubt conclude that Madison's concerns are correct and
that parties have had a deleterious impact on government. However, no serious alternative has emerged to challenge the prominence of organized political parties, and, today, political parties are the complex, multifaceted connective tissue of the body politic. They link individuals, organizations, and
their policy preferences with the governmental infrastructure in an attempt
to operate and change governmental action to their benefit. Parties, more so
than any other civic and social organizations, have become the preeminent
linkage between the people and the political structure. According to Samuel
Eldersveld and Hanes Walton, this has occurred for three reasons:

> First, [parties] provide a basis for interaction and cohesion within legisla-
> tures, such as Congress, and often, but not always, between legislative and
> executive leaders, such as between Congress and the president. Further, a

13

party provides some basis for cooperation between national, state, and
local institutions and leadership. Second, the party is a forum within which
interest groups can (but not all do) present their views about governmental
policies as well as press for particular types of candidates for offices, both
elective and appointive. The party is, therefore, an arena for the development of compromises by interest groups as well as the agent in creating
interest group coalitions working for particular goals. Third, a party constitutes a medium or channel for communication linking citizens, organizational leaders, and governmental officials. Parties bring the citizen into
contact with government and, conversely, are used by leaders to communicate with the public.[2]

Beyond this, political parties can encourage a type of behavior that furthers
their own interests. For example, loyalty and substantial work on behalf of a
party yields benefits such as political patronage and ensures the party's continued existence.

African Americans have often had fractious relations with US political
parties that were caused by what Walton referred to as the "ambiguity,
ambivalence, tension, paradox, irony, contradiction, and schizophrenia [that
has] always governed the status of [African Americans] in the American
political system and process."[3] Also, political parties have not been able to
effectively address issues of concern to African Americans because of their
inclination to "appeal to the median voter, who is White and frequently
indifferent or hostile to the interests of Blacks."[4] At best, African Americans
can hope for a partial, regional airing of grievances in certain parts of the
nation.

Throughout US political history, political parties have alternately
shunned and embraced, supported and demonized, and bullied and feared
African Americans. Consequently, African Americans have had difficulty
finding a comfortable and sustained place in these constantly changing
political environments. African Americans have had notable successes, as
evidenced by the Reconstruction-era Republicans or contemporary
Democrats. More often than not, there has been failure and difficulty in
establishing for African Americans coherent, sustained, and mutually
respectful relationships with US political parties, such as the "lily white"
Republican movement and the Democratic Party effort to have white-only
primary elections.[5]

The relationship between African Americans and the Democrats and
Republicans has almost always been lopsided. African Americans have
alternately given the overwhelming majority of their support to Republicans
or Democrats, but rarely equally to both parties. The movement back and
forth has resulted from one party using African American votes to gain
power, such as Reconstruction-era Republicans and World War II/civil
rights–era Democrats, or from one party opposing African American interests because of outright racism and hostility (Reconstruction-era

Democrats) or a party responding to the political charge that it was too close to, and supportive of, black interests (post-Reconstruction–era Republicans).

Contemporary African American politics exists within the framework of the two-party system. The Democratic and Republican parties have dominated US politics for more than 150 years and have been the only consistent, albeit often unsatisfactory, options for African American political participation. As the parties became more entrenched around the nation, they wrote election laws to perpetuate their own existence, making it virtually impossible for alternative parties to emerge. The winner-take-all method of US elections, coupled with onerous ballot access requirements—written by Democrats and Republicans—effectively discourages support for "third parties." This has frustrated US political discourse, limited voter choice, and contributed to the apathy that is too prevalent in US electoral politics.

The result of this system is that the political behavior of subgroups of US voters, be they organized by race, religion, or single issues, is complex and multifaceted. First, these subgroups of voters have to align themselves with the party that is closest to them philosophically and ideologically, even though the political space between the voter and the party could be significant. Second, it means that there is no real choice if the parties share issue positions or take issue positions that are largely indistinguishable. This happens increasingly in US politics where, on a seemingly growing list of issues, the Democrats and Republicans take similar positions. Last, it means that any calls for political changes that bring about more competition for the parties will have to go through party officials who are unlikely to support efforts that could result in the weakening of the parties.

The Republican Party

The Republican Party was formed in 1854 by a coalition composed of members of the American, Free Soil, and other parties, along with Northern Democrats who sought to restrict the expansion of slavery.[6] Their success was immediate, and in six years a Republican was president. Abraham Lincoln's election proved a seminal milestone in US politics as the Republican Party overtook the Whig Party to become the primary rival of the Democrats and the second party in the two-party system that exists to this day.

The origins of the Republican Party were very much in line with black aspirations. Its most important initial policy position was the call restricting the expansion of slavery in the wake of the passage of the Kansas-Nebraska Act. The controversy surrounding the act spawned protest within the Democratic and Whig parties that focused on Stephen Douglas, the

Democratic senator from Illinois. Douglas sought to nullify the Missouri Compromise and open the soon-to-be-created territories of Kansas and Nebraska to slavery. As historian Eric Foner noted, "Belief in the superiority of the 'free labor' system of the North and the incompatibility of 'free society' and 'slave society' coalesced into a comprehensive world view or ideology."[7] In that regard, the party represented "republican thought in the 1850s [that extolled] the values of individual liberty, legal equality, and government restrained by law, while it stressed the existence of internal conspiracies designed to overthrow republican government and eradicate liberty."[8]

Republicans seized the most important issue of the day—racial equality—and quickly established themselves as a party with which to be reckoned. They did so by providing a clear alternative to the conservative Democratic Party of that era. The most liberal members of the party came to be known by their critics as "Radical Republicans" (or "Radicals"), a faction that supported racial equality and was able to establish some rudimentary lawmaking designed to improve the general condition of African Americans. The Radicals also fought for African American employment in the federal bureaucracy and helped pave the way for the election of many African Americans during Reconstruction. The establishment of the Freedman's Bureau—an agency created to help newly freed slaves with economic, educational, and other benefits—and the adoption of the so-called Reconstruction Amendments to the Constitution, which abolished slavery, granted US citizenship to former slaves, and established voting rights for former slaves, were among the most important legislative contributions of this subset of Republicans. These actions helped win a comprehensive black allegiance to the Republican Party.

Following the post-Reconstruction era, the Republican Party evolved through a number of periods that shaped its politics and changed its ideology from liberal-moderate to conservative: the Progressive era, the New Deal era, the post–World War II era, and the conservative era. During the Progressive era, moderates and progressives engaged in a great deal of infighting for party control. Progressives sought to balance federal power and business advancement, while moderates sought as little federal involvement as possible. It was also during this period that federal officials began to rein in monopolistic business practices to protect individual consumers and advance business competition.

The New Deal era was a recovery and reassessment period for the GOP. The disastrous wake of the Great Depression, which occurred on the Republicans' watch and was viewed by many as the result of the party having too close a relationship with business interests, led to Democratic control of Congress and the White House and built a multigenerational political coalition that dominated US politics.

The post–World War II era saw moderates briefly take charge of the GOP. They were involved in a power struggle with the newly reemerging conservative wing of the party. President Eisenhower, in particular, moved the party toward racial reconciliation; he signed into law two civil rights acts that built upon previous civil rights efforts. But a disconnect emerged during this period. Within Congress, Republican votes were vital to the enactment of the civil rights acts of the period, but outside Washington, the GOP moved away from its identification with black rights and toward a sympathy for the concerns of white voters in the South and West.[9] Conservatives criticized moderates for not taking a sufficiently tough stance in opposition to the New Deal and wanted the party to focus more intently on social issues.

The conservative takeover of the GOP, which began in the late 1940s, would not be solidified for nearly a generation, but it was this period that helped set the party on its current course. The rise of the conservatives became official in 1964 with Barry Goldwater winning that year's party nomination to challenge incumbent Lyndon Johnson for the presidency. Although Goldwater lost in a landslide to Johnson, the Goldwater campaign led to an enormous ideological change for the party. In the 1960s, particularly when Ronald Reagan became president, moderate Republicans began being isolated in the party and are now considerably less influential than they have ever been.

The GOP evolved away from its progressive roots. The party that was built on radical reform of government, on nationalism and positive government, on protective tariffs, and on anti-imperialism moved into directions that its founders would only see as antithetical to its roots. The party now champions states' rights and limited federal power and supports free trade instead of tariffs.[10] On foreign policy, the party has shifted from isolationism to anticommunism to unilateral interventionism. Nowhere is the change more profound than in its current position on racial issues. As Gould notes, "Modern Republicans who find appeal in the neo-confederate arguments for states' rights and limited government separate themselves from the founding traditions and moral high ground of their party."[11]

The Republican Party was founded not only on racial moderation, but also on a strong probusiness platform, which guided much of its early development: "The Republicans associated themselves, without apology, with business and with the presumption that growing industrialization would improve the general welfare."[12] Continued economic strength, as exemplified by the growth of household incomes during the early twentieth century, helped place the Republicans and their connection to business interests in a position of political dominance. While the Great Depression dampened much of the public's favor toward such a tightly connected relationship between the GOP and large business interests, Republicans have at their core an abiding reliance on business and economic solutions to cure the nation's ills.

Paleoconservatives vs. Neoconservatives

Conservatives, moderates, and liberals do not struggle for party control as in decades past. That debate was settled in favor of conservatives, who now control virtually every part of the party's apparatus, including—but not limited to—policy development, political strategy, and fundraising activities. Liberal and moderate Republicans do not control the levers of power within the party to the extent that they once did. That is not to say no factionalism exists within the Republican Party. It does, and contemporary Republican factionalism can best be seen as a struggle between two sides of the same conservative ideological coin: "paleoconservatives" and "neoconservatives."

The paleoconservatives are the old-line conservatives in the classic context who view themselves as "real conservatives." Their domestic agenda is led by a strong bent toward states' rights, repeal or limitation of civil rights laws, opposition to immigration, and cultural homogeneity. They view cultural diversity and efforts to promote it as undermining America's cultural purity and heritage. Moreover, paleoconservatives embrace traditionalist Christian morality, Eurocentric monoculturalism, isolationist nationalism, and a complete end to social programs.[13]

Paleoconservative foreign policy is characterized by isolationism and opposition to the existence of multinational organizations such as the United Nations. Their opposition is based on their belief that membership in these organizations diminishes US sovereignty and thus weakens the nation. Prominent paleoconservatives include President Ronald Reagan; former adviser to Presidents Nixon and Reagan and two-time Republican presidential candidate Patrick Buchanan; columnist Robert Novak; columnist Paul Craig Roberts; and former Reagan administration deputy assistant attorney general and publisher Alfred Regnery. The paleoconservative faction also has a number of organizations through which it networks, such as the John Birch Society, the Council of Conservative Citizens, and the John Randolph Club. The birth of groups like Birch has been seen by some in Republican circles as the "emergence of the radical extreme right" in the party.[14] Some paleoconservatives are seen as racist, anti-Israel, or both, given their views and organizational associations.

Neoconservatives are considered to be "new converts" to conservatism; some were New Deal supporters or otherwise disaffected liberals who came to see "big government" as the problem, not the solution.[15] Neoconservative domestic policy, while certainly not to be confused with liberalism, is more accepting of certain government welfare spending than paleoconservative policy and does not oppose the use of federal legislation to help ensure civil equality for minorities to the same extent as does paleoconservative policy. This is a major point of contention with paleoconservatives, who want to end social welfare spending and who oppose government intervention to enforce civil rights. Neoconservatives are generally more interested in international affairs, and its roots are in liberal Cold War anticommunism. Neoconservative foreign policy advocates the use of unilateral, preemptive military force to facilitate the creation of democratic governments or the removal of unfriendly leaders around the world. The willingness to intervene in the affairs of other nations is the source of much criticism from paleoconservatives, who are isolationist at their core. Neoconservatives are also forceful proponents of free trade as a mechanism to undermine hostile regimes around the world. Notable neoconservatives include Jeanne Kirkpatrick, Irving Kristol, Paul Wolfowitz, and Norman Podhoretz. Neoconservatives are prominent in policy think tanks such as the American Enterprise Institute and in organizations such as the Project for the New American Century.

The term *neoconservative* is not without controversy. Many who espouse views that are linked with neoconservatism consider the term to be used against them derisively, like a slur. This is because many critics of neoconservatism see the movement as elitist, driven by New York intellectuals, many of whom are Jewish. They are viewed with suspicion by old-line conservatives, much as conservative African Americans are viewed by the general black population. The most hard-line paleoconservatives accuse neoconservatives of using US military power to further the aims of the Israeli government.

The distinctions between paleoconservatives and neoconservatives and their impact on the relationship between African Americans and the Republican Party are significant. A paleoconservative return to power would mean less international intervention, which theoretically could mean more funding available for domestic projects. However, paleoconservatives also loathe domestic social spending and the use of federal intervention to protect and advance civil rights. If neoconservatives remain in charge, there will be more international intervention. That, of course, will mean greater increases in military and related spending and less money available for domestic social spending, further exacerbating problems related to health care, public education, and housing.

Republicans and Religion

No examination of the history of the Republican Party can be complete without examining the role religion has played and continues to play in party politics. The rise of religious conservatism is a significant contributor to contemporary Republican success. For more than a generation, religious conservatives have sought a closer link between faith (particularly Christianity) and government. They came to see the GOP as more attuned and welcoming to their beliefs and began to engage more fully in the political process through the Republican Party. That engagement was facilitated by the creation of organizations such as the Moral Majority and the Christian Coalition. These and other groups served as rallying points for religious conservatives who, believing that faith should guide policy, helped push the GOP rightward. In the estimation of some analysts, this movement has made the party more ideologically rigid than it has ever been.[16]

As religious conservatives became more involved and influential in politics, candidates shaped their messages to reflect the interests of these new voters. As this evolution continued, some religious leaders became more overt in their desire to impact politics on *their* terms. According to one such leader, "If a person is trying to live for the Lord, then their life should be dominated in all areas by that principle, politics included."[17] Consequently, culturally explosive issues such as school prayer, abortion, women's rights, gun control, and gay rights became just as important political issues as jobs, the economy, civil rights, national defense, and anticommunism had been in previous decades. Because the GOP was better positioned and more willing than the Democrats to embrace these issues, it won the overwhelming majority of religious conservative votes. Over time, and particularly in the South, religion became a seminal feature of Republican politics.

The link between Republicans and the Religious Right, as Christian conservatives came to be known, was solidified at the national level with Ronald Reagan's 1980 election to the presidency. Reagan actively courted religious conservatives and saw them as a large, untapped reservoir of voters. He publicly met with prominent religious conservatives who eventually signed on to support his candidacy. These efforts opened the door so that "thousands of fundamentalist Protestant churches became political centers for Mr. Reagan and other Republican candidates, as politicized evangelical groups moved into the political arena."[18] With these new voters entering the political ranks as Republicans, the GOP shifted further right than it had ever been before in an effort to ideologically accommodate this new critical element in the party's electoral success. It also made the GOP the recipient of landslide majorities of white voters and initiated a period of sweeping conservative Republican victories, particularly in the South.

By the end of Reagan's presidency, religious leaders and Republican political leaders had, in some ways, become one and the same. Christian Coalition leader Pat Robertson sought the 1988 GOP presidential nomination. Christian Coalition executive director Ralph Reed became a key link between religious voters and the politicians who sought their votes. Reed later left the Christian Coalition to become a political consultant, chair of the Georgia Republican Party, and, later, candidate for lieutenant governor of Georgia, losing in the party's primary. Many conservatives who ran for local, state, and national office sought out Christian Coalition and Moral Majority support. Many of these office seekers ran campaigns in which they tried to "out-morality" their opponents, presenting themselves as the "most Christian" candidate and the most worthy of conservative network support. Moreover, it is no longer unusual for the GOP to prepare voters' guides comparing Republican and Democratic candidates on issues important to Religious Right voters and to distribute them in or around churches.[19]

There is a certain irony that Reagan would be the spark that lit the political fire that burned down the barriers between the GOP and religious conservatives. The irony lies in the fact that, as Charles Dunn and J. David Woodward noted, Reagan "attended church only on the rarest occasions and certainly never Sunday School and absolutely never with a Bible in his hand."[20] Indeed, Reagan focused far more assiduously on economic and international affairs than on issues pushed by the faithful.

African American Politics: A Brief History

African American politics have been shaped by the unique experiences that have characterized black life in the United States. Generations of slavery, involuntary family disconnections, legal mandates that prevented access to education, legal and cultural barriers to upwardly mobile employment, the segregation of public accommodations and housing, and a criminal justice system that targets blacks have, among other issues, informed the African American political experience. Also, African Americans share a legacy of oppression, segregation, economic and political intimidation, and repression. This exists to varying degrees because of socioeconomics, but wealth is not a complete innoculator. Many upper-middle-class and wealthy African Americans feel the same concerns about the political and social structure in which they exist.

A key variable in understanding African American politics is the notion of a "linked fate" among African Americans of various backgrounds, without regard to geography or socioeconomic status.[21] Linked fate refers to the belief held among a substantial majority of African Americans that what happens generally to black people in America will impact what happens to all black Americans in their individual lives. In other words, what affects one group of African Americans in one part of the country will likely have an impact on groups throughout the country. This helps explain why so many African Americans are concerned when they watch the news and a black mug shot is put on the screen of someone wanted for a crime. Linked

fate explains why many African Americans believe they will be viewed negatively by black criminal imagery that has nothing to do with them as individuals. This shared legacy exists, in part, because the larger white society
often did not distinguish between various types of blacks on issues such as
segregation; for their purposes, a well-educated black with "middle-class
values" was no different from an illiterate sharecropper. Consequently,
blacks responded to white society in a largely bonded fashion.

For generations, white racial conservatives have sought to remove or
limit black political behavior and rights—to make African Americans politically invisible.[22] For example, legislation designed to "redeem" the South
following Reconstruction completely removed African Americans from the
political process. This is the framework through which black politics exists
and has engendered a black response that has centered on efforts to make
African Americans visible, relevant, and strategically effective in the larger
political system. It has also highlighted the importance of charismatic black
leaders who can garner the attention of the black masses and the larger
white media. The black community has had a long list of individuals who
have played a large role in shaping and fostering black politics. Included
among them are Frederick Douglass, Booker T. Washington, W. E. B.
DuBois, Marcus Garvey, Adam Clayton Powell, Martin Luther King Jr., and
Jesse Jackson.

Current GOP efforts to increase the support it receives from African
Americans can be seen as an effort to make visible a largely forgotten or
ignored portion of the electorate. It can be argued, though, that these efforts
either misunderstand the notion of linked fate or seek to create a new para-
digm by removing race as the linkage and replacing it with something new,
such as religion. Recent GOP attempts to connect with black voters have
been based on religion and morality. This is, in some ways, a tactical shift.
Until the 1980s, the GOP attempted to connect with black voters in two
ways: first, by being willing to compete with Democrats on civil rights
issues; and, second, by creating black leaders who can be positioned as
legitimate alternatives to the traditional, civil rights–era leadership. If successful, the new strategy—to try to connect on religion and morality—has
the potential to deracialize African American politics. If this happens, race-
based discrimination and other forms of racism that still exist in America
can be seen as occurring with the complicity and tacit approval of African
Americans.

African American Politics Defined

While African American politics is seen in numerous ways, Hanes Walton's
definition, as explained in his book *Black Politics: A Theoretical and
Structural Approach* is the most comprehensive:

> [African American] politics springs from the particular brand of segrega-
> tion practices found in different environments in which [African
> American] people find themselves. In other words, the nature of segrega-
> tion and the manner in which it differs not only in different localities but
> within a locality have caused [African American] people to employ politi-
> cal activities, methods, devices, and techniques that would advance their
> policy preferences. In short, [African American] politics is a function of
> the particular brand of segregation found in different environments in
> which black people find themselves.[23]

Black politics, particularly during and since the "black power" era, may
also be "characterized by the transformation of protest politics into electoral
politics with high levels of Black political unity."[24]

Contemporary African American politics, while still greatly influenced
by segregation and racism, may also be seen as the continued struggle to
access the levers of government to ensure that preferences on issues that
speak to the unique African American experience in the United States be put
into policy. This struggle takes place within the context of interest group
behavior in which limited resources are sought by numerous contenders.
The best organized and resourced groups are more likely than not to get
their way in the policy process. So for African Americans, the struggle for
organization and resources determines access to the levers of government.

African American politics has moved through four stages: (1) nonpar-
ticipation, (2) limited participation, (3) moderate participation, and (4) full
participation.[25] It should be noted that these stages are not chronologically
fixed so that one period clearly transitions into another. Indeed, there are
some periods that may exemplify characteristics of multiple stages. In the
first stage, the overwhelming majority of African Americans were excluded
from all aspects of the political process, both electoral and nonelectoral.[26]
Legislation and societal customs froze all black political participation and
created an environment in which African American social, political, and
economic policy preferences went unconsidered or were not acted on.

The second stage of African American politics was characterized by
"extremely low participation—electoral and nonelectoral."[27] Activity in this
stage is scant and is limited to the small cadre of black elites that operated
when allowed to do so by the larger white power structure. Participation in
this stage took place primarily in northern states. To the extent that it did
occur in the South, blacks were often coerced into supporting Democrats,
the same party that fostered the segregated society in which African
Americans suffered.

Stage three "is characterized by more than 50 percent Black political participation."[28] External pressures on the larger political structure, such as black
migration to the North, encouraged more black participation. This period saw
the formation of organizations such as the National Association for the

Advancement of Colored People and the Brotherhood of Sleeping Car Porters. These and other groups gave African Americans a sense of unity that had not existed since Reconstruction and a belief that collective action could yield political rewards. This activity begat new activity in which new organizations began to emerge at the local, state, and national levels.

Full political participation characterizes the fourth stage of black politics. Here, African Americans are significantly engaged in all aspects of the political process—electoral and nonelectoral. African Americans run for office, organize policy think tanks, and intensify organizational activities designed to influence the political process. Particularly notable is the elevation of African Americans to high-level appointed office, such as membership in presidential cabinets. Further, "Blacks not only have access to the avenues of power, but tools and devices to make some impact on the power holders, and full participation represents the final stage of political development."[29]

Political Context as a Variable in African American Politics

One cannot understand African American politics and political behavior without understanding the role of political context. African American politics is a phenomenon that often operates in response to external stimuli. These external stimuli take the form of political context and are among the most important variables in black politics. Political context is a dynamic and static variable that "postulates that political behavior at either the individual or the group level is not independent of the political environment (a particular time period and a particular place) in which it occurs."[30] Political context is an amorphous phenomenon that eludes easy identification and analysis because it can be altered and transformed to meet the needs of those controlling the context in which politics and governance occur. The alteration of political context can exhibit racial tolerance, inclusiveness, and pluralism on the one hand, or abrasive intolerance, exclusivity, and hierarchical stratification on the other.[31]

Too often, context is an overlooked phenomenon because, as it relates to African Americans, it requires the consideration of inconvenient and uncomfortable facts. For example, state-sponsored economic and political violence against African Americans through the institution of slavery, racial segregation, educational deprivation, and economic poverty has created the context in which African Americans live. To ignore that these forces explain why the general black condition is what it is is an unfortunate but all too familiar fact of political analysis in the United States. Conservatives who criticize African Americans for general social dysfunction, high poverty, high incarceration, low educational achievement, and disproportionately high unemployment and welfare rates without acknowledging the overarching context in which blacks live—and the contribution of conservative public policy to these conditions—make a fatal stylistic and political mistake that contributes to their unpopularity with African Americans. Too often, conservatives are seen in the black community as "blaming the victim" for their station in life. If the political context in which blacks operate were as favorable to them as it is to whites, then an "apples to apples" comparison could be made. Failing that, an "apples to oranges" comparison presented as an "apples to apples" one is unfair.

Political context also has legislative implications for African Americans. When the majority of the black members of a city council, state legislature, or the US Congress are in the minority party, their ability to deliver resources to their constituents is hampered by the political context in which they operate. A contemporary example can be found in the Congressional Black Caucus (CBC) of the US Congress. CBC members are limited in what they can do for their constituents because they are in the minority party. Because they do not chair committees or subcommittees, they are left out of the process of defining the legislative agenda—this despite the fact that the caucus is larger than it has ever been.

The GOP's Monopoly on African American Support

The contemporary relationship between African Americans and the Republican Party has taken a nearly 180-degree turn since the party's birth. Upon its founding, the Republican Party took a progressive stance on racial issues, most notably supporting civil rights and limiting the expansion of slavery. Even though the GOP was not willing to go as far on the slavery issue as antislavery parties like the Liberty Party and the Radical Abolitionist Party, Republican policy positions earned a political debt from African Americans that was repaid with consistent and overwhelmingly high levels of support throughout much of the balance of the nineteenth century. Organizations such as the New England Colored Citizens Convention endorsed the Republican Party and urged its followers to do likewise.[32] Black support for the GOP stemmed from the call by "Radical Republicans" for black freedom and equality and the reconstruction of southern society. Republican platforms during the late nineteenth century called for the enforcement of the Fourteenth and Fifteenth Amendments, the protection of "honest voters," and the free exercise of every citizen's "civil, political, and public rights."[33] Congressional Republicans "led investigations of fraud and violence in Southern elections and accused Southern Democrats of holding their seats illegally."[34]

The GOP adroitly combined political symbolism with policy substance to create a network of legislation and organizations that supported newly freed slaves. As Walton noted, "Beyond symbolic legislative acts and charismatic and impelling personalities, the Republican party had organizations like the Union League and the Freedman's Bureau which reached even the most illiterate and remotely isolated Blacks."[35] These organizations were advocates for the GOP and reinforced at the local level what the party was doing in Washington, DC. They "carried the news of Republican greatness to places where Black leaders and newspapers had no sway, where 'word of mouth' needed reinforcement, proof that it was really true."[36]

This is not to say that Republican motivations were completely pure. More than a few Republicans believed that blacks were inherently inferior to whites. This complicated their willingness to go to any extent necessary to support black empowerment and equality and positioned some to be only grudgingly supportive of Reconstruction policies. As Gould noted, "Southern Republicans were not saints, but their days in power represented a better chance for the region than the ideology of the Democratic Party at that time."[37] Further, while the party platforms may have called for political equality and voting rights, what was happening in the states through the lily white movement—the systematic purge of African American Republicans from state parties throughout the nation that began in the post-Reconstruction era—was a clear indication of the conflict at work and the lack of unanimity among Republicans.

The Abolition Movement

The abolition movement was dedicated to ending the Atlantic slave trade that supplied the US economy with free labor for more than three centuries. It was also part of a larger international effort to end the practice of slavery and was influenced by evolving views of human rights and Christian morality. Abolitionists viewed slavery as ungodly and against the moral teachings of the church. While the roots of the abolition movement predate the founding of the Republic and the formation of the Republican Party, its principles challenged the prevailing status quo and proved attractive to many who eventually became Republicans. The movement to abolish slavery in the United States became most fervent during the mid–nineteenth century. Many of the adherents to the tenets of abolition found their way into the Republican Party.

The origins of the movement in the United States lie in the religious teachings of the Quakers, who believed all people were equal in the eyes of God. Abolitionist Quakers were also moved by the barbarity of buying human beings and selling them into slavery. Quakers were joined by Christian fundamentalists who were influenced by the Second Great Awakening, which sought devout Christians to help bring about a moral regeneration in America. Slavery was among the many societal ills that were identified for abolition.

Quakers and Christian evangelicals helped form the American Anti-Slavery Society (AASS), which called for the immediate emancipation of slaves and the provision for their equality under law. The AASS engaged in a number of activities, including petitioning the government and distributing antislavery propaganda into the South. While the society eventually succumbed to internal strife and division, it is notable as the first major organization dedicated to the abolition of slavery. As such, it helped shape the slavery debate and led to the creation of other organizations to advance and continue the movement, including the Liberty Party, which sought to get abolitionists elected to public office, and the Foreign Anti-Slavery Society, which sought support for abolition from the nation's churches.

Although Republicans were at the forefront of the abolition movement, the party was divided on the issue of how African Americans should be treated. Internal tensions concerning black freedom and equality divided the party into three camps during the Civil War: the "Radicals," who favored black freedom and equality; the conservatives, who wanted to win the Civil War but not do much for blacks; and the moderates, who stood between the two poles.[38] These tensions slowed racial progress, complicated efforts to bring full freedom and equality to African Americans, and revealed that some Republicans doubted the ability of African Americans to share the responsibility for governing the country. It also demonstrated that some Republicans had clear limits on their positions on racial equality. Abraham Lincoln, considered by many to be the epitome of racial progressivism of his era, underscored this in a debate with Stephen A. Douglas, when he stated, "I am not nor ever have been in favor of making voters or jurors of Negroes, nor of qualifying them to hold office, nor to intermarry with white people."[39] Lincoln continued by noting that physical differences between blacks and whites would prevent the races from "living together on terms of social and political equality."[40]

Radical Republicans

The liberal Republicans during the Civil War and Reconstruction eras, who strongly believed in the abolition of slavery and the social, economic, and political equality of African Americans with whites—including full citizenship and voting rights—were thought to be "radical" in their thinking. These Radical Republicans, as they were called, were also at the forefront of the abolition movement and were the precursor to the Eastern Establishment—the patrician New England Republicans who were characterized by their social moderation and financier families whose business interests were significant.[41] Most Radicals were from the northeastern United States and believed, as Reconstruction scholar Eric Foner noted, that "the driving force of Radical ideology was the utopian vision of a nation whose citizens enjoyed equality of civil and political rights, secured by a powerful and beneficent national state."[42] Radicals also supported the expansion of federal authority as a necessary component of remaking the society and protecting citizen rights. The controversial nature of their positions often left them "under fire as militants who sought to impose racial egalitarianism on the South despite evidence that white southerners did not want such a social change, and convincing proof, at least in the minds of those who assailed the Radicals, that African Americans had not been ready for self-government during Reconstruction."[43]

Prominent among these pro–civil rights Republicans were Massachusetts senator Charles Sumner and Pennsylvania representative Thaddeus Stevens. They led pro-Reconstruction efforts in their respective chambers and personified the kinds of Republicans who earned unyielding support in the African American community through their vocal support for blacks. Sumner, perhaps the most controversial of the Radicals, not only supported emancipation but also led the fight to create the Freedman's Bureau and to enlist African Americans in the Union army. He was also a strong voice in support of repealing the Fugitive Slave Act—which required federal marshals and other officials to arrest escaped slaves—and "he opposed the annexation of Texas in 1845 because it meant the extension of the slave system."[44]

Stevens was considered to be one of the most effective House leaders of his era, and his success was the result of "his force and energy of mind and will and the strength of the cause he represented."[45] He was a supporter of black freedom and equality and made a name for himself as a lawyer who defended runaway slaves. He was also a leading advocate for southern reconstruction, including the use of military force to ensure southern recognition of both the abolition of slavery and black political activity. Legislatively, he helped develop the Fourteenth Amendment and the Reconstruction Act of 1867, and he also proposed the resolution for Andrew Johnson's impeachment. Johnson, a Democrat who ascended to the presidency following the assassination of President Lincoln, opposed the Republicans' reconstruction program and vetoed important legislation (some of which was overridden). His impeachment was largely driven by his unwillingness to enforce Reconstruction policies. He was lenient toward Confederates, offering amnesty to almost all who would take an oath of allegiance, and he quickly returned political rights to former Confederates. He voided Special Field Order 15, which ordered abandoned land to be divided among former slaves, and called for land to be returned to its former owners. These and other decisions, including Johnson's overall contempt for blacks, hampered the Reconstruction effort and set back many Radical plans.

The Radicals achieved some important legislation, including passage of the Civil Rights Act of 1866, legalization of interracial marriage, and, most important, passage of the military Reconstruction Act of 1867. The success of the Radicals in Congress was, however, tempered. While Republicans controlled both houses of Congress by better than three-to-one margins, it was not easy to get Radical legislation passed. The lack of Republican unanimity forced Radicals to curtail their legislative ambitions, which had a chilling effect on the movement for freedom and equality. Historically, the Republican Party has basked in reflected sunlight because of their relative progressivism during that era; however, many of their actions were far from unanimously progressive. While the GOP is rightfully credited for its actions during that era, one may argue that it also benefited from the role of the Radicals more than is warranted by history. There is no question that the GOP was clearly better on race than the Democrats. The Democrats, however, set a very low bar, and one must not overlook the racial divisions that existed within the GOP. It should also be noted that Radical power in Congress was enhanced by the secession of eleven southern states. When the seceding states removed their representatives from the US Congress, they eliminated the Radicals' most strident opposition.

Many Republican political activists take the position that the Republican Party was comprehensively pro-black and point to Radical legislation and Reconstruction for proof. That position is overstated because the Republican record on race, even during Reconstruction and in comparison to the dominant Democrats of that era, was mixed and revealed the conflicted racial positions held by most of the GOP. There were Republicans during that period who argued that blacks should not be allowed to vote or hold office; those same Republicans contended that in the exercise of other political and legal rights, blacks should be treated the same as all other citizens.[46] While the efforts of the Radicals are rightly seen as the most significant and progressive in US history until the civil rights movement—and certainly better than the Democrats' efforts—one would be mistaken to believe that Radical thinking was totally resistant to its political and social environment. Many Radicals believed the regnant racial stereotypes that governed conservative thought and politics of the day and "accepted the common stereotypes of the manly and vigorous Anglo-Saxon, the religious, 'feminine' Black, and the intelligent mulatto, and assumed Blacks were naturally suited to warmer climes."[47] The important distinction between Radicals and conservatives was, of course, that the former fought for black equality despite their inherent doubts, while the latter used those same beliefs to justify the subordination and exploitation of a race. Some Radicals could even accept some level of segregation while still arguing in favor of equality. Thaddeus Stevens, a leading Radical, contended that "Negro equality . . . does not mean that a Negro shall sit on the same seat or eat at the same table with a White man. That is a matter of taste which every man must decide for himself."[48]

While Radical success was significant and critical to black political and social freedom, it was also short-lived and incomplete. The Radicals' crowning achievement, the reconstruction of the American South, was the result of numerous political compromises that occurred because they did not have enough strength in Congress to ensure the implementation of their policies. The compromises that led to a watered-down Reconstruction also contributed to the relative brevity of its implementation. Reconstruction did not last long enough to establish a long-standing black presence in US politics. Indeed, it would take nearly a century before there were African Americans elected in the South on the same scale as during Reconstruction. Be that as it may, the Radicals' legislative acts, including the creation of the Freedman's Bureau and "the Thirteenth, Fourteenth, and Fifteenth Amendments were the chief measures through which the Republican Party secured the allegiance of the Black community."[49] This legislation had such an impact on black freedom and provided so many tangible results that "even the illiterate Freedmen could make the connection between these positive features and the benefits of Republicanism and the party."[50]

Reconstruction

Reconstruction refers to the period beginning in 1865 and ending in 1877 that was instituted to reconstruct southern and, by extension, US society.[51] Reconstruction proved to be a significant milepost in the political and social development of African Americans. It, at least temporarily, opened the doors to freedom and equality for a group of people that had been purposefully and legally prevented from enjoying these core tenets of US society. Radical Republicans were responsible for initiating Reconstruction in the face of conservative opposition and pushed to make it a reality.

Initial historical accounts of Reconstruction were written from a racially conservative perspective and reflected hostility to the notion of black freedom and equality. They described the period as a failure, the product of black mental incompetence and corrupt northern interference. The writing and scholarship, based on racist interpretations of black humanity, "documented, denounced, and derided African-American ignorance, venality, and exploitation under Reconstruction."[52] Conservative scholars portrayed the era as a blight on US history and an unjust occupation of the South by northern troops. The troop presence, which ranged from a high of over 17,600 at the start of Reconstruction to just over 6,000 in 1876, was a major point of contention that created a hostile environment throughout the occupied South.[53] Conservative scholars also portrayed the era as having no redeeming value for the nation: "Vindictive Radical Republicans fastened black supremacy upon the defeated South, unleashing an orgy of corruption presided over by unscrupulous carpetbaggers, traitorous scalawags, and ignorant freedmen. Eventually, the white community overthrew this mis-government and restored Home Rule."[54] This dim view of Reconstruction was, no doubt, informed by a resistance to the change that was brought on by the Civil War and its aftermath. To consider the societal good that occurred because of Reconstruction would counter the conservative view that blacks were intellectually and otherwise inferior to whites. This school of Reconstruction historiography reigned for more than sixty years.

Later historical studies challenged this bigoted writing and scholarship by describing and analyzing Reconstruction's black successes. Howard Beale, A. A. Taylor, W. E. B. DuBois, Francis Simkins, Joel Williamson, and Robert Woody are among those credited with revisiting and reinterpret-ing Reconstruction more accurately. Williamson "depicted Reconstruction in South Carolina as a time of extraordinary progress for blacks in political, economic, and social life."[55] DuBois's *Black Reconstruction in America, 1860–1880* was the first of a number of such works that presented a more complete view of Reconstruction and identified many positive outcomes. The mere presence of this new wave of research challenged the dominant and prevailing wisdom concerning Reconstruction and introduced the notion of black humanity to a society largely ignorant of and resistant to such imagery.

Reconstruction primarily used the ballot to open the door to black par-ticipation in many new aspects of southern society. From the ballot, all other advances, such as public education and employment, emanated. According to one Reconstruction scholar, "Black participation in Southern public life after 1867 was the most radical development of the Reconstruction years, a massive experiment in interracial democracy with-out precedent in the history of this or any other country that abolished slav-ery in the nineteenth century."[56] It has been estimated that by 1870, nine of the reconstructed states had a black male voter registration rate of at least 85 percent.[57] This opened the door for the election of African Americans, all of whom were Republicans. African Americans were elected as Republicans to public offices throughout the South during Reconstruction, including as mayors, sheriffs, and judges. The first twenty-two African American mem-bers of the United States Congress were elected during Reconstruction, all as Republicans from the Old Confederacy. They had varied backgrounds and although more than half were former slaves, by the time they were elected to Congress, the group included lawyers, ministers, teachers, college presidents, a banker, and a publisher; half of them had previous experience in state legislatures.[58] Frederick Douglass, an African American civil rights pioneer, ran for the 1871 Republican nomination for the newly created posi-tion of District of Columbia Delegate to the House of Representatives, los-ing by four votes. At one point, Louisiana had a black governor, and the South Carolina House of Representatives had a black majority. Other state legislatures had near majorities or a substantial black presence. African Americans understood who supported Reconstruction and its improvement of black life—the Republicans—and who did not—the Democrats—and cast their ballots accordingly.

Ultimately, the amalgamation of consistent conservative opposition, violent confrontations, and growing Republican ambivalence and weakness ended Reconstruction. The end opened the door to the dismantling of the legal structure that was established to help bring about freedom and equality to former slaves. The "redemption" of the South, as the return of white power was termed, came about through violence and intimidation and led to the reintroduction of white supremacy. Southern redemption also led to the construction of numerous barriers designed to stop the participation and election of African Americans: literacy tests, grandfather clauses, poll taxes, and other impediments. Once in place, conservative governments began to rewrite their constitutions and laws to eliminate blacks from the political process. Table 2.1 illustrates the devastating impact southern "redemption" and "home rule" had on post-Reconstruction black political officeholding. The table clearly demonstrates that black officeholding declined as southern conservatives regained control of state governments.

The elimination of black elected officials was the result of removing virtually all African Americans from voter registration rolls. In Louisiana, over 130,000 blacks had gone to the polls in 1896. They were a voting majority in twenty-six parishes. In 1900, two years after the adoption of a new state constitution modeled on Mississippi's, Negro voter registration dropped 96 percent. A bare 5,000 blacks now voted in Louisiana; in not a single parish could their votes carry an election. In Alabama, a state with an adult Negro population of nearly 300,000, the number of blacks permitted to vote in the new century hovered around 3,500. In Georgia, some 10,000 out of an adult population of 370,000 blacks now voted. In Virginia, it was about 15,000 out of a possible 250,000. Fewer than 1,000 blacks voted in Mississippi; some 300,000 were by white standards qualified to vote.[59]

Table 2.1   Post-Reconstruction Black Officeholding

	1876	1878	1880	1882	1884	1886	1888	1890
Number	162	74	75	71	66	56	45	35
Percentage change		−54.3	+1.3	−5.3	−7	−15	−19.6	−22

Source: J. Morgan Kousser, "The Voting Rights Act and the Two Reconstructions," in Bernard Grofman and Chandler Davidson, eds., *Controversies in Minority Voting: The Voting Rights Act in Perspective* (Washington, DC: Brookings Institution Press, 1992), pp. 135–176, table 1, quoted in Richard Vallely, *The Two Reconstructions: The Struggle for Black Enfranchisement* (Chicago: University of Chicago Press, 2004).

Concomitant with the political evisceration of African Americans, southern conservatives took a further step toward restricting social and economic movement by instituting a series of "black codes," which constricted the rights of newly freed slaves.

The return of blacks to a subservient role in America was accelerated by a number of notable court decisions. *United States v. Cruikshank, United States v. Reese,* the *Slaughter-House Cases,* and *Plessy v. Ferguson* were among the most important in rolling back black progress and solidifying the white supremacy long sought after by southern conservatives who wanted to continue slavery and who opposed Reconstruction. In the *Cruikshank* and *Reese* cases, the Supreme Court denied blacks the protection of the Fourteenth Amendment in all cases except those of official state discrimination and affirmed the power of the individual states to control voting requirements.[60] *Slaughter-House* held that the Fourteenth Amendment only gave Congress the power to outlaw public, not private, discrimination.[61] *Plessy* allowed for state-level segregation provided that it was "separate but equal."[62] These decisions codified second-class citizenship for African Americans, and in little more than a generation after Reconstruction began, it was again legal to exclude blacks from jury service, prohibit interracial marriage, segregate schools and public accommodations, and disenfranchise black voters.[63]

The stage also was set to allow hate groups to form and operate with impunity. The Ku Klux Klan, the Knights of the White Camelia, and the White Brotherhood were among the groups that became a way of life in the South. These groups facilitated violence against and intimidation of black southerners. Without the presence of federal troops to curb their activities, their reign of terror had a chilling effect on African American political participation and social life. Overt racism and a eugenics movement reemerged, fueled by pseudoscientific biological studies that purported to support the notion of black genetic inferiority.

Conclusion

The turning back of the political, social, and economic clock for African Americans during GOP government control is significant in understanding the mistrust that characterizes the relationship between blacks and the Republican Party. The GOP ceased to fight the changes that were being put in place by conservatives throughout the South and acquiesced to conservative Democratic racism; in some cases, Republicans joined the Democrats in repressing African Americans. By this point in the history of the nation, the Republican Party had completely capitulated to the opposition and, in the process, turned its back on some of its most fundamental founding principles.

The evolution of African American political support reflects the changing nature of US politics, most notably the way the Republican and Democratic parties switched their positions on racial and social issues over the years. This switch placed the GOP on the wrong side of the political fence from most African Americans. It did not start out that way. In the abolition and Reconstruction eras, African American support for the Grand Old Party was virtually unanimous. The relationship between African Americans and the Republican Party during the Civil War and Reconstruction eras was the progeny of a simple political quid pro quo: Republicans wanted southern black votes to secure their burgeoning political dominance and, in exchange for such support, African Americans wanted protection from discrimination, the enforcement of Reconstruction constitutional amendments and laws, and a greater share of freedom and equality. White northern Republicans and black elites coalesced and demanded full legal and political equality for African Americans. Their efforts culminated in the Republican-led Reconstruction, the launching point for an unprecedented era of black social and political opportunity. Given conservative Democratic racism of the day, African Americans had only one political option—the Republicans. The Democrats of that era were racial and social conservatives and used racism to justify undemocratic public policy. The political needs of Republicans and African Americans thus forged an alliance that produced (temporary) political dominance for Republicans, unprecedented access to the political process for African Americans, and historic numbers of black elected officials. These fruitful political results also created "a vexatious problem" that went unresolved for decades.[64] Over time, the GOP and African Americans moved in different directions.

Notes

1. Lorenzo Morris, "Race and the Rise and Fall of the Two-Party System," in Lorenzo Morris, ed., *The Social and Political Implications of the 1984 Jesse Jackson Presidential Campaign* (New York: Praeger, 1990), p. 67.

2. Samuel Eldersveld and Hanes Walton, *Political Parties in American Society*, 2nd ed. (Boston: Bedford/St. Martin's Press, 2000), pp. 4–8.

3. Hanes Walton, *Black Political Parties: An Historical and Political Analysis* (New York: Free Press, 1972), p. 1. See also Hanes Walton, *Black Politics: A Theoretical and Structural Analysis* (Philadelphia: J. B. Lippincott, 1972). There have been numerous political parties in America's political history. However, for the purposes of this study, "political parties" refers to the Republicans and Democrats unless otherwise noted.

4. Robert C. Smith, *Encyclopedia of African-American Politics* (New York: Facts on File, 2003), p. 264. See also Hanes Walton, *Black Republicans: The Politics of the Blacks and Tans* (Metuchen, NJ: Scarecrow Press, 1975).

5. See *Nixon v. Condon*, 286 US 73 and *Smith v. Allwright*, 321 US 666. The lily white movement is discussed in detail in Chapter 3.

6. A useful examination of the early years of the Republican Party can be found in Robert Engs and Randall Miller, eds., *The Birth of the Grand Old Party: The Republicans' First Generation* (Philadelphia: University of Pennsylvania Press, 2002). See also William Gienapp, *The Origins of the Republican Party, 1852–1856* (Oxford: Oxford University Press, 1987).

7. Eric Foner, "The Ideology of the Republican Party," in Engs and Miller, *The Birth of the Grand Old Party*, p. 9.

8. Gienapp, *The Origins of the Republican Party*, p. 4.

9. Louis Gould, *Grand Old Party: A History of the Republicans* (New York: Random House, 2003), p. 489.

10. Ibid., p. 483.

11. Ibid., p. 23.

12. Stanley B. Greenberg, *The Two Americas: Our Current Political Deadlock and How to Break It* (New York: Thomas Dunne Books/St. Martin's Press, 2004), p. 14.

13. Chip Berlet and Matthew Lyons, *Right-Wing Populism in America: Too Close for Comfort* (New York: Guilford Press, 2000), p. 243.

14. Robert Finch, interview by Ed Edwin, June 19, 1967, Columbia Oral History Project, Columbia University, transcript, p. 16.

15. Perhaps the most important intellectual contribution to the neoconservative movement is Irving Kristol, *Neo-conservatism: The Autobiography of an Idea* (New York: Ivan R. Dee, 1999). Other important contributors include Irwin Stelzer, *The Neocon Reader* (New York: Grove Press, 2005); Murray Friedman, *The Neoconservative Revolution: Jewish Intellectuals and Public Policy* (Cambridge: Cambridge University Press, 2005); and Christopher Demuth and William Kristol, *The Neoconservative Imagination: Essays in Honor of Irving Kristol* (Washington, DC: American Enterprise Institute Press, 1995).

16. See Earl Black and Merle Black, *The Rise of Southern Republicans* (Cambridge: Belknap/Harvard University Press, 2002); and Gould, *Grand Old Party*.

17. Black and Black, *Southern Republicans*, p. 228, quoting *Atlanta Constitution*, March 1, 1996.

18. Ibid., p. 215, quoting *New York Times*, November 6, 1980.

19. Ibid., p. 251.

20. Ibid., p. 214, quoting Charles Dunn and J. David Woodward, "Ideological Images for a Television Age," in Dilys Hill, Raymond Moore, and Phil Williams, eds., *The Reagan Presidency* (London: Macmillan, 1990), p 123.

21. The preeminent discussion of "linked fate" has been developed by Michael Dawson. Dawson argues that linked fate is the result of the shared history and common lived experience among African Americans and the various differences between blacks and other groups, specifically white Americans. See Michael Dawson, *Behind the Mule: Race and Class in African-American Politics* (Princeton: Princeton University Press, 1994), pp. 76–84.

22. The most significant book that explains the "invisible" nature of black politics is Hanes Walton, *Invisible Politics: Black Political Behavior* (Albany: State University of New York Press, 1985).

23. Walton, *Black Politics*, p. 11.

24. Dawson, *Behind the Mule*, p. 4. See also Michael Preston, Lenneal Henderson, and Paul Puryear, eds., *The New Black Politics: The Search for Political Power* (White Plains, NY: Longman, 1987); and Katherine Tate, *From Protest to Politics: The New Black Voters in American Elections* (Cambridge: Harvard University Press, 1993).

25. Walton, *Black Politics*, p. 12.

26. Ibid.

27. Ibid., p. 13.

28. Ibid.

29. Ibid., p. 15.

30. Hanes Walton, *African American Power and Politics: The Political Context Variable* (New York: Columbia University Press, 1997), p. 7.

31. Ibid., p. xxi.

32. Herbert Aptheker, ed., *A Documentary History of the Negro People in the United States* (New York: Citadel Press, 1969); Benjamin Quarles, *Black Abolitionists* (New York: Oxford University Press, 1969), quoted in Hanes Walton, *Black Republicans*, p. 15.

33. Vincent DeSantis, "The Republican Party and the Southern Negro, 1877–1897," *Journal of Negro History* 45, no. 2 (April 1960): 73.

34. Ibid.

35. Walton, *Black Republicans*, p. 22.

36. Ibid.

37. Gould, *Grand Old Party*, p. 52.

38. Eric Foner, *Free Soil, Free Labor, Free Men: The Ideology of the Republican Party Before the Civil War* (New York: John Wiley, 1978), pp. 266, 269; Michael Johnson, ed., *Abraham Lincoln, Slavery and the Civil War: Selected Writings and Speeches* (Boston: Bedford/St. Martin's Press, 2001), p. 73, quoted in Gould, *Grand Old Party*, p. 20.

39. Gould, *Grand Old Party*, pp. 34–35.

40. Ibid.

41. An excellent discussion of the Eastern Establishment can be found in Kevin Phillips, *The Emerging Republican Majority* (Garden City, NY: Anchor Books, 1970), pp. 83–93.

42. Eric Foner, *Reconstruction: America's Unfinished Revolution, 1863–1877* (New York: Harper & Row, 1988), p. 230.

43. Gould, *Grand Old Party*, p. 34.

44. Carl Frasure, "Charles Sumner and the Rights of the Negro," *Journal of Negro History* 13, no. 2 (April 1928): 126.

45. Mildred Bryant-Jones, "The Political Program of Thaddeus Stevens, 1865," *Phylon* 2, no. 2 (1941): 147.

46. Gould, *Grand Old Party*, p. 21.

47. Foner, *Reconstruction*, p. 231.

48. *Congressional Globe*, 40th Cong., 3rd sess., p. 1326; Foner, *Free Soil, Free Labor, Free Men*, pp. 291–297; *Congressional Globe*, 39th Cong., 2nd sess., p. 252, quoted in Foner, *Reconstruction*, p. 231.

49. Walton, *Black Republicans*, p. 21.

50. Ibid., pp. 21–22.

51. Some scholars date the start of Reconstruction to before the end of the Civil War. Examples in this regard are Eric Foner, who dates the start of the period to 1863, and W. E. B. DuBois, who cites 1860 as the start of Reconstruction. I acknowledge their start dates as fair and representative of the period in which there was widespread discussion of "reconstructing" southern society and do not take substantial issue with them. However, for this work, I settled on 1865, because that is the year in which the Thirteenth Amendment to the Constitution was adopted. The amendment, which abolished slavery, was the first of numerous laws and constitutional amendments designed to "reconstruct" the South and, by extension, the nation.

52. W. E. B. DuBois, *Black Reconstruction in America, 1860–1880* (New York: Free Press, 1992), p. viii.

53. Richard Vallely, *The Two Reconstructions: The Struggle for Black Enfranchisement* (Chicago: University of Chicago Press, 2004), p. 95.

54. Eric Foner, "Reconstruction Revisited," *Reviews in American History* 10, no. 4 (December 1982): 82. In the context of Reconstruction-era southern society, "home rule" was a euphemism for white supremacy.

55. Foner, "Reconstruction Revisited," p. 83.

56. Foner, *Reconstruction: America's Unfinished Revolution*, p. xxv.

57. US Bureau of the Census, Ninth Census, 1870 (Washington, DC: Government Printing Office, 1872), table 23; William C. Harris, *The Day of the Carpetbagger: Republican Reconstruction in Mississippi* (Baton Rouge: Louisiana State University Press, 1979), p. 76, note 30; William Russ, "Registration and Disfranchisement Under Radical Reconstruction," *Mississippi Valley Historical Review* 21 (September 1934): 177, quoted in Vallely, *The Two Reconstructions,* p. 33.

58. William L. Clay, *Just Permanent Interests: Black Americans in Congress, 1870–1991* (New York: Amistad Press, 1992), p. 13.

59. Harvard Sitkoff, *A New Deal for Blacks: The Emergence of Civil Rights as a National Issue,* vol. 1: *The Depression Decade* (Oxford: Oxford University Press, 1978), p. 4.

60. Ibid., p. 8; *U.S. v. Cruikshank*, 92 U.S. 542 (1876); and *U.S. v. Reese*, 92 U.S. 214 (1876).

61. 83 U.S. 36 (1873).

62. 163 U.S. 537 (1896).

63. Sitkoff, *A New Deal for Blacks,* p. 5.

64. DeSantis, "The Republican Party and the Southern Negro, 1877–1897," p. 71.

3

The Republicans
Fall Out of Favor

THE SUCCESSFUL COALITION OF NORTHERN WHITES AND southern blacks that put a Republican in the White House six years after the party's formation was not enough to overcome charges lodged by their opponents that the GOP was the "party for blacks." The post-Reconstruction Democratic resurgence led the GOP to seek ways to strengthen its southern standing by appealing to Democratic voters in hopes of maintaining control of the Senate and truly becoming a national party. In so doing, it began to support or acquiesce to policies that it had previously opposed. The Reconstruction era marked the zenith of African American support for the GOP, but when GOP policies began shifting, black support for the GOP began shifting as well.

In response to these policy shifts, concern developed in some segments of the black community about whether African American support should continue at such high levels—concern that contributed to the erosion of black support for the Republican Party. This appeal had been driven largely by feelings for "the martyred Lincoln and numerous outspoken radicals like Sumner and Stevens, whose names became associated in the Black community with the cause of freedom and liberty."[1] Blacks were disconcerted not only by the GOP's backtracking on many of its pre-Reconstruction promises but also by the political patronage and rewards bestowed on Carpetbaggers—northern whites who came to the South to take advantage of political, social, and business opportunities—and Scalawags—white southern natives who acceded to and joined northern whites for political control from which they were largely excluded. Blacks, while better positioned than they had ever been, were not seeing benefits commensurate with their overwhelming support for the Republican Party. Blacks began to see GOP promises as political expediency as the party capitulated to Democratic efforts to overturn Reconstruction and limit black voter participation. They also began to question the ability of the GOP to deal quickly

39

with the race question.[2] Reconstruction historiography has also suggested war weariness, bitter intra- and interparty strife, increased concern for economic expansion and capital accumulation, as well as race prejudice as factors that caused the "party of Lincoln" to fall short of its promises.[3]

Abraham Lincoln's presidency also led some blacks to question their fealty to the GOP. Though Lincoln was able to work with Radicals, he did not share their fundamental belief in racial equality. While Lincoln is credited with freeing the slaves with the Emancipation Proclamation, his views on African Americans alternated between ambivalence and contempt. He did not expend any political capital to support African Americans until he was forced to, and he looked for ways short of complete freedom and equality to deal with black issues. He even supported the repatriation of blacks to Africa to establish a colony, telling a White House gathering of black leaders that he was prepared to raise funds for the cause. His justification was fundamental:

> You and we are different races. We have between us a broader difference than exists between almost any other two races. Whether it is right or wrong, I need not discuss, but this physical difference is a great disadvantage to us both, as I think your race suffers very greatly, many of them by living among us, while ours suffers from your presence.[4]

Congress appropriated $100,000 in 1862, at Lincoln's request, to aid in the resettlement process and met with and encouraged black leaders who supported African emigration. Lincoln also overturned an order freeing slaves in Missouri, explaining:

> My paramount object in this struggle is to save the Union, and is not either to save or destroy slavery. If I could save the Union without freeing any slave, I would do it; and if I could save it by freeing all slaves, I would do it; and if I could do it by freeing some and leaving others alone, I would also do that. What I do about slavery and the Colored race, I do because I believe it helps save this Union.[5]

Lincoln's ambivalence toward African Americans did not inspire among Republicans the kind of fortitude they needed in the face of dedicated opposition to fulfill their promises to blacks throughout the South—to those who had won the GOP so many important elections during this period. It further convinced black leaders that the GOP would not, or could not, deliver for African Americans on the important social, economic, and political issues of the day.

The failure of land reform was the most significant economic contributor to blacks becoming disenchanted with the GOP. Special Field Order No. 15, issued on January 16, 1865, by Maj. Gen. William T. Sherman, promised to distribute abandoned white-owned land to blacks who lived along coastal South Carolina and Florida. There is little evidence that any land distribution ever occurred. Also important was the failure of the Freedman's Bureau, which was formed to assist distressed former slaves with basic job training and education. The bureau, which had the potential to add thousands of new workers to compete with white laborers, was constantly opposed by conservatives, never sufficiently funded, and closed with achievements far below its potential.

African Americans responded in a number of ways when the post-Reconstruction GOP turned away from them. Some accepted the new Republican policies toward African Americans and rejected the notion that they represented an abandonment of blacks. Many among this group worked to prevent a mass black exodus from the party and received personal recognition from President Rutherford Hayes. Some continued to fight for respect and position within the Republican Party and return it to its former racial policies. Others took the step of petitioning President Hayes for government funds to transport them to Liberia, an idea that had actually been previously floated by President Lincoln. Some simply withdrew from politics altogether.

A number of political episodes, decisions, and elections contributed to the GOP's falling out of favor with African American voters. Each of these instances had the effect of repelling black support for the party; some were due to Democrats actively competing for black support. One can see a push-pull effect. Some Republicans began to push away from blacks for fear of being seen as too close to them, while some Democrats began to try to pull in black voters—a move brought on, in part, by the migration of millions of southern blacks to northern cities, changing the political dynamics and demography in many large cities. The most important among these events were the 1877 Hayes-Tilden Compromise; the lily white movement; Franklin D. Roosevelt and the New Deal; Harry Truman and the Dixiecrats; the Republican embrace of conservatism, including the 1964 nomination of Barry Goldwater for the presidency and his ensuing campaign; and the party switching of a number of conservative Democrats who jumped to the Republican Party.

Hayes-Tilden Compromise of 1877

The political crisis that followed the 1876 presidential election set off the multigenerational deterioration of the relationship between African Americans and the GOP. While Democrat Samuel Tilden led the popular vote, Republican Rutherford B. Hayes was initially named winner of the

Electoral College vote. Democrats challenged the validity of the electoral count in Florida, Louisiana, and South Carolina, and the resulting controversy sent the election to Congress. This was significant because state and local elections were similarly contested and created a tense, tinder box–like environment that left many believing the country could return to civil war if the election controversy were not quickly settled. As the controversy continued, concern began to emerge that violence would occur as competing groups vied for control of state governments. The concern was a function of both parties' claiming victory and organizing separate governments in each state.

In January 1877, Congress set up a special electoral commission composed of ten members of Congress (five from each party) and five Supreme Court justices to decide the disputed votes. The tie-breaking vote went to Hayes, and the commission awarded all disputed votes to him. Southern Democrats planned to use a filibuster to block congressional approval of the commission's report, thereby preventing Hayes from being named president. The ensuing constitutional crisis led to the Hayes-Tilden Compromise of 1877. The deal provided for Democratic acceptance of Republican Hayes as president if a number of provisions were met, most notably the removal of the remaining federal troops from the former Confederate states and the appointment of at least one southern Democrat to Hayes's cabinet.

When Hayes began his presidency, he removed the remaining federal troops who were guarding the Louisiana and South Carolina statehouses. The soldiers were protecting the legislatures from being overrun by mobs of Tilden supporters who wanted "home rule" to decide the important state races and further their attempts to "redeem" southern government. This was a critical decision, because it was the military presence that was the primary bulwark for enforcing Reconstruction, protecting black civil rights, and creating an environment whereby blacks could pursue freedom and equality with a reduced fear of physical, economic, or social retribution.[6] This compromise effectively ended Reconstruction by allowing white racists into the leadership of those states and began a period of racial retrenchment and the reestablishment of the pre-Reconstruction status quo. Hayes's southern troop removal was part of a larger strategy to win more white conservative votes in the region. Hayes hoped the troop removal "would reconcile North and South, conciliate Southern Whites, and ingratiate the Republican Party with them."[7]

The Compromise of 1877 proved to be a perverse surgery on the US body politic. Surgery is designed to fix a problem, but the compromise had the opposite effect. It actually inserted a malady—race-driven de jure segregation that existed in various forms for nearly a century—into the US body politic. Once they regained congressional control, southern conservatives went about the business of undoing Reconstruction. By 1911, they repealed nearly 94 percent of Reconstruction legislation.[8]

The Lily White Movement

The post-Reconstruction "redemption" of the South set off a political fight for control of southern governments and their attendant patronage. Democratic racial appeals to white voters and Republican capitulation to conservative racial preferences ended Republican political domination of the era and returned Democrats to control of southern governments. Democrats were successful for two reasons. First, they made overt racial appeals to the considerable racial hostility and anxiety that existed among whites during the period. Second, Republicans responded to the new competition by mimicking Democrats in hopes that they could maintain control of southern governments. The appeal was simple: Democrats charged that the Republican Party was the "party of the Negro" and that it had to be crushed to return the South to its pre-Reconstruction white supremacist roots. Democrats argued that those who supported the Negro and the notion of black social, political, and economic equality also supported the idea of black domination of the white man—and voted Republican. Those who opposed the Negro voted Democrat. The perception that the GOP was too supportive of black freedom and equality and its electoral implications became a political albatross for Republicans, who began to fear being marginalized by the Democrats.

Many Republicans feared the charge would undermine their efforts to nationalize the party and responded by accelerating their efforts to back away from their support for and commitment to blacks. The shift created a schism that split Republicans into two factions—the "lily whites" and the "black and tans"—both seeking control of the party and its attendant power. Their battles for party control were critical components of the long, slow decline in black support for the GOP.[9] By the end of the nineteenth century, the lily white Republican movement had taken the upper hand in solidifying control of the party throughout the South, rendering the black and tans a valiant but increasingly impotent political faction.

The lily white faction represented white Republicans only, opposed black political participation, and supported the return of segregation and white supremacy.[10] It was the product of conservative-racist ideology and the "inherent demands and the customs of southern life-styles and occurred at a time when Republicans sought to expand their base of support into the South."[11] It also emerged out of frustration with black control of many state Republican parties, as this short period of black control affected white access to patronage. In many cases, lily whites worked with Democrats to disenfranchise African Americans.

Black and tan parties, which represented blacks and liberal whites, were established in response to and were born of two similar forces that required them to fight for control of their party.[12] First, black and tans had no viable party alternative to the GOP. Democrats were largely driven by racism and could not be seen as hospitable to blacks. Second, the memory of progressive GOP public policies was still sufficiently fresh in the minds of many blacks that there was reason to believe that the party could return to its roots. Black and tans supported Reconstruction-era policies such as racial equality and political participation. Black and tan Republican organizations developed differently throughout the South. Some were born in the 1880s, while others did not appear until the 1920s.[13] In some states, such as Tennessee and Arkansas, the black and tan movement was short-lived, whereas in others, such as South Carolina and Mississippi, "black and tanism" lasted until 1960.[14]

The contentiousness between the two factions occasionally turned violent, as evidenced in 1888 by a race riot that broke out in Texas when white Republicans tried to wrest party control from blacks at that year's state convention.[15] For African Americans, this factional conflict came to characterize the racial power struggle over who would lead the party—the multiracial coalition of blacks and tans or the conservative lily white faction. The formation of these schisms, coupled with the increasing support given to lily whites by national Republicans, confirmed in the eyes of many African Americans that their presence and support were unwanted.

This period was particularly vexing for Republicans seeking to establish southern strongholds. On the one hand, black migration north presented new opportunities for the GOP to add support in that part of the country; on the other hand, southern white migration meant that the GOP could begin to make inroads there.[16] However, as Gould noted, "The dilemma was that the policies that spoke to one group alienated the other."[17] President Warren G. Harding angered African Americans during the 1920 campaign by saying, "You can't give one right to a white man and deny it to a black man. But I want you to know that I do not mean that white people and black people should be forced to associate together in accepting their equal rights at the hands of the nation."[18]

The irony of the lily white movement lies in the fact that the GOP lost control of the South anyway, even though they capitulated to southern conservative racial preferences. Their attempts to compete with Democrats on racial repression by mimicking conservatives were viewed as phony and insincere to many white southerners who viewed the Democratic Party as most serious about protecting their political, social, and economic position. By walking away from its historic commitment to blacks, the party alienated a substantial part of its support base and rendered itself impotent throughout the South. Consequently, the Republican Party's multigenerational southern irrelevance began, in part, because it sought to be seen as a conservative alternative to the Democrats, who had long before established its conservative credentials.

Franklin D. Roosevelt and the New Deal

While southern Democratic race baiting led southern Republicans to purge African Americans from the party, northern Democrats were beginning to make faint, halting moves toward the black community. The moves were due less to a sincere change of heart regarding African Americans than to the changing demographic realities of the 1930s. Millions of black southerners uprooted themselves and moved to eastern seaboard cities like Washington, DC, Baltimore, Philadelphia, New York, and Boston, as well as to Midwest industrial centers like Cincinnati, Cleveland, Chicago, Detroit, and Pittsburgh looking for work and a new life free from the codified bigotry that ruled their lives in the South. These new voters forced northern Democrats to rethink some of their racial positions for fear of losing elections to Republicans, who were still viewed by many African Americans of the day as the lesser of two evils.

The new demography and the economic crisis of the Great Depression changed the political calculus of the nation, and it was northern Democrats who began to seize the opportunity. The Depression disproportionately damaged African Americans. Black unemployment, already higher than any other group in the country, became, in many cities, two- to fourfold their black population proportions. Nearly one-third of black Baltimoreans were unemployed in March 1931, almost twice the black proportion of the city's population. According to the Urban League, by 1931, one-third of southern urban blacks were jobless; a year later, that figure grew to more than one-half.[19] The persistent unemployment only increased antagonism and economic desperation in black communities around the nation.[20] Jobs that had customarily been considered "Negro jobs," such as janitorial and sanitation work, were now being filled by whites upended by the economic downturn. The firing of blacks so that their jobs could be given to whites became accepted policy.[21]

Republican president Herbert Hoover's inability to remedy the crisis only intensified questions about the party's ability to successfully govern the country. Hoover's economic failures, coupled with his disbanding of the black Tenth Cavalry, his refusal to be photographed with black leaders, the smallest-ever percentage of black delegates to the 1932 Republican National Convention, and a weak plank on black rights all helped set the stage for a sea change in black support for the party.[22] Even with the erosion of black support for the GOP, most blacks stood with Hoover in the 1932 election, because the thought of supporting a Democrat—the party that did so much to overturn Reconstruction and return blacks to second-class citizenship—was still not palatable.

Franklin D. Roosevelt stepped into the void and proved to be a major factor in drawing African Americans away from the Republican Party.

Roosevelt's New Deal economic policies were seen as more favorable to black interests than those of previous administrations and "confirmed the importance of the link between politics and economics for African Americans."[23] Many of Roosevelt's policies designed to deal with the Great Depression and its impact on the larger white economy aided African Americans, too. Particularly noteworthy was Roosevelt's creation of the Fair Employment Practices Committee (FEPC) and the Work Projects Administration (WPA). The FEPC had a favorable effect on the structure of the labor market and was credited with providing "basic earnings for one million Black families."[24] The WPA was among the first federal government projects to include nondiscriminatory clauses in its operating guidelines.[25] As a consequence of these and other policies, Roosevelt's presidency helped African Americans view the Democrats more favorably. Like African American support for the GOP during Reconstruction, black support for Roosevelt and the Democrats was a rational act—the community responded favorably to the party that best spoke to their needs.

This is not to say that Roosevelt was especially progressive on racial issues. He resisted efforts to desegregate the armed forces, and the majority of his key advisers were given to appeasing the "Southern branch of the party and actively tried to insulate the campaign and the early presidency from black leaders."[26] Roosevelt refused to meet with the National Association for the Advancement of Colored People (NAACP) and had no staffers in his administration devoted solely to racial issues.[27] Given this, it can be argued that African Americans became Democrats in response to the economic benefits of the New Deal, and they voted for Roosevelt while overlooking his modest racial record.[28] In this regard, the New Deal's significance in generating black support for the Democrats was largely ancillary—a by-product of other efforts. Roosevelt's administration was far more concerned with effectively responding to the economic collapse brought on by the Depression than with addressing racial issues.

President Franklin Roosevelt made it palatable for African Americans to consider voting for a Democrat. The New Deal had an additional attraction to African Americans: it provided white-collar work to African Americans and created a small class of black bureaucrats. This change provided "important evidence of the New Deal's role in stimulating new kinds of politicization and involvement with government on the part of Black Americans."[29] For the first time since Reconstruction, African Americans began to see themselves in government, and the presence of these new black bureaucrats became one of the reasons the larger black community took a more sympathetic view of the Democratic Party. The addition of African Americans to the New Deal coalition of blue-collar workers, farmers, and ethnics congealed the party into congressional dominance that lasted until the 1994 congressional elections.

Two other important Democrats during the Roosevelt administration are notable for helping move blacks toward the Democrats: First Lady Eleanor Roosevelt and Secretary of the Interior Harold Ickes. Mrs. Roosevelt was seen as far more progressive on civil rights than her husband and has been credited with prodding the reluctant president to move toward a more conciliatory racial posture. Eleanor Roosevelt, like her husband and many nonsoutherners, had little contact with blacks and little understanding of the raw reality of racism, discrimination, and segregation. Her meetings with black leaders led her to understand more fully the realities of being black in America, and she responded favorably within the context of her contemporary existence. Her public friendships with prominent black leaders, particularly Mary McLeod Bethune of the National Council of Negro Women, while politically embarrassing for the president, were symbolically significant to African Americans. Mrs. Roosevelt became a forceful voice in favor of civil rights legislation, and her advocacy helped open White House doors to black leaders for meetings with the president so they could personally make their case for more governmental involvement in ending racial discrimination.

Ickes ended segregation in the Interior Department cafeterias and restrooms in 1933, a move that other cabinet secretaries followed.[30] He also required Public Works Administration (PWA) construction projects to hire blacks as skilled and unskilled laborers. To that end, "Ickes stipulated that all PWA contracts include a clause specifying that the number of Blacks hired and their percentage of the project payroll be equal to the proportion of Negroes in the 1930 occupational census."[31] Under Ickes, nearly 30 percent of PWA low-rent housing projects were reserved for blacks, and the US Housing Authority, between 1937 and 1942, reserved 34 percent of its 122,000 housing units for African Americans.[32] Millions more were spent on building or repairing black schools, hospitals, and recreational facilities. While the new public housing supported existing segregated housing patterns and the repaired schools, hospitals, and recreational facilities were still segregated, the mere fact that blacks and their communities were getting substantial government commitments was viewed positively by African Americans and became a magnet for the Democrats.

Harry Truman and the Dixiecrats

President Harry Truman and the political events of 1948 are an underappreciated milepost in the movement of African Americans away from the GOP. This period was important to the political shift of African Americans for two reasons. First, President Truman expanded on Roosevelt's limited and tentative steps toward racial moderation and reconciliation. Truman established the President's Committee on Civil Rights (CCR) in 1947, which helped set the civil rights agenda for the next two decades. The CCR called for guaranteed voting rights and equal employment opportunity, the first time since Reconstruction that an official federal government organ made such a statement. The CCR also called for legislation to prohibit racial violence, segregation, and poll taxes. The Justice Department, also in 1947, began submitting briefs to courts in support of civil rights. A year later, Truman signed Executive Order 9981, which desegregated the armed services.

Second, southern racial conservatives walked out of the 1948 Democratic National Convention to protest the efforts of Truman and others to include a pro–civil rights plank in that year's party platform. The conservative protesters, who came to be known as Dixiecrats, left to form the States' Rights Democratic Party; their slogan was "Segregation Forever!" They nominated South Carolina governor J. Strom Thurmond to run as their presidential nominee and Mississippi governor Fielding Wright to be his running mate. Thurmond's campaign called for stronger states' rights and opposition to any form of racial desegregation.[33] The 1948 walkout represented a repudiation of racial liberalization that had begun to take root in the Democratic Party.

While Truman narrowly overcame the Dixiecrats to win reelection, the victory validated his tentative racial policies and positioned him to build upon them. His reelection was attractive to African Americans who felt that they had a president who would attempt to be fair with them. The 1948 election also proved to be the beginning of the end of racial conservative domination of the Democratic Party. While the final ending of racial conservative domination of the Democratic Party lay two decades away from the 1948 election, Truman's reelection led to the remaking of US public policy with the passage of landmark legislation that guaranteed civil rights, voting rights, and fair housing. Many of the Dixiecrats of that era began to rethink their allegiance to the Democratic Party; some eventually made their way to the Republican Party—yet another wedge driven between African Americans and the GOP.

While many analysts have pointed to 1964 as the major turning point in the movement of African Americans from the GOP to the Democratic Party, 1948 may actually be a more significant year. It is understandable to view 1964 as *the* turning point; the civil rights act of that year, coupled with the Goldwater presidential campaign and the widely followed civil rights movement were critical. However, the efforts of 1948 were significant and accelerated the movement of black public opinion away from the GOP. It was in 1948 that a majority of African Americans (56 percent) first shifted their party identification to the Democrats.[34] The electoral movement in 1964 simply took African American support for the Democratic Party from a solid majority to a near monopoly. Within a century, the Republicans went from near monopoly support from African Americans to near unanimous rejection.

The GOP Embrace of Conservatism

The GOP did not respond to the shifting party alignment of African Americans by redoubling its efforts to win black support; instead, the party moved further right ideologically.[35] While the party always had conservative elements, it wasn't until the 1960s that the "Republican Right" evolved into a dominant, complex, organized, and effective political force.[36] These conservatives loathed acceptance of New Deal policies by liberal and moderate Republicans and wanted to seize control of the party to overturn such public policy. An uneasy alliance developed among conservative intellectuals, local groups, journalists, traditionalists, libertarians, anticommunists, and right-wing politicians to wrest control of the Republican Party from the liberal and moderate Eastern Establishment, those Republicans with the common bond of Ivy League educations, exclusive club memberships, and financial success who had dominated the party from its inception.[37]

For generations, the Eastern Establishment controlled the party because they controlled party purse strings. That began to change when increasingly impatient southern conservatives who began to develop financial strength sought to play a more critical role in party activity, and "by the 1950s . . . businesspeople and political leaders from the South and West increasingly challenged these power brokers within the GOP."[38] These coalescing Republicans created organizations and communications mechanisms such as the *National Review* to promote conservative ideas. Racial conservatism was one of the areas in which this alliance was able to generate consensus. Over time, the party became a comfortable place for racial conservatives who opposed the developing racial moderation and liberalism of the Democratic Party on issues such as civil rights and segregation. This racial conservatism was embraced rather than rebuffed because it was seen as a way to make political inroads in the South.

In the context of this study, racial conservatism refers to an ideological philosophy held by whites that seeks to shape the racial status quo to their benefit and resist any changes in the social, political, and economic status quo that benefit minorities. Racial conservatives oppose policy changes that would result in an enhanced position for African Americans or a perceived diminution of status for whites, or both. The importance of race as a social, political, and economic motivator cannot be ignored:

> Race looms large with respect to the other issues and concerns of American politics because our society is organized around race. It is certainly no exaggeration to say that race is the primary social cleavage within the population. Thus the political salience of race is so high because it galvanizes and mobilizes the electorate along social boundaries that are deep and thoroughgoing in the social life of the nation . . . there are very few cross cutting cleavages with respect to race—whites and Blacks continue to live in separate social worlds.[39]

The racial question in the United States has been the subject of considerable research and study since the early years of our nation, and it is generally conceded that institutional racism, in various amounts, permeates segments of the general society of the United States.[40] The GOP greatly benefited from the change in racial attitudes in the Democratic Party. As one former county commissioner in rural North Carolina noted, "The Democratic party left the white people. When they left, that is what caused the new wave of Republicanism."[41]

Previous research demonstrated how racial conservatism plays a role in congressional partisanship. One of the most important works in this regard is that of political scientists Edward Carmines and James Stimson, who show that in terms of racial voting, there has been clear movement toward racial conservatism on the part of Republicans in Congress. They refer to it as "secular realignment of partisan voting patterns on race."[42] As political scientist V. O. Key notes, racial conservatism is greatest in states with the highest proportions of blacks, and where white supremacy demagogues seem to be most strident:

> The harshness and ceaselessness of race discussion in South Carolina are not matters of coincidence. It is but a short time, as time must be measured, since the state had three [African Americans] for every two White persons. In 1900, the population was 58.4 percent [African American]; in 1910, 55.2; in 1920, 51.4; in 1930, 45.6. In 1940 the state's population was 42.9 percent [African American], a ratio exceeded only by Mississippi's 49.2 percent.[43]

Given Key's thesis—race has been a political and social constant in the American South—it is no surprise that the South is where the Republican Party has been most successful in attracting conservative white voters.

Racial conservatism has traditionally, though not exclusively, been grounded in the American South, a region of the country that has seen the most partisan change. Historically known as a Democratic stronghold, the American South is now solidly Republican. While the name of the dominant party has changed, the dominant ideology—conservatism—remains the same. The southern Democratic racial conservatives of the first sixty years of the twentieth century are now Republicans. This change began to take shape in the mid 1960s:

> Racial conservatism evolved from [1964 Republican presidential nominee Barry] Goldwater's conservatism, not from traditional racism, and it depended for its expression upon the new conservative dominance of the Republican party. We can even date its origin with some confidence, for it arises from Goldwater's coherent statement of the issue in *Conscience of a Conservative* (1960), very widely read and undoubtedly influential in the months before the 1964 election.[44]

This racial conservatism emerged in the form of "opposition to strong federal intervention in civil rights," which was beginning to become a dominant issue in Congress.[45] This becomes even more apparent when one considers the results of the 1964 presidential election. Goldwater made a name for himself among racial conservatives in the South with his opposition to the Civil Rights Act of 1964 (Goldwater was one of eight nonsoutherners in the Senate to vote against the act) and his general position on civil rights issues. He campaigned in stark racial terms, particularly in the South. His Texas campaign tried to exploit white racial economic fears with a poster that targeted employees and employers. The poster had images of an unsmiling white man with the word "fired" placed below his face and a smiling black man with the word "hired" placed below his face. The language was stark:

> Employees read this: Did you know that Lyndon Johnson's Civil Rights Bill can get you fired from your job and give it to a person of another race? No matter what ability you have to do your job . . . or how much seniority you have on your job . . .you can lose your job because of Johnson's Civil Rights Bill. This is your last chance. Vote to put an end to racial favoritism . . . vote to protect your job . . . your family . . . your home. Employers read this: THIS IS YOUR LAST CHANCE TO SAVE YOUR FREEDOM TO RUN YOUR OWN BUSINESS AS YOU CHOOSE![46]

The tagline of the poster implored voters to support Goldwater, stating, "In your heart, you know he's right."

The South repaid his ideological support and hardball racial politics in the 1964 presidential election. Goldwater lost to President Lyndon Johnson by an overwhelming margin nationally, winning the electoral votes of just six states. However, five of those states were in the South, and he won those states with, in some cases, overwhelming percentages of the vote: 87 percent in Mississippi, 70 percent in Alabama, 59 percent in South Carolina, 57 percent in Louisiana, and 54 percent in Georgia. Goldwater's southern triumph demonstrated the stark contrast between the South and the rest of the nation in terms of its racial conservatism.

Goldwater's defeat, however, was the birth of the "Southern Strategy" that Richard Nixon successfully implemented in the 1968 election. This Southern Strategy, which is discussed in more detail in Chapter 6, played on growing southern dissatisfaction with the Democratic Party on racial issues and was a landmark in the partisan realignment of the South. Despite the fact that, as of 1972, Republicans trailed Democrats in party identification by 15 percentage points, twelve seats in the US Senate, and seventy-five seats in the US House, Nixon swept every state of the Old Confederacy in defeating George McGovern for the presidency.[47] As political scientists Merle Black and Earl Black have noted, the GOP's willingness to use and, in many elections, rely on the Southern Strategy has "continued to make the GOP a fundamental unattractive and hostile institution to many southern Blacks."[48]

Party Switchers

What may seem like a 1990s phenomenon of southern Democrats becoming Republicans, party switching has a long history that dates back to the earliest days of political parties in the United States. Indeed, the Republican Party was created when members of the American, Free Soil, and Whig parties and some Northern Democrats left their parties and organized under the newly created Republican banner.

Party switching is seen as less controversial now than in the early days of the Republican Party. According to historian William Gienapp, "For many antebellum Americans a party identity, once formed, established a lifelong loyalty that became more powerful with age."[49] Extended support for a party tended to reinforce "emotional links between a voter and that party."[50] While some voters may still rely on historical connections to explain support for a particular political party, the extensive party shifting of voters in the last two decades—particularly southern whites who left the Democrats to affiliate with the GOP—suggests that individuals are more flexible with their party preferences. It is difficult to imagine the wholesale disruption that switching parties caused in the immediate antebellum period. In that period, it was not unusual for friendships and associations to end if one were to switch parties.

Party switching occurs for three primary reasons. First, legislative redistricting may create a circumstance in which a district takes on a critical mass of new voters registered in the opposition party. In such circumstances, certain candidates may feel that their best, or only, chance to win is to run under a different party banner. Incumbents in this situation can innoculate themselves from significant challengers in either primary or general elections.[51] While the new party may have leaders and potential candidates who are bothered by possible implications of the switch on their personal electoral chances, they tend to overlook those concerns if the switcher is a popular incumbent who is all but assured of victory.

Second, some officials may believe that they are no longer in ideological agreement with the party. This is a particularly common explanation for conservatives who leave the Democrats to align with the Republicans. Since the 1960s, virtually all of the southern Democrats who became Republicans cited growing Democratic liberalism as a factor in their decision; many charged that they didn't leave the Democratic Party, the party left them. They argued that the Democrats no longer represented their conservatism and that they found a better fit with the increasingly conservative GOP. As

Strom Thurmond noted when explaining his switch, "After I got up here [in the Senate], I soon found that the Republican Party was more in line with my thinking and the philosophy of the people of South Carolina than the Democratic Party at the national level."[52]

Third, elected officials may seek greater political power by aligning with the majority party. This may be the deal maker for certain legislators who have been in the majority party but now find themselves in the minority. In such circumstances, the maintenance of seniority and ability to continue chairing a committee with all its attendant power and influence by switching parties may prove too attractive an offer for some being wooed to switch. The House Republican Conference offered such benefits to southern Democrats to encourage party switching during the 1990s.

In some cases, party switchers cite multiple reasons when explaining their decision. Alabama senator Richard Shelby, who became a Republican in 1994, stated upon leaving the Democrats that he felt alienated from the national Democratic Party and that all his relatives, previously solid Democrats, were "moving to the Republican party step by step."[53] He concluded that there was no future for any conservative southern Democrat in the Democratic Party. His sentiment was representative of many Democratic Party switchers in the mid-1990s. Shelby, in this regard, could have been seen as following his constituents. Because these Democrats were so conservative, their new allegiance to the GOP was often seen by African Americans as further evidence that Republicans were turning "right" ideologically. Since African Americans, as a group, have never been uniformly conservative, any party that becomes more conservative will necessarily be less attractive to them.

It should be noted, however, that contemporary party switching rarely occurs in a vacuum or appears out of thin air. Both parties seek to identify and cultivate potential party switchers in hopes that, when the time is appropriate for the target, a switch can be easily facilitated. Often, back-channel negotiations have been undertaken to settle on certain perks to be given to the switcher, such as maintaining seniority, chairing a committee or subcommittee, or both. Additionally, covert steps are taken to smooth the transition in the legislator's district to help mitigate any political problems that are likely to arise from a party switch.

As it pertains to the evolution of African American support for the Republican Party, a creeping moderation on racial issues began to emerge among Democrats in the World War II era. The shift toward a more inclusive Democratic Party that actively sought black support ran counter to the interests of racial conservatives who preferred the continuance of the racial status quo. These southern conservatives were, for more than a century, members of a party that opposed the racial equality and freedom on which the Republican Party was formed. Those conservatives began to feel that they were being pushed out of a party that no longer held some of the same policy stances.

The 1960s marked the beginning of an era when many conservative Democrats—voters and elected officials—shifted their allegiance and became Republicans. Some of these new Republican officeholders had earned reputations for opposing public policy that was friendly to African Americans; some came to office on platforms that were hostile to black interests. So while their moves were good for the GOP in attracting conservative white voters, they also served as an additional signal that the party was no longer hospitable to African Americans or their interests. Indeed, the Republican Party came to welcome, rather than repudiate, this brand of conservatism. From a purely electoral standpoint, this is not a problem for the GOP, because it has allowed the party to dominate the South and much of the nation. However, it is bad for US political race relations, because it reflects a resistance to civil rights equality.

Among the notable southern congressional Democrats who switched parties after 1960 were Floyd Spence (1962), Strom Thurmond (1964), Albert Watson (1965), Jesse Helms (1971), Trent Lott (1972), Phil Gramm (1983), Andy Ireland (1984), Bill Grant (1989), Tommy Robinson (1989), Mike Parker (1994), Richard Shelby (1994), Billy Tauzin (1995), Jimmy Hayes (1995), Nathan Deal (1995), Greg Laughlin (1995), Wes Watkins (1996), Ralph Hall (2002), and Virgil Goode (2002—he spent about two years as an Independent before joining the Republicans).[54] Over time, "many of the region's most prominent Republicans, men such as Thurmond, Helms, Lott, Gramm, and Shelby, were conservatives who had been born and raised as Democrats but who had come to view the Republican party as their appropriate ideological home."[55]

These congressional Democrats were joined by other prominent southern Democrats, including Mills Godwin (1973), then Democratic governor of Virginia who later served as a Republican in the same office; former Texas governor John Connally, who later sought the Republican presidential nomination; Rick Perry (1990), who switched parties while campaigning to become the Texas agriculture commissioner; Louisiana governor Buddy Roemer (1991); and Amy Tuck, lieutenant governor of Mississippi (2002).[56]

It is quite possible that party switching among conservative Democrats could have extended well beyond the relatively few, but prominent, examples at the national level that have emerged in the past few decades. Many veteran conservative Democrats who were nearing the end of their careers in the late 1960s and early 1970s may have decided to just ride out the balance of their time in Congress comforted by the power—in the form of committee and subcommittee chairs—they accumulated from years in the majority even though they became increasingly estranged from their party. For example, given his racism and hostility to his black constituents, it is difficult to believe that Representative James L. McMillan (D-SC) would have remained a Democrat if he had entered the House in 1978 instead of in 1938. Given the perquisites and power derived from being in the majority, it would not have been in the political interest of these long-serving southern Democrats to go from the well-entrenched majority to a weak minority. Also, the number of conservative Democrats to leave the party and align with the Republicans would have been higher if the GOP had taken control of the House sooner than they did (1994). By the mid-1990s, many conservative Democrats had already switched parties—in many cases, even before running for office.

The party switching of many conservative Democrats simply reinforced the emerging view among many African Americans that the GOP was turning away from its historic support for black America. After all, Republicans were more hostile to black interests than were Democrats. The open arms that welcomed these new Republicans represented a philosophical and ideological switch in the party. It had the same impact that the lily white movement had on African Americans—it chilled black support for the GOP. It is notable to African Americans that some of the Republicans who became notorious for their use of race to generate racial hostility in their campaigns and who opposed legislation deemed helpful to African Americans were one-time Democrats, including Strom Thurmond, Jesse Helms, and Trent Lott. The Democrats look better relative to Republicans when a Democrat with a history of racism becomes a Republican. These prominent party switchers made the Democrats more attractive to African Americans.

The 1990s round of party switching was politically devastating to Democratic and African American political interests. For Democrats, it helped break the hold the party had on southern votes, which, by extension, meant loss of its control of Congress and, to a lesser extent, the presidency. This was a critical development, because Democrats had controlled all southern Senate seats for half a century. This domination gave them a twenty-two-seat head start, requiring them to win fewer seats to control that body and forcing Republicans to overwhelmingly dominate the rest of the nation to control the Senate. By breaking the Democrats' southern stranglehold, Republicans were able to win control of Congress. By 2005, Democrats were in the reverse position. They controlled four southern Senate seats, requiring Democratic dominance of the rest of the nation to control that body.

To many African Americans, this change represented the "enemy" in charge, much like during the post-Reconstruction era. In both eras, the party that was more resistant to black progress controlled the government. African Americans were additionally hurt, because black members of Congress were overwhelmingly Democrats and the party's minority status meant that senior black Democrats would not chair committees and wield the significant power that goes with being in the majority. We now have a situation in which the Congressional Black Caucus is at its largest but, arguably, has far less power than it did when it was half its current size but with Democrats controlling the House.

Black Votes for GOP Presidential Nominees

The effect that African American support for the GOP has had in its 150-year evolution can be seen electorally in a number of circumstances, most prominently in the percentage of African Americans who vote Republican in presidential elections. Table 3.1 shows the African American support for Republican presidential nominees in vote percentages from 1936 to 2004 and tracks the decline in black support for the GOP. The table clearly demonstrates that black support for the Republican Party declined as the party became more conservative. As it became more conservative, particularly relative to the Democratic Party, it welcomed party switchers, some of whom had previously established reputations as racists. The more the party became viewed as supportive of racists, the less African American support it received.

Table 3.1 Percentage of Black Vote That Went to GOP Presidential Nominee, 1936–2004

Year	Nominee	Percentage	Year	Nominee	Percentage
1936	Alfred Landon	28	1972	Richard Nixon	13
1940	Wendell Willkie	32	1976	Gerald Ford	15
1944	Thomas Dewey	40	1980	Ronald Reagan	12
1948	Thomas Dewey	23	1984	Ronald Reagan	9
1952	Dwight Eisenhower	24	1988	George H. W. Bush	10
1956	Dwight Eisenhower	39	1992	George H. W. Bush	11
1960	Richard Nixon	32	1996	Bob Dole	12
1964	Barry Goldwater	6	2000	George W. Bush	9
1968	Richard Nixon	15	2004	George W. Bush	11

Sources: David Bositis, *Blacks and the 2004 Republican National Convention* (Washington, DC: Joint Center for Political and Economic Studies, 2004), p. 9, citing 1936–1956 data from Everett Carll Ladd Jr. and Charles D. Hadley, *Transformations of the American Party System: Political Coalitions from the New Deal to the 1970s* (New York: Norton, 1975); 1960–1980 partisan identification from Paul R. Abramson, John H. Aldrich, and David W. Rohde, *Change and Continuity in the 1984 Elections;* 1960–1980 presidential preference data from Gallup Opinion Index 1980; 1984 presidential preference data from CBS/*New York Times* exit poll, November 1986; 1988 presidential preference data from ABC News/Capital Cities; 1988 party identification data from JCPES Gallup Survey; 1992 party identification data from Home Box Office/Joint Center Survey; 1992 presidential preference data from Voter Research and Surveys; 1996 vote data from Voter News Service; 1996 party identification data from 1996 JCPES National Opinion Poll; 2000 vote data from Voter News Service; 2000 party identification data from 2000 JCPES National Opinion Poll.

Three presidential elections warrant particular attention, because the Republican nominee's performance was directly affected by GOP efforts to push away black support in an effort to win white conservative votes or by increased Democratic efforts to win black votes. First, Republican Thomas Dewey's 23 percent of the black vote in the 1948 presidential election was a seventeen-point decline from his 1944 performance. The change was less about Dewey than about what his Democratic opponent, Harry Truman, did as president. Truman's desegration of the military and his establishing of a civil rights committee proved irresistible to many African Americans, particularly given the weak Republican response to these events. Second, Republican Barry Goldwater's "states' rights" campaign for the 1964 presidency was a substantial turnoff for African Americans and the primary reason why he received fewer black votes (26 percentage points) than Richard Nixon received in 1960. Third, President Reagan's receipt of 9 percent of the black vote in 1984, 3 percentage points fewer than in 1980, was brought about by a number of his policy positions, including, but not limited to, his stances on South African apartheid, opposition to the Martin Luther King holiday bill, and his willingness to use racial symbolism, such as "welfare queens," to deride African Americans.

Conclusion

While the parties have largely realigned and remade themselves on social and racial issues, African Americans are what they have always been: a community of citizens who are, with exceptions, liberal to moderate and tied together by a linked fate. As such, given "the preferences of Blacks on salient policy questions, and the electoral strategies of the rival parties, nearly all calculations of self *and* group interests have positioned most Blacks far closer to the Democrats than to the Republicans."[57] Given this reality, it is unlikely that there will be a large-scale movement of African Americans to the Republican Party without a realignment of the parties on these same issues. There have always been pockets of African American conservatives, and their presence will continue. However, given historical trends in public opinion, conservatism is unlikely to ever become the dominant ideology among African Americans. Unless the GOP becomes more moderate and brings its party's positions closer to African Americans, there is no reason to believe that a critical mass of African Americans will take on the conservative positions that they have so far resisted—no matter how well they are packaged and marketed.

The GOP's lock on the African American vote eroded not solely because of Democratic entreaties, but also because of conscious decisions made by the Republican Party to seek southern support. That necessarily meant embracing conservatism, an ideology that has never been at the fore-front of black interests. While some may argue that blacks are conservative on certain issues—abortion and same-sex marriage, for example—this situational conservatism does not overwhelm the traditional liberalism and moderation that has characterized African American political behavior for more than 150 years.

Notes

1. Hanes Walton, *Black Republicans: The Politics of the Black and Tans* (Metuchen, NJ: Scarecrow Press, 1975), p. 22.

2. Peter Klingman and David Geithman, "Negro Dissidence and the Republican Party, 1864–1872," *Phylon* 40, no. 2 (June 1979): 174. Klingman and Geithman also cited the "Southern intransigence" as a major creator of obstacles to racial progress in 1866.

3. Kenneth Stampp and Leon Litwack, *Reconstruction: An Anthology of Revisionist Writings* (Baton Rouge: Louisiana State University Press, 1969), quoted in Klingman and Geithman, "Negro Dissidence," p. 172.

4. William L. Clay, *Just Permanent Interests: Black Americans in Congress, 1870–1991* (New York: Amistad Press, 1992), p. 4, quoting *New York Times*, August 15, 1862, p. 1. Lincoln revealed a different view two years later in a letter to the interim governor of Louisiana in which he proposed "that some African Americans be allowed to vote, especially the 'very intelligent.'" Lincoln also alluded to the possibility of linking black military service to voting. See also Benjamin Quarles, *Lincoln and the Negro* (New York: Oxford University Press, 1962).

5. Abraham Lincoln, letter to Horace Greeley, August 22, 1862, quoted in Clay, *Just Permanent Interests*, p. 3.

6. Other components of the compromise included the appointment of at least one southern Democrat to Hayes's cabinet, the construction of a transcontinental railroad in the South, and federal assistance in industrializing the South.

7. Vincent DeSantis, "The Republican Party and the Southern Negro, 1877–1897," *Journal of Negro History* 45, no. 2 (April 1960): 74.

8. For a detailed discussion of the impact of the end of Reconstruction on black politics, see Vallely, *The Two Reconstructions*.

9. According to *The Handbook of Texas Online*, the term *lily white* apparently originated at the 1888 Republican state convention in Fort Worth, when a group of whites attempted to expel a number of black and tan delegates. Norris Wright Cuney, the black Texas leader who controlled the party, promptly labeled the insurgents "lily whites," and the term was soon applied to similar groups throughout the South. See *Handbook of Texas Online*, "Lily-White Movement," www.tsha. utexas.edu/handbook/online/articles/LL/wfl1.html (accessed August 12, 2005).

10. While the "lily whites" represented only white Republicans, it should be noted that they did seek token black membership so as to avoid the charge of racism. It can be said that those black conservatives that espoused the accommodationist principles of Booker T. Washington were seen as acceptable to the lily whites because they would not challenge white authority and power.

11. Walton, *Black Republicans*, p. 29.

12. Ibid., p. 39.

13. Ibid., p. 137.

14. Ibid.

15. Clay, *Just Permanent Interests,* p. 72.

16. Louis Gould, *Grand Old Party: A History of the Republicans* (New York: Random House, 2003), p. 224.

17. Ibid., p. 225.

18. Richard B. Sherman, *The Republican Party and Black America from McKinley to Hoover, 1896–1933* (Charlottesville: University of Virginia Press, 1973), pp. 137, 140, quoted in Gould, *Grand Old Party,* p. 225.

19. T. Arnold Hill, "Briefs from the South," *Opportunity* 11 (February 1933): 55, quoted in Harvard Sitkoff, *A New Deal for Blacks: The Emergence of Civil Rights as a National Issue: The Depression Decade* (Oxford: Oxford University Press, 1981), p. 36.

20. Nancy Weiss, *Farewell to the Party of Lincoln: Black Politics in the Age of FDR* (Princeton: Princeton University Press, 1983), p. 15.

21. National Urban League, Department of Industrial Relations, "How Unemployment Affects Negroes," National Urban League Papers, Department of Industrial Relations files, Manuscript Division, Library of Congress, March 1931, quoted in Weiss, *Farewell to the Party of Lincoln,* p. 15.

22. Sitkoff, *A New Deal for Blacks,* p. 39.

23. Michael Dawson, *Behind the Mule: Race and Class in African-American Politics* (Princeton: Princeton University Press, 1994), p. 72.

24. William H. Harris, *The Harder We Run: Black Workers Since the Civil War* (Oxford: Oxford University Press, 1982); Sitkoff, *A New Deal for Blacks,* p. 70. Dawson also notes the role of Democratic presidents Harry Truman, John F. Kennedy, and Lyndon B. Johnson: Truman desegregated the armed forces and created a civil rights commission; Kennedy and Johnson followed with a combination of executive orders and legislation in 1961 (Kennedy's executive order barring employment discrimination in federal employment) and in 1964 (the Civil Rights Act), which broadly extended employment antidiscrimination law, quoted in Dawson, *Behind the Mule,* p. 23.

25. Sitkoff, *A New Deal for Blacks,* p. 103.

26. Ibid.

27. Weiss, *Farewell to the Party of Lincoln,* p. 35.

28. Ibid., p. xiv.

29. Ibid., p. 78.

30. Sitkoff, *A New Deal for Blacks,* p. 66.

31. Ibid., p. 67.

32. Ibid.

33. The irony of Thurmond's position is unmistakable, given the revelation after his death that he fathered a child with a black teenager when he was in his twenties.

34. David Bositis, "Blacks and the 2004 Republican National Convention" (Washington, DC: Joint Center for Political and Economic Studies, 2004), p. 9, citing 1936–1956 data from Everett Carll Ladd Jr. and Charles D. Hadley, *Transformations of the American Party System: Political Coalitions from the New Deal to the 1970s* (New York: Norton, 1975), pp. 60, 112.

35. See David Lublin, *The Republican South: Democratization and Partisan Change* (Princeton: Princeton University Press, 2004).

36. Mary Brennan, *Turning Right in the Sixties: The Conservative Capture of the GOP* (Chapel Hill: University of North Carolina Press, 1995), p. 2.

37. Ibid., pp. 1–18.

38. Ibid., p. 8.

39. Robert Huckfeldt and Carol Weitzel Kohfeld, *Race and the Decline of Class in American Politics* (Urbana: University of Illinois Press, 1989), pp. 183–184.

40. For a discussion of institutional racism and its relationship to racist policies, see Louis Knowles and Kenneth Prewitt, *Institutional Racism* (Englewood Cliffs, NJ: Prentice Hall, 1969), pp. 5–6. For a detailed discussion of racism, see Robert C. Smith, *Racism in the Post–Civil Rights Era: Now You See It, Now You Don't* (Albany: State University of New York Press, 1995).

41. Rob Christensen and Jack Fleer, "North Carolina: Between Helms and Hunt No Majority Emerges," in Alexander Lamis, *Southern Politics in the 1990s* (Baton Rouge: Louisiana State University Press, 1995), p. 88.

42. Edward Carmines and James Stimson, *Issue Evolution: Race and the Transformation of American Politics* (Princeton: Princeton University Press, 1989), p. 76.

43. V. O. Key, *Southern Politics* (New York: Vintage Books, 1949), p. 130.

44. Carmines and Stimson, *Issue Evolution,* p. 191.

45. Ibid., p. 190. See also Thomas Edsall and Mary Edsall, *Chain Reaction: The Impact of Race, Rights, and Taxes on American Politics* (New York: W. W. Norton, 1992).

46. Fair Campaign Practices Committee Archives, Lauinger Library Special Collections, Georgetown University. A photographic reproduction of the poster can be seen in Jeremy Mayer, *Running on Race: Racial Politics in Presidential Campaigns, 1960–2000* (New York: Random House, 2002).

47. Kevin Phillips, *Post-Conservative America: People, Politics, and Ideology in a Time of Crisis* (New York: Vintage Books, 1983), p. 57.

48. Earl Black and Merle Black, *The Rise of Southern Republicans* (Cambridge: Belknap/Harvard University Press, 2002), p. 248.

49. William Gienapp, *The Origins of the Republican Party, 1852–1856* (Oxford: Oxford University Press, 1987), p. 6.

50. Ibid. By the 1990s, the GOP had become dominant in the southern United States. Some of that dominance was due to Democrats switching parties and becoming Republicans. See Lamis, *Southern Politics in the 1990s.*

51. Timothy Nokken and Keith Poole, "Congressional Party Defection in American History," paper prepared for the annual meeting of the American Political Science Association, San Francisco, August 29–September 2, 2001, p. 2.

52. Jack Bass and Marilyn Thompson, *Strom: The Complicated Personal and Political Life of Strom Thurmond* (New York: Public Affairs, 2005), p. 188, quoting Bass-DeVries interview with Strom Thurmond, February 1, 1974.

53. *Roll Call,* November 10, 1994; *Boston Globe,* January 20, 1995, quoted in Black and Black, *The Rise of Southern Republicans,* p. 304.

54. Trent Lott was an administrative assistant to Democratic representative William Colmer of Mississippi. When Colmer retired, Lott switched parties and ran for his seat.

55. Black and Black, *The Rise of Southern Republicans,* p. 269.

56. Prominent party switching from Democrat to Republican has not been limited to the South. Other prominent nonsouthern Democrats who became Republicans include Ronald Reagan (1960), Colorado senator Ben Nighthorse Campbell (1996), and St. Paul, Minnesota, mayor Norman Coleman (1996).

57. Black and Black, *The Rise of Southern Republicans,* p. 248.

4

Efforts to Regain and Retain African American Support

EVIDENCE OF A POLITICAL PARTY'S COMMITMENT TO CERTAIN
sectors of the electorate can be found in the human, financial, and other
resources it uses to target those voters as well as in the vitality of the organizations the party supports to target voters in these groups. The mere presence of such groups is an important sign. More important, however, is the
extent to which a party provides supportive organizations with the resources
they need to complete their task, or the groups' ability to raise such funds
themselves.

Equally important is the strength of the organizational network that
exists to work with the party to target particular voters. The presence of
long-standing relationships with consistent and substantial funding suggests
a certain seriousness on the part of the GOP and related groups in trying to
bring more African Americans into the party. The lack of such relationships
suggests systemic or other problems in trying to win more black support or
an unwillingness to commit the resources necessary to be taken seriously.
Examining these organizations provides an opportunity to assess the organizational network and impact they have had on increasing black support for
the GOP. This chapter describes, examines, and assesses the network that
exists to increase African American support for the GOP.

The Republican Party has long argued that it is serious about winning
African American support, and its efforts in this regard can be placed in
four categories. The first category concerns Republican-led policy initiatives designed to deal with issues that acutely affect African Americans.
Notable examples, elaborated in subsequent sections, are the "black capitalism" effort and the "Philadelphia Plan" during the Nixon administration;
and the public school choice efforts that began in the 1990s. The second category concerns party and political activities that have been undertaken to
increase black support. Particularly noteworthy in this regard are the efforts
of conservative philanthropic groups that have teamed with state and local

61

parties to target African Americans; the creation of official auxiliary groups within the party that have played important roles; and party support for African American Republican electoral candidates. The third category comprises the numerous black state and local organizations formed to bring in more black support for the Republican Party. There are black groups—large and small, effective and ineffective, well funded and barely functioning—in many states around the nation that are part of a network dedicated to this end. Last are the numerous national African American organizations, operating at varying levels of activity, that have worked to attract more black voters to the GOP. The Republican Party has supported a number of African American organizations—some of which are new or reconstituted—in its efforts to gain black support. An examination of these policy proposals, party and political actions, and selected state and national organizations that target African Americans sheds light on the network that exists to increase black support for the GOP and makes an assessment as to whether it can lead to significant gains.

Policy Proposals

Republican presidents and congressional leaders have offered a range of policy proposals, designed primarily to further their particular interests, that they hoped would have the additional benefit of being popular in the black community. The goal was that some of the policy positions would help turn the political tide from Democrats to the GOP or at least force the Democrats to use resources to defend their own positions with their strongest and most secure voting bloc. These policies have generally focused on economic issues, the area where Republicans have believed they were best positioned to make inroads into the black community. Noteworthy policy proposals in this regard have included Richard Nixon's black capitalism initiative to grow black wealth and his Philadelphia Plan to open employment to African Americans, and George W. Bush's school choice initiatives. While there are numerous policy programs that can be seen as having a positive impact in the African American community, these particular policies are important because they specifically targeted black America or responded to occurrences in the black community that were seen as potentially problematic for the nation or for the GOP. The public school choice movement together with a public policy initiative to create private retirement investment accounts have been offered as remedies for two important issues facing black America—educational opportunities for the young and economic security for seniors. While these initiatives were not created solely with African Americans in mind, they have been marketed to the black community in a "pro-black" way.

Nixon's Black Capitalism Campaign

President Nixon's black capitalism campaign was a political initiative that emerged from his 1968 presidential campaign to halt growing black radicalism. The radicalism began to emerge in the wake of the rise of the black power movement and the riots, anger, frustration, and hostility that gripped much of the African American community in the summer following the assassination of Rev. Dr. Martin Luther King Jr.[1] As scholars Robert Weems and Lewis Randolph noted in their study of black capitalism, "Nixon viewed an uncontrolled Black Power movement as a major threat to the internal security of the United States."[2] That view was informed by his advisers, many of whom categorically rejected black claims of being victimized by an unjust political, economic, and social structure. The advisers were motivated more by the need to comfort conservatives nervous about the potential for expanded black rioting than by the obligation to deal honestly with the reality of black life in America. According to Dean Kotlowski, author of *Nixon's Civil Rights: Politics, Principle, and Policy*, some Nixon advisers neglected white racism and blamed its black victims.[3]

The nation was angry. White conservatives were upset about crime and violence and wanted government to step in and stop it. They did not know or care about the economic, social, and political repression that led many African Americans to America's streets angrily demanding change. African Americans were frustrated that after years of the civil rights movement, change was slow or nonexistent. That, coupled with the assassination of Dr. King, led many African Americans to take a more militant approach to the larger white society. It was within this context that Nixon embraced black capitalism and voiced a message that combined repression (the use of force, if necessary, to end street rioting to appease white conservatives) with reform (new economic opportunities to appease black nationalists).[4]

In that way, black capitalism may be seen as an attempt to co-opt the nationalist, black power wing of the African American community—a group of activists who were gaining popularity throughout black America. The initiative promised to increase black entrepreneurship and wealth by developing small black businesses. The plan would have an ancillary benefit for the Republican Party in that accelerating the inclusion of African Americans into the national economy could lead to greater black support for the Republicans. As one Nixon aide noted, "Everything we can do to increase minority business holdings, minority home ownership, and more jobs for minorities, will in the long run mean more to the minorities and help increase our political favor."[5]

To facilitate this effort, Nixon, once elected, created the Office of Minority Business Enterprises (OMBE) within the Department of Commerce. The OMBE, established in March 1969 through Executive

Order 11458, was envisioned as a supplement to the work of the Small Business Administration (SBA), which covered similar ground. By creating the agency within an executive department, Nixon was able to bypass Congress and avoid many of the same conservatives who thwarted President Johnson's efforts to expand equal opportunity and affirmative action.

Nixon supporters viewed the black capitalism initiative as one of a number of examples of his sincere attempts to improve the general condition of black America and to use the power of government to make positive change a reality. The success of black capitalism lay in the willingness of the government to push minority procurement under Section 8(a), the act that suspended competitive bidding on federal contracts for small firms. The decision to use 8(a) as an instrument to facilitate black capitalism paid dividends: between 1969 and 1975, 8(a) procurement from minority firms grew from $9 million to $250 million.[6] Also, during the period 1970–1975, purchases from minority businesses increased 165 percent, to $475 million.[7] This procurement activity, along with increased federal deposits in minority-owned banks, can be seen as impressive, given the level of support that had existed before Nixon.

While Nixon's initiative may be seen as a legitimate attempt to craft policy favorable to African Americans, it drew numerous critics within the black community. Many viewed the initiative as an attempt to segregate the national economy and limit support to activities in black communities, thereby leaving the rest of the economy—larger and more lucrative—to white entrepreneurs. Further, some critics believed that black capitalism would merely set up black businesses that would ultimately be taken over by larger white businesses, particularly in areas such as apparel manufacturing. Andrew Brimmer, then a member of the Federal Reserve Board, noted that black businesspeople should not "count on nationally oriented manufacturing firms leaving the Negro market to Negro entrepreneurs" and called the initiative "one of the worst digressions that has attracted attention and pulled substantial numbers of people off course."[8] An additional criticism of the plan was that it would only benefit African Americans who were already middle and upper class.

Ultimately, Nixon's black capitalism initiative failed to live up to the high expectations it created—its solid accomplishments notwithstanding. OMBE was never able to command the resources, financial and otherwise, to be the success many hoped for and expected. The agency was plagued by poor funding, turf battles with SBA, inexperienced staff, high leadership turnover, and an amorphous implementation and enforcement mechanism.[9] Indeed, some have argued that the initiative was more rhetoric than policy to begin with, offered to African Americans as a panacea for societal ills that plagued the black community. However, remedying those ills may not have been the real goal of the Nixon administration. As some have argued, the "larger ideological goal of subverting African American radicalism" may have been more important than improving black economics, particularly if the cost of undermining black radicalism was less than creating black wealth.[10]

The Philadelphia Plan

The Philadelphia Plan was the name given to the first federal affirmative action plan. It was developed by the Department of Labor to address racial discrimination in Philadelphia's construction industry, which, like most industries around the nation, was heavily influenced by labor unions that controlled who worked and who did not. The unions had job assignment arrangements with builders that made it easier to lock out minority skilled workers. Also, "father-son traditions [passing down jobs from father to son] and guildlike patterns in the American Federation of Labor had largely excluded minorities from apprenticeships and union membership, and, hence, from high-wage construction jobs."[11]

The goal of the plan was to make the proportion of African Americans in each trade equal to their 30 percent proportion of metropolitan Philadelphia's workforce.[12] While the plan was localized to Philadelphia, it ultimately became the model for affirmative action programs around the nation. The plan was an expansion of Johnson administration efforts to enforce Executive Order 11246, which required contractors to engage in affirmative action to ensure equal employment opportunity. The Johnson administration requirements to end, or at least limit, racial discrimination in employment were ultimately ruled violations of federal contract law. The ruling, made near the end of the Johnson administration, left Johnson little time or willingness to respond and left many to conclude that such redress for racial discrimination would not be allowed or pursued with Nixon entering the White House.

Nixon resurrected the plan, a surprise to many given his 1968 presidential campaign as an opponent of racial quotas, school busing, and other attempts to use law to address structural racism. These positions earned Nixon a great deal of animus in the black community and perhaps made him the president least likely to advocate policy changes that could be seen as pro-black. Hugh Davis Graham suggests four reasons for Nixon's support of the plan: (1) a new etiology of social disadvantage that implied more radical remedies; (2) clientele control of civil rights agencies; (3) Nixon's commitment to affirmative action preferences; and (4) the intervention of federal courts in social policy.[13] Nixon's positions were also guided by his experience, as vice-president, chairing President Eisenhower's Committee on Government Contracts, which was designed to end bias in firms doing business with the government. Nixon concluded that "bias was a waste of urgently needed manpower" and that promoting equal opportunity was "the right thing to do."[14]

The assumption behind the plan was that merely requiring nondiscrimination was "inadequate to uproot white job entrenchment"; a results test was therefore necessary to determine compliance with affirmative action requirements for government contractors.[15] The new standard, effective in 1971, required government contractors with contracts of at least $50,000 and fifty or more employees to file an affirmative action plan with the Office of Federal Contract Compliance. The plan had two components. The first was an analysis of all job categories to determine whether minorities were underrepresented. The second was a specific plan with goals and timetables to correct any identified underrepresentation.

The Philadelphia Plan should be viewed less as Nixon's attempt at political moderation and more as an effort to break craft union influence over the construction industry and to please business. The injection of more minority workers could potentially drive down wages as the supply of skilled workers increased and thereby boost company profits. While the plan had obvious positive potential for black voters, it can also be seen as an attempt to curry favor or repay a political ally—big business in this case. However, the plan's political significance lay in the fact that it was the most extensive and progressive antiracism public policy in the post–civil rights movement era, and a Republican president oversaw its introduction. President Nixon had earned an anti-black reputation, and the implementation of the Philadelphia Plan was one of the few exceptions to an otherwise racially hostile administration.

School Choice

A consistent concern of many African Americans has been the quality of education their children receive. Generations ago, the fight was against underfunded, segregated schools. Now, the concern and fight are over reversing the low achievement levels among African American students. African American performance in US public schools is among the worst in the nation, and many of the states with the highest dropout rates also have large African American populations.[16] While there are many reasons for the disparity that are not necessarily a function of a particular school system, such as the need for a young person to quit school to work full-time to help support the family, the fact that black achievement is not where it could be has created frustration and presented opportunities to call for change. School choice is one alternative in this regard.

As Table 4.1 demonstrates, African Americans have historically dropped out of school at higher rates than whites. While official dropout

Table 4.1   School Dropout Rates by Race, 1987–2001

Year	Total	White	Black	Hispanic
1987	12.7	10.4	14.1	28.6
1988	12.9	9.6	14.5	35.8
1989	12.6	9.4	13.9	33.0
1990	12.1	9.0	13.2	32.4
1991	12.5	8.9	13.6	35.3
1992	11.0	7.7	13.7	29.4
1993	11.0	7.9	13.6	27.5
1994	11.5	7.7	12.6	30.0
1995	12.0	8.6	12.1	30.0
1996	11.1	7.3	13.0	29.4
1997	11.0	7.6	13.4	25.3
1998	11.8	7.7	13.8	29.5
1999	11.2	7.3	12.6	28.6
2000	10.9	6.9	13.1	27.8
2001	10.7	7.3	10.9	27.0

Source: John Wirt, Susan Choy, Stephen Provasnik, Patrick Rooney, Anindita Sen, and Richard Tobin, *The Condition of Education 2003,* NCES 2003-067 (Washington, DC: US Department of Education, National Center for Education Statistics, 2003), table 17-1.

data show that the African American dropout rate has been relatively stable—in the low- to mid-teens—there are many public school districts around the nation in which more black students drop out of school than graduate. Unofficial estimates place African American dropout rates far higher than official state data. According to Education Trust, a Washington, DC–based education think tank, nearly half of African American high school students in North Carolina do not finish high school, and 75 percent of African American males do not graduate from the Indianapolis, Indiana, public schools.[17] Of the forty states (plus the District of Columbia) that provided data for a 2004 Urban Institute study on school dropout rates, thirteen had an African American dropout rate of at least 50 percent.[18] New York had an African American graduation rate of 35 percent.

The profound and deleterious impact that failing schools have had on the black community can be seen in a number of areas, including employment, family household wealth, community cohesion and stability, and crime. African Americans constitute nearly half of the 2 million people incarcerated in US prisons, and a majority of those are high school dropouts. There is a multitude of social science research that demonstrates the role education plays in one's life. The better one is educated, the more opportunities one has, including a relatively stable employment future. Without education, employment opportunities are limited and neighborhoods suffer and run the risk of destabilization. Chronic high unemployment has been shown to have devastating effects on communities. As

William Julius Wilson noted in his 1996 study of the effects of unemployment, "Many of today's problems in the inner-city ghetto neighborhoods—crime, family dissolution, welfare, low levels of social organization, and so on—are fundamentally a consequence of the disappearance of work."[19] Blacks are unemployed at higher rates than whites.

Activists and policymakers have focused on public education as a means of dealing with this societal dysfunction. Here, the Republicans have offered a collection of school choice policies they argue are designed to improve public education. Among these policies are education vouchers, which provide government funds to pay tuition for selected students to attend private, parochial, or charter schools (public schools created outside the traditional system). Such vouchers have heavily targeted African Americans. The targeting of African Americans is designed to show that the Republican Party is interested in the general well-being of the black community. To that end, Republican activists have pushed education initiatives designed to implement voucher programs and to open the door for charter schools around the nation.

The District of Columbia has been a primary battleground for school choice initiatives for at least two reasons. First, Congress has ultimate constitutional jurisdiction over the District and can legislate there in ways it is prohibited from doing in the fifty states. Second, the District is a significant city for African Americans and has been a majority-black city since the 1950s. Consequently, Congress can more easily pass controversial legislation for the District than it can for the rest of the nation. Politically, if the GOP can make school choice work in the District, then it can more easily pass national legislation. As one voucher supporter and founder of a private school in the District noted, "For school choice to succeed [nationally], it has to succeed in D.C.; it's in the backyard of Congress. If it doesn't work here, vouchers are dead for a long, long time."[20]

Congress required the local school system to establish a system for creating charter schools. The DC School Choice Initiative is the first federally funded school choice demonstration program. The Republican congressional majority passed the plan over the objections of the majority of the District's elected officials. According to the Department of Education,

> Students who are residents of the District and who come from households whose income does not exceed 185 percent of the poverty line are eligible to apply for scholarships from a grantee under this program. These scholarships may be used to pay the tuition and fees and transportation expenses, if any, to enable students to attend the participating District private elementary or secondary school of their choice.[21]

The plan grants scholarships of up to $7,500 per school year to District residents who want to send their children to private or parochial schools. By

2006, the program was a mixed success. In the first year of the program, the general criticism was that too few students from low-performing public schools and too many already enrolled in private schools had received vouchers.[22] Further, the program also failed to draw enough students for a congressionally mandated evaluation to be conducted. [23] The second year was more successful, with over 500 applicants for 271 available scholarships.[24]

Some critics argue that GOP advocacy for school choice is less about providing opportunity and more about prying open the door to a business opportunity potentially worth billions nationally: elementary and secondary education. According to one such critic, Republican strategists want to privatize education for five reasons:

- Education is a multibillion-dollar market, and the private sector is eager to get its hands on those dollars.
- Conservatives are devoted to the free market and believe that private is inherently superior to public.
- Shrinking public education furthers the Republican Party goal of drastically reducing the public sector.
- Privatization undermines teacher unions, a key base of support for the Democratic Party.
- Privatization rhetoric can be used to woo African American and Latino voters to the Republican Party.[25]

Be that as it may, school choice initiatives can be an attractive option for African American parents who are desperate for better education opportunities for their children.

Nixon's black capitalism initiative and the Philadelphia Plan, coupled with Bush-era school choice initiatives, represent the three most significant Republican-led policy proposals that have targeted African Americans in the hope that they would favorably respond to the GOP and begin to support the party at the ballot box. While the proposls have met with limited success, the Republican Party can point to them to demonstrate its sincerity in improving the general condition of African Americans.

Party and Political Actions

The Republican National Committee and conservative philanthropic foundations and think tanks also play roles in efforts to attract more African Americans to the GOP and to solicit support for African American Republican electoral candidates. When taken in total, these entities help provide leadership, guidance, and consultation in crafting and marketing policies designed to convince black voters that GOP policies are favorable to black interests.

Republican National Committee

As the central party apparatus, the Republican National Committee (RNC) plays the primary role in crafting African American outreach efforts, setting the tone for state and local groups. If the national party is aggressive and consistent in its recruitment and outreach efforts toward a segment of the electorate, then a signal is sent throughout the party structure around the nation that that voting bloc is appreciated, welcomed, and worthy of significant attention. Conversely, a national party that treats a voting bloc with apathy and ambivalence sends another message: We'll gladly accept your votes, but won't work too hard to get them.

Staffing problems have undermined the RNC's African American outreach efforts. Inexperienced activists with limited staff support have been a consistent problem for the RNC for much of the last three decades. One former Republican activist and consultant described the consistent staff turnover as a "revolving door" of people who are unable to make progress:

> They're [the RNC] getting these people, these black folks, they get them wherever they find them. They come in thinking that it's going to be different because for one they're in there, and the people before them weren't smart enough or aggressive enough. And they simply did not know how to get it done. . . . We've got all kinds of Ivy League graduates who have come before you and have gotten nowhere.[26]

The lack of staff stability complicates the task of building and developing relationships with African Americans and the groups to which they belong around the country, thus rendering the party largely impotent in the competition for black votes. It also contributes to the belief held by some, including some African American Republican activists, that party outreach efforts to blacks have been inconsistent and unfocused.[27]

While the GOP is still not doing as well as it can, it is closer to where it needs to be than it has been in decades. Past RNC chairs Jim Nicholson, Mark Racicot, and Ed Gillespie, and current chair Ken Mehlman, are cited by some party elites as being serious about outreach to the African American community.[28] Others say Lee Atwater was a significant player in trying to get the Republican Party to understand the need for more African American support.

One mechanism the GOP has used for African American outreach was the National Black Republican Council (NBRC). The group was formed in 1972 following the Republican National Convention when then chairman George H. W. Bush was able to implement a rule change that would allow for the creation of auxiliary groups designed to target specific segments of the electorate. NBRC was charged with building black support for the party throughout the country. It was during this period that Professor Ronald Walters, an expert in black political behavior, noted unease among the black Republican leadership. Walters took note of what he concluded was the great "extent to which black Republican leaders felt disenfranchised" at the Republican National Convention:[29] "They would be roaming the halls talking about the fact that the party wasn't paying any attention to them or listening to them, and they couldn't get the attention of key leaders and they couldn't get a voice."[30]

While the organization had the official backing of the national party, it never had the sustained administrative and financial support necessary to build strong black Republican organizations throughout the country. By the late 1990s, the organization barely existed and ultimately "died on the vine." NBRC is not a significant factor in the effort to bring more African Americans to the GOP and does not appear to have a large presence in the black conservative movement. When asked, many black Republican elites are unaware of NBRC's activities. This is a major shortcoming for an organization that is an official affiliate of the RNC and would presumably have an easier time than any other group in getting support for the national party.

Rather than reconstitute and rebuild NBRC, the RNC created the African American Advisory Committee in 2005 to advise the national party chair on ways to reach out to African Americans. The purpose of the committee is to bring together respected community leaders, who meet regularly with the RNC leadership and provide a sounding board to assist in strategic implementation of the RNC's outreach efforts in the black community.[31] According to RNC chair Ken Mehlman, "This is an endeavor I take very seriously and I look forward to working with this outstanding group of individuals to share ideas, grow our party and continue to achieve progress for all Americans."[32] The panel also helps keep the chair apprised of particular issues around the nation and suggests ways to position the party to make the most of potential political situations.

The members of the committee constitute a "who's who" of prominent black Republicans, including former members of Congress, federal cabinet officials and agency directors, state elected and appointed officials, and religious leaders. One member described the organization as "a broad cross-section of folks from elected officials to future candidates, to people who have been in this endeavor for a long time, to young folk who are just now in, businesspeople, pastors."[33] The committee holds biweekly conference calls (more frequently if the need arises) during which they discuss "where we need to go, what we need to do, what we need him [Mehlman] to do, where we need him to be."[34] While it is too early to assess the success of the organization, some are concerned that its informal structure renders it less effective than it could be—and more vulnerable to cronyism.

The prominence of many of the members has caused some concern among some black grassroots Republican activists that the group represents the same top-down approach to outreach that has failed to work in the past. It also reflects a reliance on black Republican "celebrities"—well-known black activists who hold office or advise on outreach (or both) without having engaged in many of the grassroots activities needed to build a lasting organization. One activist noted that there is some resentment around the nation concerning the membership of the committee: "My colleagues who grew up within the party and came up through the party as precinct chairs and city district chairs, worked on campaigns and volunteered and wrote checks, they didn't like it one bit."[35] These black Republican critics of the committee also see as a problem the RNC's reliance on "black Republican celebrities" to serve on the committee even if they have little organizational experience.

Conservative Philanthropy and Think Tanks

Conservative philanthropy—the network of right-wing foundations—has had a two-sided relationship with black America. On the one hand, conservative foundations have poured millions of dollars into efforts to win over conservative African Americans, particularly on issues such as school vouchers, charter schools, and gay marriage. On the other hand, conservative foundations have funded think tanks and have supported black and other scholars who produce research that often takes anti-black positions. Related to this is the impact conservative philanthropic funding has had on the operation of many notable black organizations.

With regard to winning over and expanding the number of black conservative voters, conservative philanthropic foundations have focused their funding on groups that target social issues, such as gay marriage, and they have worked through black churches to attract new black voters. These foundations have poured millions of dollars into such efforts, primarily in two ways. First, they have made financial contributions to black churches to gain favor with prominent and popular ministers. These foundations were greatly boosted by President George W. Bush's Faith-Based Initiative, which has given billions of dollars in grants to churches and religious groups for a range of purposes. African American churches in some parts of the country have particularly benefited from such grants.

Second, they have created, or funded the creation of, ostensibly black organizations that seek to win black support for the GOP, for conservative public policy, or both. The Lynde and Harry Bradley Foundation, the Coors family Castle Rock Foundation, the Richard and Helen DeVos Foundation, the Koch Family Foundations, the John M. Olin Foundation, the Randolph Foundation, and the Scaife Family Foundation are among the numerous organizations that fund these efforts. These foundations also have been benefactors for organizations and individuals that have taken anti-black policy positions and have sought to end public policies that benefited African Americans, such as affirmative action. They have also supported efforts to block important Clinton political appointees and have funded research that has been used to reinforce negative racial stereotypes of African Americans and other minorities.[36]

One example is the Black Alliance for Educational Options (BAEO), a Milwaukee, Wisconsin–based group that was created in 2000 to generate support for tax-funded voucher programs, private scholarships, tuition tax credits, charter schools, and public/private partnerships. While BAEO's board and leadership are almost entirely African American, it is financed, almost entirely, through the contributions of conservative white philanthropists. The Bradley, Friedman, and Walton foundations, along with the American Education Reform Council, have contributed the largest proportion of BAEO's budget since its formation, and although all are prominent supporters of education privatization, all also oppose affirmative action.[37]

While it is difficult to uncover definitive dollar amounts, it is clear that these foundations have spent millions of dollars to sponsor prominent African American commentators, academics, and others who espouse conservative principles, hoping that their heightened media and scholarly presence will resonate with blacks. An ancillary hope is that these groups and individuals will rise to such prominence that they will be seen as legitimate alternatives to traditional African American leadership. Examples include Walter Williams, who is the John M. Olin Distinguished Professor of Economics at George Mason University, and Thomas Sowell, the Rose and Milton Friedman Senior Fellow at the Hoover Institution. Williams, who is also a senior fellow at both the Heritage Foundation and the Hoover Institution, has received at least twenty-eight grants since 1985, amounting to at least $1.9 million.[38] Twenty-four of the grants came from the Olin Foundation and four from the Bradley Foundation—all disbursed through George Mason University. Sowell has received numerous foundation grants that have supported the research of many of his books. He is also the recipient of the 2003 Bradley Prize, awarded by the Bradley Foundation, which recognizes conservative scholars and thinkers who demonstrate outstanding achievement consistent with the foundation's mission.[39] The prize included a $250,000 stipend.

Conservative foundations have also supported the research of nonblack scholars, including Charles Murray and Dinesh D'Souza, who research issues that affect African Americans. Murray, coauthor of the *The Bell Curve: Intelligence and Class Structure in American Life*, argued that intelligence is predicated on race and that African Americans, because of their race, have a lower ceiling on their intellectual abilities than whites and other racial groups. The book set off a wave of discussion and debate on intelligence and race-based inferiority, with Murray arguing that, because of this genetic defect, African Americans cannot be helped by increases in social program spending. The thesis of his research has been challenged in many quarters as being racist and as using racial stereotypes to justify certain public policy positions. He also authored *Losing Ground: American Social Policy, 1950–1980*, which called for the abolition of social programs. Murray has received at least $3.5 million in grants from conservative foundations since 1985 to support his research.[40] The Bradley Foundation funded at least twenty-three of Murray's grants; the remaining funds originated at the Olin Foundation and were disbursed by the American Enterprise Institute and the Manhattan Institute.

D'Souza, the Robert and Karen Rishwain Research Fellow at the Hoover Institution at Stanford University, "perfectly illustrates the rightwing foundation goal of cultivating the next generation of conservative leaders by . . . linking them with conservative networks and internships, placing them with think tanks and guiding them toward high-level government positions."[41] D'Souza emerged from conservative circles when he authored *Illiberal Education*, a book that attacked affirmative action, and *The End of Racism*, which argued that black culture is pathological in its criminal and social behavior. D'Souza has received at least $1.6 million in grants to support his research since 1988 from foundations such as the Hoover Institution, the American Enterprise Institute, the Intercollegiate Studies Institute, the Madison Center for Educational Affairs, the Brownson Institute, and the Institute for Educational Affairs.[42] The funds for these grants originated in the Olin, Scaife, and Bradley foundations.

The prominence of philanthropic organizations' support for black conservatives and groups seeking to bring more African Americans to the GOP naturally leads to concerns over the legitimacy and independence of the funding recipients. The close relationship leaves the recipient groups open to the charge that they are influenced, if not controlled, by the donors. As one elite noted, "Their positions follow their funding and there is little daylight between the two."[43]

According to one study of conservative philanthropy, virtually every significant conservative think tank and advocacy group and the most significant conservative scholars have received some funding from the largest conservative foundations.[44] Some groups, such as the Heritage Foundation, were actually founded by and received their startup funding from conservative foundations. Other groups, such as the American Enterprise Institute and the Cato Institute, have received millions of dollars from conservative foundations during the past two decades to house, during Democratic administrations, conservative officials and conservative research scholars. As a consequence of this consistent and significant funding, the think tanks and advocacy groups have been able to focus more of their energy on research and advocacy without having to worry as much about fundraising. This is a consistent advantage over liberal think tanks, which do not benefit from such a strong and willing network of foundations.

The importance of this network with regard to African Americans and the Republican Party lies in the legitimacy that is attached to the conservative scholars' negative opinions regarding public policy that disproportionately affects African Americans. The opinions are often given additional credence because they are espoused by black authors and commentators who help provide political cover for conservative policymakers who would prefer to eliminate or reduce support for the kinds of social programs that have been helpful to African Americans. Also, the strategic promotion of these opinion leaders gives the impression that their views are more popular than they really are and thus worthy of more coverage. This could lead some African Americans to give those views more serious consideration than they would otherwise have given them. In this regard, the funding gives the commentators a legitimacy that they would unlikely have without the support.

Support for African American
Republican Electoral Candidates

A critical area in which the GOP can make inroads in the black community is in its support for African American Republican electoral candidates, particularly challengers to African American Democratic incumbents. While this is an opportunity for the GOP, the fact is that there are very few African Americans winning GOP nominations for House and Senate seats. Many black Republican elites see this as an area in which the Republican Party has been lacking and has not been as effective as it could be in targeting and recruiting black candidates with great potential.[45] To correct that, Washington, DC–based party operatives have begun promoting a few African American Republicans for office in an effort to build a candidate pipeline that will, ultimately, compete with Democrats. Too often, however, these black GOP candidates are running in districts or jurisdictions in which they have no real chance of victory. This may actually make it more difficult to win black support, as these candidates may be viewed by voters as political "sacrificial lambs" offered up by the Republican Party to appear as though the party supports black candidates. Furthermore, the party is not effective in cultivating black "favored candidates"—candidates with so much potential to be electoral winners or "stars" that they become worthy of extra party assistance.

While some candidates may be promoted as having star potential, they have rarely translated that attractiveness to ballot box victory. Sixty-four African American Republicans captured their party's nomination for the US House or Senate during the 1998, 2000, 2002, and 2004 congressional election cycles (this figure includes multiple counting for candidates who ran in more than one election cycle). Table 4.2 demonstrates the lack of electoral success selected African American Republican candidates have had in winning general elections. All but one—J. C. Watts of Oklahoma—lost The table also demonstrates how few African American Republicans have come even reasonably close to winning. Fifty-two of the sixty-four nominees (81 percent) lost by at least 25 percentage points.

While each race had unique dynamics and characteristics—for example, partisan makeup of district, candidate experience and quality, and fundraising ability—two important observations can be made regarding these races. First, most African American GOP nominees did not come close to winning; between 50 and 93 percent of these nominees lost by at least 25 percent; there were numerous races in which the GOP nominee lost by more than 50 percentage points. Second, many of the multiple nominees, those who run in more than one election, did worse in subsequent elections than they did in their first race.

These observations are important because they go to the perceived viability of black Republican candidates. The consistent and overwhelming defeat of black Republican candidates may leave skeptics of GOP efforts to win black support to conclude that these candidates are merely political "sacrificial lambs" and "cannon fodder" and that these candidates are promoted because it gives the RNC cover to defend itself against charges that it is not interested in black candidates or votes, but they are not supported

Table 4.2   Success of Black GOP US Congressional Nominees, 1998–2004

Year	Number of Races	Number of Black GOP Winners	Number of Black GOP Nominees Within 10 Percentage Points of Winner	Number of Black GOP Nominees Who Polled in Single Digits	Number of Black GOP Nominees Who Lost by 25 or More Percentage Points
1998	17	1	0	2	15 (88.2%)
2000	22	1	1	2	18 (81.8%)
2002[a]	10	1	1 .	0	5 (50%)
2004	15	0	0	0	14 (93%)

Source: Table created by author using data from the Joint Center for Political and Economic Studies, Washington, DC.

Note: a. J. C. Watts did not seek reelection in 2002.

enough to be competitive. The lack of success may also give the impression in the African American community that black Republican candidates are "losers," which can have a chilling effect on recruitment of future quality candidates and voters. Few want to be associated with losers.

It is on the issue of nominee support that a comparative criticism can be made with regard to other minority Republican candidates. Political parties understandably maintain neutrality policies in primaries. However, in some cases, they do make it clear when they have an unofficial "favored candidate," and the party may clear a path for the nomination of that candidate. One such example was Mel Martinez in the 2004 GOP Florida Senate primary race. A former Bush administration secretary of housing and urban development, Martinez was seen as an opportunity to curry favor with Florida Hispanics, a key constituency in that year's presidential election. The expectation was that Martinez's candidacy would bring in more Hispanic voters and that they would also vote for Bush, thereby solidifying his chances to win the state.

While the party and the White House political team were not able to completely clear the field—former representative Bill McCollum ran as well—they did make it clear whom they preferred, effectively securing the nomination for Martinez. McCollum ran well in the 2000 Florida Senate race against Democrat Bill Nelson, losing by fewer than 5 percentage points. The expectation among many following that race was that McCollum was the frontrunner for the 2004 race. That was so until the national party and the Bush White House decided that a Martinez candidacy was more helpful to their national goals. The significance here, though, is that the party apparatus was able to keep out of the race enough potential candidates who could have made it more difficult for Martinez to win the nomination.

The "favored candidate" policy was not in place, however, for Herman Cain, a wealthy African American businessman who, unlike Martinez and most other GOP candidates, could self-finance his 2004 Senate race. Seeking the GOP nomination in a crowded field that included two sitting members of the House of Representatives, he lost, garnering 26 percent of the vote. An argument can be made that the state and national GOP could have convinced the sitting representatives to forgo the race and give the party an opportunity to make real progress with African Americans. They took the step with Martinez in Florida, but not with Cain in Georgia.

The policy also was absent in Dylan Glenn's 2004 House race. Glenn, a promising young African American, twice has sought a seat in the US House. Glenn established his conservative credentials as an aide to Mississippi senator Thad Cochran and as a research assistant in George H. W. Bush's 1988 presidential campaign. Glenn worked in the Bush White House and as deputy chief of staff to Georgia governor Sonny Purdue. Because he was seen as a potential trail blazer who could win elections and serve as a magnet for young African Americans to support the GOP, he was able to garner consistent support from the Washington-based GOP establishment.

He ran in 2000 for the southwest Georgia (2nd District) seat held by Sanford Bishop, losing by 8 percentage points. Glenn moved to the 8th Congressional District, where he ran and lost in a 2004 four-candidate primary race to Georgia state representative Lynn Westmoreland. The importance of Glenn's election to GOP outreach efforts was not lost on him, when he noted, "I believe in my heart of hearts that if the Republican party is going to reach out, it will have to start electing folks that look like me."[46]

The race was notable because Glenn had the support of national Republicans such as former speaker of the House Newt Gingrich, while Westmoreland was backed by state Republicans. The national Republicans did not exercise the requisite influence to ensure that their favored candidate was in a position to win the nomination, though they made clear their candidate preference throughout the campaign. Glenn lost and, as a two-time loser, no longer engenders the same potential for political stardom that he once did.

The year 2006 may prove to be a turning point in party support for African American Republican candidates. It was in that year that a number of African American Republicans ran for prominent positions around the country. Gubernatorial campaigns by J. Kenneth Blackwell in Ohio and Lynn Swann in Pennsylvania, US Senate bids by Michael Steele in Maryland and Keith Butler in Michigan, and US House of Representatives races, including Sherman Parker in Missouri, can be seen as evidence that the GOP is now serious about recruiting and supporting viable African American candidacies. Among these candidates, Blackwell, Swann, and Steele won their party nominations. It may also reflect a growing sophistication among black Republicans who are interested in running serious campaigns without being used as tokens. As Steele noted in describing his decision to seek the Senate seat, "I had a very long and frank conversation with the leadership of the Republican Party [and] I told them: 'This has to be real. This can't be tokenism.'"[47]

In the case of Blackwell and Steele, in particular, national and statewide Republican officials have supported the campaigns with substantial funding and infrastructure support virtually unseen in decades for an African American Republican candidate. Given Steele's background as state party chair and lieutenant governor, it did not take long for high-level support to materialize once he announced his candidacy. President George W. Bush and top aides, including Karl Rove and Andrew H. Card Jr., hosted fundraisers for him, and former RNC chair Ed Gillespie agreed to serve as

Steele's national finance chair. He held a fundraiser at his home that raised $100,000 for Steele, who raised more than $2.6 million in the first six months of his campaign.[48]

African American Organizations
Working to Increase Black Support for the GOP

The network in place to expand black support for the GOP exists at the national, state, and local levels; many of the state-level organizations are auxiliaries of the state Republican Party. Some organizations are officially independent of the party and exist on their own initiative and resources. Most focus on political organizing, while others seek to increase the media presence of African American conservatives. Still other organizations focus on research and policy development, trying to bring black conservative policy preferences to the general policy debate, particularly on issues that impact African Americans. What most of these organizations have in common, however, is that they either emerge from or rely on white foundation grants for a substantial part of their funding. The African American Republican Leadership Council, Black America's Political Action Committee, the Black Republican Council of Texas, the Center for New Black Leadership, Colorado Black Republicans, the Harlem Republican Club, the Pinchback Society, and Project 21 are representative of efforts in this regard. These organizations are important because they are, or have been, at the forefront of recent efforts to expand black support for the GOP and are viewed as among the most significant group-based mechanisms for targeting the African American community. Examining and assessing these organizations provides important insights into the structure and impact of the network that exists to bring more African Americans into the GOP.[49]

African American Republican Leadership Council

The mission of the African American Republican Leadership Council (AARLC) is to "break the liberal Democrat stranglehold over Black America."[50] The AARLC purports to be the "only national organization to raise and increase support for common sense Reaganite Republican public policies and candidates" and has set a target of 25 percent for black support of GOP candidates.[51] The target is to identify sufficient numbers of African American Republican voters to "give the edge to closely contested races for victory when they support Reaganomic public policies, challengers or incumbents."[52]

The AARLC identifies, recruits, and trains local, state, and federal candidates to run in open seats or against Democratic minorities. The AARLC claims to be the only nationwide conservative Republican organization dedicated to electing African American Republicans to local, state, and national government. The group seeks to leverage and provide critical early financial support, issue advocacy, public education information, and independent campaigns to complement particular races.

While the AARLC's leadership is well known among black Republican elites, its work is not; some acknowledged a passing understanding of what the group is intended to do but could not point to any concrete efforts that would establish the AARLC as a significant player in efforts to win black support for the GOP. One prominent black Republican who lent his name to the organization as a board member indicated that (as of April 2005) there had never been a meeting of the board of directors and "there hasn't been a teleconference of the board to have a discussion about where we're going, what we're doing."[53] Another prominent black Republican noted that the group has done "nothing that I've really noticed frankly" and that they have been unimpressive.[54] As such, the group has not made much of a mark.

Black America's Political Action Committee

Black America's Political Action Committee (BAMPAC) is the largest African American political action committee dedicated to supporting conservative candidates for federal, state, and local office. BAMPAC recruits African American voters to support its endorsed candidates, and its work has five major components: candidate support, issue advocacy, national polling, civic political action, and international political education.

BAMPAC's candidate support activities include financing candidates the organization endorses, developing candidate marketing packages, and introducing its most viable candidates to other Republican donors. BAMPAC supported forty candidates for office in 2004, all of whom were Republicans. The organization, unlike most other similar political action committees, also supports challengers in Republican primary elections. While BAMPAC is registered as a nonpartisan organization, its support goes overwhelmingly to conservative Republican candidates. BAMPAC president and chief executive officer Alvin Williams estimates that 99 percent of its support goes to GOP candidates.[55]

BAMPAC's issue advocacy goes hand in hand with candidate support because it decides if it will or will not support someone as a candidate. The organization is particularly active in advocating for conservative social policies, such as outlawing abortion and other "values" issues such as gay marriage and the role of faith-based organizations in community development.

BAMPAC conducts an annual national opinion poll to assess black thought on a range of issues and individuals. According to Williams, the poll applies "research methods to critical questions today to find out where African Americans are in their current political opinions on the two major political parties."[56] He explains that another purpose of the poll is to make "sure that we're in synch and aware of what those top issues are on a yearly basis and also to detect those issues that we may be completely unaware of."[57] There is also a public relations component to this poll, as BAMPAC feels the need to "get out the word" regarding African Americans and the GOP.

And then there is international political education. BAMPAC works with sub-Saharan African countries that are studying US-style politics and figuring out how, if at all, they can be applied to their particular nations. According to Williams, "They are quite interested in how we do things and hoping that we can help export that; we want to encourage countries toward democracy and capitalism as best as possible."[58]

BAMPAC is the most widely known organization and has won praise from a number of prominent African Americans for its efforts to raise awareness in the black community of the Republican Party and conservative principles. Michael Steele, the first African American lieutenant governor of Maryland, noted that BAMPAC "has done a tremendous job developing and providing the kind of political/financial infrastructure for candidates across the country."[59]

Black Republican Council of Texas

The Black Republican Council of Texas (BRCT) is an organization of about 350 Texans dedicated to elevating black support for Republicans to at least 35 percent of the vote in each election cycle in state and local elections within targeted counties or districts in Texas.[60] The BRCT targets the thirty-two counties in Texas where approximately 85 percent of the state's African Americans live. According to BRCT president Bill Calhoun, "Our goal is to have a club in each of those counties, develop African American Republicans at the precinct level, bring those people up through the ranks, let them find offices to run for, be it city council, be it school board, mayor, whatever."[61] The group also identifies districts ideal for the election of black Republican candidates; identifies black voters within targeted counties; identifies potential Democratic Party switchers; assists faith based organizations in expanding their outreach; and recruits and trains the next generation of African American leaders.[62] The BRCT receives little financial support from the RNC and relies almost entirely on member-driven contributions. However, some efforts are envisioned to widen its donor base, because "the work that [the BRCT] want[s] to do is going to require being able to tap into Republican funds."[63] BRCT's initiatives are hindered by the lack of extensive financial support from outside sources.

Although the BRCT was officially organized in 1986, the impetus for its creation dates to the 1972 Republican National Convention. Party chair George H. W. Bush initiated a rule change that allowed for the creation of official auxiliary organizations to reach out to selected voters. That move led to the creation of the National Black Republican Council and the creation of state-level organizations around the country to work with it. The BRCT was one of the state-level organizations created in support of this effort.

The BRCT uses four criteria to measure its success: first, the number of black voters who vote for the Republican ticket in general elections; second, the number of precinct chairs they are able to recruit and train and get working in precincts; third, the number of African American clubs they are able to establish in targeted counties around the state of Texas and how well those clubs work with their county party leadership; and, finally, the number of African Americans they are able to get elected.

Center for New Black Leadership

The Center for New Black Leadership (CNBL) was started in 1994 by the Center of the American Experiment (CAE), a Minneapolis-based conservative think tank. The group was formed at the suggestion of Mitchell Pearlstein, founder of the CAE, who with Boston University economics professor Glenn Loury and CAE board member Peter Bell put together the initial meetings that led to the founding of the organization. According to one of the founders, CNBL was an outgrowth of the fight to confirm Clarence Thomas to the Supreme Court, and "there were a lot of individuals who watched those proceedings and felt that somehow they were no longer alone."[64] Within a short period following the hearings, "people were just coming out of the woodwork" wondering if there were black organizations they could join that espoused conservative values.[65]

CNBL is a policy organization that offers conservative policy prescriptions on issues such as education, economic development, and the role of faith-based organizations in social service delivery. While it is ostensibly a think tank, it also played an important symbolic role as challenger of the black organizational status quo. Consequently, it was seen as a leader and ally in efforts to bring more African Americans into the GOP. The organization has operated almost exclusively through contributions from conservative philanthropists and through grants and corporate gifts. The Richard and Helen DeVos Foundation, the Randolph Foundation, the Scaife Family Foundation, the Lynde and Harry Bradley Foundation, and the John M. Olin Foundation have been among its most significant funders.[66]

CNBL gained a great deal of publicity and attention in its early years and claimed a role in fighting for school choice and other social issues; the group, among the first organizations to support the Milwaukee school choice plan, filed a brief before the Supreme Court in support of that plan. It was also "one of the first out of the chute that talked about the role of faith-based organizations and community-based organizations in transforming the black community."[67] Its members were highly sought after to provide a counterbalance to liberal voices in debates on issues of importance to African Americans. In that regard, the center's biggest success may have been in voicing policy prescriptions that had not necessarily been heard presented by blacks.[68]

Currently, though, the organization no longer plays a prominent role among African American organizations espousing conservative principles and seeking black support for the GOP, nor does it have much of a media presence. According on one officer, CNBL did not have the "skills sets and the budget" to impact debates to the extent that the Joint Center for Political and Economic Studies, the premier black issues think tank, does.[69] The organization may exist on paper, but it is practically inactive. Its importance lies in its position in the vanguard of organizations created or funded by larger white foundations for the purpose of targeting black voters.

The organization appears to have receded in significance for two reasons: funding and internal struggle. While initially well funded by conservative philanthropy, the CNBL ultimately found itself unable to continue gaining foundation support. Although conservative philanthropists were enthusiastic about helping launch the group, their commitment to consistent giving waned, putting the organization in a precarious position. With no meaningful membership base, the organization found itself unable to garner the resources necessary to effectively undertake initiatives and other activities targeting its goals. Basic organizational mechanisms, such as a website and administrative staff, do not exist. The need for CNBL to focus so heavily on fundraising detracts from its focus on "thinking and writing and learning more about promising programs."[70]

Regarding internal struggle, Roy Innis, one of the founding members, was forced out of the organization in a power struggle that included Glenn Loury and, to a lesser extent, Phyllis Berry Myers and Peter Bell. The controversy that led to Innis's departure contributed to the destabilization of the organization. Loury's break with the organization is also seen as a major factor in its deterioration as a policy player. Loury, one of the key founders of the organization, broke with the group over its endorsement of the California Civil Rights Initiative, a conservative-backed measure that·called for an end to affirmative action in university admissions and in hiring by any state public employer, school, or contractor. Loury contended that his unwillingness to endorse the initiative in a speech before the Federalist Society in San Francisco just before the vote caused a problem between him and the rest of CNBL's leadership, particularly Shelby Steele. Loury came to believe that, from his perspective as an economist, the "absolutist" position against preferences was not helpful to black interests.[71] The departures of Innis and Loury began a period of descent that saw the CNBL recede from significance. From that point to now, the CNBL has been decreasingly operational.[72] It is unclear if the funding problems led to the internal strife, or vice versa, but both factors have combined to render the Center for New Black Leadership largely ineffective.

Harlem Republican Club

The Harlem Republican Club (HRC) is the official Republican District Club for the 70th Assembly District, covering historic Central Harlem and parts of Manhattanville, Hamilton Heights, and Sugar Hill. The club has a long history of activity designed to win black support. The current version of the club is actually a reincarnation of the HRC that shut down in 1942. The group was reborn in 2002 in a community where fewer than 4 percent of its residents were registered Republicans.[73] The original Harlem Republican Club was established in 1886, after the Civil War. The organization began to wane in the 1940s as the African American northern migration developed, when southern blacks moved to the north and were courted by the city's Democratic leaders.[74] A further complication in HRC support emerged when Adam Clayton Powell, a prominent African American minister, was elected as a Democrat to the New York City Council and, later, to Congress. Powell's presence as a black Democrat in the US House of Representatives proved to be a magnet that drew African American New Yorkers away from the GOP. Powell, for many of his early years in House, was one of just two African Americans in Congress. As such, he was often seen as representing black America, not just his Harlem constituency; blacks from all over the nation who couldn't get help from their own representatives called on him.

The HRC has a number of goals, most notable of which are to increase the level of participation in the Republican Party and the party's contribution to the advancement and achievement of both blacks and the community at large; to identify and cultivate viable candidates for elective office on the city, state, and national levels; to work with other Republican Party clubs and organizations to formulate and implement community-based programs to address local issues and generate local visibility that helps promote the relevance of the Republican Party; and to help the Republican district leaders build a strong political organization within the respective Assembly District and establish viable programs.[75]

The HRC is one of a number of black Republican organizations around the country that exists on paper but does not appear to meet any of its publicly stated goals. According to one prominent black Republican, the HRC is more moderate than traditional black Republican groups and does not take advantage of the opportunities that exist in Harlem to increase black support for the Republican Party.[76] The group has yet to make a mark in New York. One prominent New York–based black Republican was even unaware of the group's existence.

National Black Republican Association

The National Black Republican Association (NBRA) is an organization that has the potential to be an important player in efforts to increase African American support for the GOP. The group was formed in June 2005 with the mission of "returning Black America to its Republican roots"; it also seeks to "increase the number of Black Republican voters and, for those already in the party, provide information and networking opportunities."[77] Another goal of the group is "to be a resource for the black community on Republican ideals and promote the traditional values of the black community which are the core values of the Republican Party: strong families, faith in God, personal responsibility, quality education, and equal opportunities for all."[78] The NBRA plans to develop local chapters throughout the country, sponsor events to raise the profile of black Republicans, lobby, and access the media to spread its message. It also publishes a magazine, *The Black Republican*, to tout the activities and successes of prominent African American Republicans; and it operates a political action committee, National Black Republicans for Freedom, to support black Republican electoral candidates.

The NBRA was started with funds provided by each of the founding members and takes a different approach to fundraising in that it does not focus on large foundations to the extent that other groups do. According to Frances Rice, the founding chair of the NBRA, "All the money that we have gotten so far has come from ordinary middle-class Republicans—black and white."[79] This approach reflects the overall philosophy of the organization: that bringing more African Americans into the GOP has to be about efforts in the black community, not simply focusing on what the party does.[80]

The organization does, however, face substantial threats to its potential success. One occurred within a month of its official founding when two disagreements led to the resignation of six of the ten founders. The first was over a "statement of commitment" to the organization that NBRA chair Frances Rice requested board members to sign. According to one report, the loyalty oath concluded with the following statement: "My failure to sign this statement confirms that I am not a member in good standing of the NBRA and am not eligible to be an officer in the NBRA or a member of the NBRA Board of Directors."[81] The second disagreement concerned an NBRA-issued statement addressing the federal response to Hurricane Katrina. The press release commended President Bush for "deploying all of the resources of the federal government to help the refugees" and noted that the "President turned an unacceptable situation in New Orleans into a massive relief effort."[82] The press release charged Bush critics with seeking to "politicize, for their own partisan agenda, a disaster that affects so many of our fellow African American citizens."[83] The tone of the press release led one board member to note in his decision to resign that "the organization and its current leadership is heading down a much different direction than was envisioned by myself and other board members."[84]

Pinchback Society

The Pinchback Society is Louisiana's Black Republican Council and serves as a statewide business and political networking organization that engages registered black Republicans in Louisiana.[85] To that end, the group's plan is to establish a statewide infrastructure of black Republican activists throughout Louisiana's sixty-four parishes.[86]

The group is named after P. B. S. Pinchback, a Reconstruction-era Republican governor of Louisiana. Pinchback served as governor from December 9, 1872, to January 9, 1873, being elevated from lieutenant governor after the impeachment of Republican governor Henry Clay Warmouth. Pinchback and L. Douglas Wilder of Virginia are the only African Americans to have served as governor of a US state.

The Pinchback Society is not particularly well known among black Republican elites, and those interviewed were not able to identify any activities undertaken by the group that have made a significant difference in drawing blacks to the Republican Party.

Project 21

Project 21, an initiative of the National Center for Public Policy Research, a conservative think tank, bills itself as the "national leadership network of Black conservatives."[87] As such, it promotes "the views of African-Americans whose entrepreneurial spirit, sense of family and commitment to individual responsibility has not traditionally been echoed by the nation's civil rights establishment."[88] According to those familiar with the organization's founding, the group was created as a response to the frustration felt by a number of black conservatives who were offended by media coverage of the April 1992 Los Angeles riots following the verdict in the Rodney King–Los Angeles Police Department brutality case. They took umbrage at the traditional liberal voices called upon by the media to analyze what was going on in Los Angeles. The organization concluded that the media did not sufficiently focus on the lawlessness of the rioters, excusing their illegal behavior in favor of focusing on the controversy that led to the riot.[89]

The founders of Project 21 concluded that alternative views of African Americans were not being effectively presented, in contrast to the media's penchant to publicize the views of the civil rights establishment. They see Project 21 as filling a void by serving as a clearinghouse for black conservative political opinion and cultural commentary. Unlike most other conservative black organizations, Project 21 focuses its activities more on public relations than on voter organization. Their goal has been to promote the widespread placement of African American conservatives in media positions to advance black conservative viewpoints on the salient issues of the day. They send faxes and e-mails to media outlets, assist in getting opinion columns placed in newspapers and magazines, and provide infrastructure and technical assistance to black conservative individuals and groups. One member of the black Republican elite called Project 21 a "very important group" whose role "is to promote that eclectic group [black Republicans and conservatives] coalition, if you will, and get them [promoted in the media] by whatever means."[90] Project 21 is among the best-known black Republican organizations.

While Project 21 is less organizational than the other groups, it does play an important role in influencing media coverage of black conservatives and black Republicans. Their ability to access media is critical to airing the black conservative message. The more black conservatives on the air and in print, the greater the possibility that their message will find an audience with black viewers, listeners, and readers. Project 21 members are published in numerous outlets around the country, including some of the nation's largest black newspapers.

Analysis

It is easy to look at African American vote totals for Republican candidates and conclude that these organizations have had little or no impact on increasing African American support for the GOP. This conclusion, however, does not tell the entire story of GOP efforts to win African American support. Identifying why these organizations have been ineffective is critical to understanding where the GOP has fallen short and where it must go if it really wants to win black votes.

The Policies and Politics

Republican policy proposals intended to win black support have generally focused on economic development and income questions. They have had minimal impact on attracting black votes because they do not deal with the issues on which African Americans are most likely to be swayed—namely, social justice issues. While economic development is critical to black progress, one may wonder what good it would do if structural disparities such as incarceration rates and disparate sentencing, public education funding, and drug control policy, to name a few, continue to go unaddressed. A major problem from a policy standpoint is the fact that for every Republican-led policy initiative that can be seen as even indirectly pro-black, there are numerous other policy initiatives that can be seen as anti-black. In this regard, the good is far outweighed by the bad.

Politically, these outreach efforts are seen as less than sincere in many ways and reflect a commitment to developing effective political strategy rather than seriously going after black votes. The ultimate aim of these efforts is to force the national Democratic Party to expend resources to maintain its standing with African American voters—particularly the prominent engagement with popular black party leaders such as Jesse Jackson and Al Sharpton—efforts that would surely alienate white racial conservatives. Others have concluded that the outreach strategy is not aimed at African Americans but rather at "upper middle class suburban voters who agree with Republican economics but don't feel comfortable voting for a party that has a reputation for apathy—or worse—toward blacks; a Republican minority outreach program, even if it doesn't accomplish much, will help assuage their consciences."[91]

The Network

There is not yet a strongly coordinated network of state and local organizations seeking to increase black support for the party. For example, some states have Black Republican Councils (BRCs), while others do not. It is understandable if states with small percentages of black voters do not have such organizations, less so in states with significant black populations. The work of the network of national organizations—to the extent that it exists—is loosely organized, and its work is marginal at best. As Walters noted, "Most of these organizations are relatively small and not that great, either in terms of their function or in terms of their role."[92] Indeed, many of the organizations that exist do so on paper only and are actually one-person operations.[93] Some of these organizations are not well known even among the elites. While there is evidence that more organizations are forming, they have yet to have a measurable impact.

Some evidence of network weakness may be found in the fact that President George W. Bush, exceptionally well regarded among black conservatives, won 11 percent of the African American vote in 2004, a 2 percentage point increase from 2000. That George W. Bush could gain only 2 percentage points among African Americans in four years after having placed a number of African Americans in important cabinet positions, including the historic appointments of Colin Powell as secretary of state and Condoleezza Rice as national security adviser and later as secretary of state, is a major shortcoming that speaks less about the candidate (Bush) and more about the inability of the network to translate goals into accomplishments.[94]

The numerous reasons for the national network's inability to successfully draw black voters to GOP candidates include poor coordination and cooperation among groups, limited funding, and the perception that these groups lack legitimacy in the black community. According to one prominent black conservative activist, many of these organizations compete with one another rather than work together to obtain financial and other resources:

> There is no coordination and cooperation between black Republicans and black conservatives, blacks who are willing to say I [am not] for the status quo and I'm fighting against that status quo. There's not. Worse than that, we're crabs in a barrel, a small barrel, a 9 percent barrel, an 11 percent barrel. We're crabs in a barrel when there is no damn barrel! That's the biggest problem. And so when you've got that problem, the RNC is, like, well, you guys have got to get your stuff together. And when the RNC says, well, all right, we're going to try to help you get your stuff together, they select from one or two elements within the black Republican community, and if those one or two elements only represent one faction or one group within the black Republican agenda, if you will, then you're going to get limited support.[95]

These groups do not readily share donor, mailing, and membership lists, which could be helpful in solidifying the network of individuals who might agree on the issues and be willing to contribute to multiple organizations. Moreover, some organizational leaders are engaged in "turf battles" to seek a favored position in the eyes of RNC leaders around the nation that impede the larger issue they are concerned with—winning more black support for the GOP and fostering a movement of black conservatism generally.

Funding is a major issue for all of these organizations, particularly those that seek to operate nationally. Many of the national organizations are overly dependent on foundation grants or large individual donations to fund their operations, because they do not have significant community support in terms of paid memberships that can result in consistent income free from external direction. Grant dependency poses a major problem. Critics can rightfully contend that these organizations are not truly representative of black interests because their funding is not primarily derived from black sources—either black members or groups and foundations. Further, the charge that these organizations are constrained by their funding sources takes on a particular resonance when the source is white. It ultimately calls into question the legitimacy of these organizations as being "authentically black" or as seeking to further black interests; it also opens the groups to the charge that they are merely black fronts for white interests. BAMPAC appears to be the best-funded African American organization that targets black voters to support the GOP. It raises nearly $2 million annually, almost all of which comes through mail solicitations.[96] The group claims 135,000 donors nationwide and does not seek, though it may accept, contributions from large donors or foundations because of concerns over the potential restrictions that may come with the funding.

The funding problems help contribute to the perception that these organizations lack legitimacy in the African American community and in the upper echelons of the Republican Party. The perception is driven by two factors. First, many of these groups are not membership organizations; those that are have low individual participation levels. Second, these organizations receive scant media coverage, which—rightly or wrongly—is a primary contributor to the perception that an individual or organization is a legitimate spokesperson or representative of a particular segment of society. An individual or organization that professes to be working for the best interest of African Americans must be able to garner media coverage if it wants to be taken seriously. This is particularly the case for some of these organizations that criticize traditional civil rights groups, who maintain a larger media presence regarding issues that impact the black community.

One way to test the extent to which these organizations are able to garner media attention is to examine the major newspapers in some of the cities with large African American populations for mentions of these groups. A review of the major newspapers in cities such as Atlanta, Chicago, Detroit, New York, and Washington, DC, allows for a number of observations regarding the perceived legitimacy of these organizations.[97] While newspapers are far from the only form of media, they do represent a significant forum for public legitimacy.[98]

As Table 4.3 demonstrates, from 1995 through 2004, the nine largest newspapers in these cities had a total of seventy-three mentions of these organizations. Some of the mentions are obituaries, letters to the editor, and affiliation identifiers for individuals quoted in articles. None of the mentions were organization profiles or articles that described their work and effectiveness. Consequently, seventy-three mentions in 120 months is not enough to make a significant impact in the way African Americans perceive organizations dedicated to winning their favor toward the GOP.

Regarding the support of the larger Republican Party, it is notable that the black GOP organizations around the nation receive scant financial support or technical assistance from the national party. This presents a paradox for the party and the organizations: Are the groups unsuccessful because they get limited support from the party or does the party give them limited support because they are unsuccessful? One black Republican activist and former elected official indicated that because these organizations are not particularly successful in bringing in large numbers of black voters, the

Table 4.3 Selected Newspaper Citations of Black Organizations That Seek Increased Black Support for the GOP, 1995–2004

	AARLC	BAMPAC	CNBL	NBRC	P21	Total
AJC	2	6	3	2	0	13
DFP	0	0	0	0	0	0
CST	0	0	1	0	0	1
CT	0	0	0	0	0	0
NYDN	0	0	0	0	0	0
NYT	1	2	16	0	1	20
NYP	0	0	0	0	0	0
WP	3	5	25	0	6	39
WT	0	0	0	0	0	0

Source: Data compiled by author through Lexis/Nexis search.

Notes: AARLC: African American Republican Leadership Council; BAMPAC: Black America's Political Action Committee; CNBL: Center for New Black Leadership; NBRC: National Black Republican Council; P21: Project 21; AJC: *Atlanta Journal-Constitution,* DFP: *Detroit Free Press*; CST: *Chicago Sun-Times*; CT: *Chicago Tribune*; NYDN: *New York Daily News*; NYT: *New York Times*; NYP: *New York Post*; WP: *Washington Post*; WT: *Washington Times.*

Republican Party does not see these groups as viable players in the development and implementation of electoral strategy.[99] In other words, these groups have yet to make themselves politically relevant to the larger party. Comparatively, that same activist noted that the GOP goes to great lengths to support white evangelical groups because they can turn out large numbers of voters.

Notes

1. Robert Weems and Lewis Randolph, "The National Response to Richard M. Nixon's Black Capitalism Initiative: The Success of Domestic Detente," *Journal of Black Studies* 32, no. 1 (September 2001): 66.

2. Ibid.

3. Dean Kotlowski, *Nixon's Civil Rights: Politics, Principle, and Policy* (Cambridge: Harvard University Press, 2001), p. 128.

4. Ibid., p. 127.

5. Harry S. Dent Jr. to Bryce N. Harlow and John D. Ehrlichman, December 22, 1969, Box 4, Harry S. Dent Jr. files, White House Special Files, quoted in Kotlowski, *Nixon's Civil Rights,* p. 134.

6. Kotlowski, *Nixon's Civil Rights,* p. 144, quoting "Highlights of Nixon Administration Initiatives in Civil Rights and Related Programs," February 1974, Box 4, Garment Papers, Library of Congress.

7. Ibid.

8. Weems and Randolph, "National Response," p. 76, quoting Andrew Brimmer, "Trouble with Black Capitalism," *Nation's Business* 57: 78–79; Kotlowski, *Nixon's Civil Rights,* p. 139.

9. Kotlowski, *Nixon's Civil Rights,* pp. 137–140.

10. Weems and Randolph, "National Response."

11. Hugh Davis Graham, "The Origins of Affirmative Action: Civil Rights and the Regulatory State," *Annals of the American Society of Political and Social Science* 523 (September 1992): 56.

12. Ibid., p. 57.

13. Ibid.

14. Kotlowski, *Nixon's Civil Rights,* p. 99, quoting transcript of press interview by Nixon, October 25, 1955, PPS 307.70; television remarks, April 22, 1956, PPS 307.80; summary of discussion with representatives of organized labor, April 30, 1957, PPS 307.97.2 (Nixon Pre-Presidential Papers, Richard Nixon Library and Birthplace, Yorba Linda, California).

15. Kotlowski, *Nixon's Civil Rights,* p. 57.

16. Diana Jean Schemo, "Graduation Study Suggests That Some States Sharply Understate High School Dropout Rates," *New York Times,* September 17, 2003.

17. Daria Hall, "Getting Honest About Grad Rates: How States Play the Numbers and Students Lose," *Education Trust,* June 2005; Michael Dobbs, "States' Graduation Data Criticized: Independent Study Shows Disparities," *Washington Post,* June 24, 2005.

18. Christopher Swanson, "Who Graduates? Who Doesn't? A Statistical Portrait of Public High School Graduation, Class of 2001," Urban Institute, Washington, DC, February 2004.

19. William Julius Wilson, *When Work Disappears* (New York: Vintage Books, 1996), p. xiii.

20. Luiza Ch. Savage, "Private School in Washington Seeks to Capitalize on First-Ever Vouchers," *New York Sun,* March 17, 2004.

21. Department of Education, DC School Choice Initiative, available at www.ed.gov/programs/dcchoice/index.html (accessed June 8, 2005).

22. V. Dion Haynes, "2nd D.C. Voucher Lottery Gets Stronger Response," *Washington Post,* April 16, 2005. p. B2.

23. Ibid.

24. Ibid.

25. Barbara Miner, "Why the Right Hates Public Education," *The Progressive* 68, no. 1 (March 2004), www.progressive.org/jan04/miner0104.html (accessed June 8, 2005).

26. Faye Anderson, interview by author, tape recorded, December 13, 2004.

27. Bill Calhoun, interview by author, tape recorded, June 23, 2005.

28. Deroy Murdock, interview by author, tape recorded, March 17, 2005; Niger Innis, interview by author, tape recorded, March 18, 2005.

29. Ronald Walters, interview by author, tape recorded, July 26, 2005.

30. Ibid.

31. Republican National Committee press release, March 10, 2005, available at www.gop.com/News/Read.aspx?ID=5260 (accessed June 23, 2005).

32. Ibid.

33. Phyllis Berry Myers, interview by author, tape recorded, July 25, 2005.

34. Renee Amoore, interview by author, tape recorded, August 4, 2005.

35. Calhoun interview.

36. People for the American Way, *Buying a Movement: Right-Wing Foundations and American Politics* (Washington, DC: People for the American Way, 1996).

37. People for the American Way, *Community Voice or Captive of the Right? The Black Alliance for Educational Options* (Washington, DC: People for the American Way, 2003), p. 4.

38. Search of Walter Williams, *Media Transparency: The Money Behind the Media*, www.mediatransparency.org/search_results/comment_string_search_results.php?Message=Walter+E.+Williams (accessed May 5, 2005).

39. Press release announcing 2003 Bradley Prize recipients, available at www.bradleyfdn.org/PR/pr0903.html (accessed May 5, 2005).

40. Search of Charles Murray, *Media Transparency: The Money Behind the Media*, www.mediatransparency.org/search_results/comment_string_search_results.php?Message=Charles+Murray (accessed May 5, 2005).

41. People for the American Way, *Buying a Movement*, p. 32.

42. Search of Dinesh D'Souza, *Media Transparency: The Money Behind the Media*, www.mediatransparency.org/search_results/comment_string_search_results.php?Message=Dinesh (accessed May 5, 2005).

43. Anderson interview.

44. People for the American Way, *Buying a Movement*.

45. Alvin Williams, interview by author, tape recorded, June 29, 2004. See also David Almasi, interview by author, tape recorded, August 24, 2005.

46. Rachel Zabarkes Friedman, "Southern Conservative Comfort: Will Georgia Voters Embrace GOP Rising Star Dylan Glenn? *National Review Online*, July 14, 2004.

47. Dan Balz and Matthew Mosk, "The Year of the Black Republican? GOP Targets Democratic Constituency in 3 High-Profile Races," *Washington Post*, May 10, 2006, p. A1.

48. Ibid.

49. It is important to note that many of these organizations state, for tax purposes, that they are nonpartisan. However, it is clear from their issue positions and the candidates they endorse or contribute to that they are part of a network of groups that want and espouse Republican control of government.

50. African American Republican Leadership Council website, www.aarlc.org/about/index.shtml (accessed March 25, 2005).

51. Ibid.

52. Ibid.

53. Niger Innis, interview by author, tape recorded, March 18, 2005.

54. Robert George, interview by author, tape recorded, March 29, 2005.

55. Alvin Williams interview.

56. Ibid.

57. Ibid.

58. Ibid.

59. Michael Steele, interview with author, tape recorded, December 9, 2005.

60. See www.blackrepublicancounciloftexas.com/About_Us.html (accessed February 21, 2005).

61. Calhoun interview.

62. See www.blackrepublicancounciloftexas.com/About_Us.html (accessed February 21, 2005).

63. Calhoun interview.

64. Myers interview.

65. Ibid.

66. Gerald Reynolds, interview by author, tape recorded, August 4, 2005.

67. Myers interview.

68. Reynolds interview.

69. Ibid.

70. Ibid.

71. Glen Loury, interview by author, tape recorded, July 21, 2005.

72. As of August 2006, the CNBL website, cnbl.org, is not functioning. It simply reads "This Web site is coming soon."

73. Julia Levy, "GOP Reviving Its Harlem Republican Club," *New York Sun*, September 25, 2002, p. 1.

74. Ibid.

75. Harlem Republican Club website, www.nycrepublican.org/hrc/mission.htm (accessed February 7, 2005).

76. Innis interview.

77. National Black Republican Association, www.nbra.info (accessed December 28, 2005); Brian DeBose, "Black Republican Group Will Focus on Recruitment," *Washington Times*, August 15, 2005.

78. National Black Republican Association, www.nationalblackrepublicans. com/index.cfm?fuseaction=pages.aboutnbra&x=819384 (accessed December 28, 2005).

79. Frances Rice, interview by author, tape recorded, August 15, 2005.

80. Ibid.

81. John McCaslin, "Inside the Beltway," *Washington Times*, September 13, 2005.

82. National Black Republican Association press release, "Black Republican Group Praises Bush's Disaster Reaction," September 2, 2005.

83. Ibid.

84. McCaslin, "Inside the Beltway.".

85. Pinchback Society, www.blacksforgeorgewbush.org/about.html (accessed February 16, 2005)

86. Ibid.

87. Project 21, www.project21.org/P21Index.html (accessed February 16, 2005).

88. Ibid.

89. Ibid.

90. Innis interview.

91. Eric Alterman, "G.O.P. Chairman Lee Atwater: Playing Hardball," *New York Times Magazine*, April 30, 1989, p. 30.

92. Walters interview; Rice interview.

93. Anderson interview; Innis interview.

94. Innis interview.

95. Ibid.

96. Ibid.

97. The newspapers searched include *Atlanta Journal-Constitution, Chicago Sun-Times, Chicago Tribune, Detroit Free Press, New York Post, New York Daily News, New York Times, Washington Post*, and *Washington Times*.

98. Further, newspapers (and magazines) are easily searchable on various databases. As such, they are available to virtually anyone who wants to revisit a particular issue, controversy, or individual.

99. J. C. Watts, interview by author, tape recorded, October 12, 2005.

5

Public Policies Speak
Louder Than Words

THE CONSERVATIVE TAKEOVER OF THE REPUBLICAN PARTY IN the 1960s, coupled with the 1980 election of Ronald Reagan as president and the GOP's Senate takeover, pushed the party toward advocating policies that satisfied their conservative ideological supporters who, rightfully, claimed responsibility for the GOP's ascension to the White House. However, those same policy positions pushed the party further away from African Americans and became a significant impediment to the party's efforts to win black support. The GOP's consistent opposition to race-specific legislation favored by African Americans, along with its position on legislation seen as hostile to black interests, solidified the belief in the black community that the Republican Party was anti-black.

Certain public policy positions taken since the conservative takeover of the party contributed to this view, including Reagan administration budget cuts at the US Commission on Civil Rights and the Equal Employment Opportunity Commission (EEOC); Reagan's opposition to the 1982 extension of the Voting Rights Act; opposition to the Martin Luther King Jr. holiday bill; opposition to antiapartheid legislation; opposition to affirmative action; President George H. W. Bush's veto of the Civil Rights Act of 1990; opposition to minimum wage increases; and support for "mandatory minimums" and other anticrime policies. These policy areas provided an opportunity for the Republican Party to take stances that could have been seen positively by African Americans. The fact that it did not do so greatly contributed to the animus many African Americans have toward the party. This also established the public policy hurdles with which the GOP must contend if it wants to overturn its current standing in the African American community.

95

Reagan Dismantling of Federal
Civil Rights Enforcement Mechanisms

Ronald Reagan entered the White House with a civil rights record and phi-losophy that was far different from his predecessor's and that was in stark contrast to the preferences of the civil rights establishment. Reagan advo-cated states' rights and believed that the federal regulatory structure neces-sary to enforce the civil rights laws created in the 1960s was onerous and anticompetitive and that it hurt US business interests. He also believed that the laws created an environment of "reverse discrimination" and cam-paigned to overturn liberal civil rights laws and regulation. Reagan's civil rights agenda reflected traditional conservative positions—for example, anti–affirmative action and anti–women's rights. Conservatives oppose affirmative action because the existence of such programs requires the admission that African Americans continue to face discrimination—an admission that contradicts conservative claims of a color-blind society. Conservatives tend to oppose women's rights because they believe such policies undermine the traditional family structure.

Reagan's position on these issues raised the ire of minorities all over the country and brought down the wrath of civil rights organizations who concluded that his ascension to the presidency heralded a new era in which civil rights enforcement and regulation would be loosened or, if possible, eliminated. His positions also earned him the overwhelming support of white conservatives who believed that he would "put blacks in their place" by overturning affirmative action and other civil rights protections, which many Reagan supporters believed were responsible for their flattening wages or job loss. Many Republicans during this era campaigned on the notion that racial preferences, rather than conservative economic policies that encouraged the movement of jobs to cheaper labor markets abroad, were the reason for shrinking employment opportunity in the smokestack, labor-intensive industries of the Midwest and South.

Reagan faced a significant barrier to reaching his goal of remaking the civil rights status quo. Democrats, who controlled the House of Representatives, vehemently opposed his efforts and served as a backstop against him and the Republican majority in the Senate, many of whom were elected along with Reagan on a conservative policy platform and were sure to support the president's proposed changes in this regard. Overtly seeking to overturn these measures would continue to paint Reagan as a racist and continue a controversy that had the potential to bog down other areas of his domestic agenda, such as tax cuts. Reagan needed a more covert approach to get closer to his policy goals. His solution was to withdraw funding from those parts of the federal apparatus responsible for enforcing civil rights laws, thereby lessening their ability to examine and enforce them.

The dismantling of federal civil rights enforcement took two forms and occurred concomitantly. First was to freeze or reduce funding for agencies charged with federal civil rights enforcement. Rather than overtly end these programs and agencies, the Reagan administration sought to starve them to prevent them from doing their work. In this way, the administration could largely achieve its goal of civil rights deregulation without seeking the abolition of the programs and agencies, thereby providing some political cover. Second was to hire as leaders of these organizations individuals who were ideologically predisposed to not enforcing federal civil rights laws and regulations as aggressively as their predecessors. These actions deregulated federal civil rights enforcement and created an environment in which civil rights violations could occur with near impunity and certainly with much less fear of federal reprisals than before.

In some departments, enforcement either shifted in new ways, was reduced, or was discontinued. One congressional investigation concluded that the EEOC shifted away from class action lawsuits, elevated the standard of proof to establish reasonable cause, orally directed staff not to recommend the use of goals and timetables and not to intervene in cases in which goals and timetables were proposed as a remedy for discrimination, and accelerated closure of cases at the expense of quality of investigations.[1] The Justice Department filed no cases under the Fair Housing Act of 1968 during its first year under Reagan; it filed two in 1982. Under Presidents Nixon, Ford, and Carter, the department averaged thirty-two cases a year.[2]

Particularly notable in this regard were budget cuts and personnel changes at the US Commission on Civil Rights and the EEOC. These changes signified a clear move away from traditional civil rights enforcement and toward a less active federal role in ensuring that these laws were followed. To those who sought more stringent enforcement of US civil rights laws, the budget cuts and personnel changes were seen as an attempt to roll back government regulation in this area. That they were initiated at the urging of a Republican president and a Republican Senate majority is a significant variable as it relates to the relationship between African Americans and the GOP.

President Reagan's personnel moves at the Civil Rights Commission began a period of political bloodletting that ultimately rendered the organization unable to meet its historic role. Reagan dismissed longtime chair Arthur Flemming and angered civil rights activists when he proposed nominating to the commission B. Sam Hart, a black Philadelphia radio evangelist who opposed busing, the Equal Rights Amendment, and gay rights.[3] Hart ran into bipartisan opposition and was never nominated. Reagan fired three civil rights commission members—Mary Frances Berry, Blandina Cardenas Ramirez, and Rabbi Murray Saltzman—so that he could replace them with conservative supporters of his civil rights ideology and enforcement philosophy. Mainline civil rights groups opposed the replacements and charged Reagan with trying to undermine the commission and politicize its work.

The replacement commissioners led the agency in a new direction. The public statements of the chair and others on the commission began to echo the White House. The commission produced fewer enforcement reports and, to the extent that they did prepare such reports, contracted out the projects to external groups that were likely to draw the conclusions favored by the administration. In so doing, they bypassed the experienced career civil servants who had long served the commission and had "institutional memory" as to how the agency operated. At one point, the contracting was so significant that it constituted more than three-quarters of the commission's budget.[4] The House responded to Reagan's action by moving to extend the commission's life and allow for the removal of a commissioner only for neglect of duty or official malfeasance.

After months of negotiating between Congress and the White House, the commission was restructured and extended. Under the compromise, the existing six-member commission was replaced by a new eight-member panel, with four commissioners named by the president and four by Congress. Unlike the previous incarnation, appointees would not require Senate confirmation. Berry, whom Reagan had fired, successfully sued the president—joined by Ramirez, who had also been fired—and returned to the commission in 1984. The controversy surrounding these appointments and the increased politicization of the commission marked the beginning of the end for the agency as a significant, independent, credible body that could conduct the research necessary to appropriately advise Congress and the president on the full range of civil rights issues.[5]

As Table 5.1 shows, appropriations for Civil Rights Commission operations were cut during the Reagan years. The commission's funding, adjusted for inflation, declined by about 58 percent from fiscal year (FY) 1980 through FY1995.[6] The largest cuts in funding occurred between FY1986 and FY1988, when funding was reduced by 56 percent. Since FY1991, funding has hovered around $9 million. These cuts were even more significant when one factors in variables such as inflation and personnel costs. The budget cuts forced drastic personnel reductions. By FY1987, the commission workforce was cut in half. In 1983, it had 256 employees and ten regional offices; by 1991, it was reduced to seventy-nine employees and four regional offices.[7] The commission has never recovered from the gutting it took at the behest of President Reagan. Even by 2005, its budget was about three-quarters of what it was in 1982. The cuts hurt staff morale and effectiveness, and the result was a commission that existed on paper but was largely a shell of its former existence unable to significantly investigate civil rights in the United States—aggressively or otherwise.

Regarding the EEOC, the Reagan philosophy of the agency favored

Table 5.1   Civil Rights Commission Actual and Inflation-Adjusted Appropriations, FY1980–FY1995 (dollars)

Fiscal Year	Actual Appropriation	Inflation-Adjusted Appropriation[a]	Fiscal Year	Actual Appropriation	Inflation-Adjusted Appropriation[a]
1980	$11,230,000	$20,748,000	1988	5,707,000	7,576,000
1981	11,719,000	19,749,000	1989	5,707,000	7,323,000
1982	12,318,000	19,529,000	1990	5,707,000	7,078,000
1983	11,626,000	17,747,000	1991	7,075,000	8,318,000
1984	11,887,000	17,654,000	1992	7,159,000	8,240,000
1985	12,747,000	18,294,000	1993	7,776,000	8,606,000
1986	12,300,000	17,223,000	1994	7,776,000	8,310,000
1987	7,500,000	10,277,000	1995	9,000,000	9,224,000

Source: US Commission on Civil Rights: Agency Lacks Basic Management Controls (Washington, DC: General Accounting Office, 1997), citing *Economic Report of the President: February 1997* (Washington, DC: Government Printing Office, 1997), Table B-3.
    Note: a. Inflation-adjusted appropriation in 1996 dollars.

reducing the number of lawsuits filed against suspected violators of equal employment statutes and lessening penalties against those who were convicted. That the Reagan administration sought to relax civil rights enforcement is confirmed in 1981 transition documents that set a goal of rescinding Executive Order 12067, which established authority for affirmative action in hiring.[8] The documents established a number of objectives designed to reduce federal civil rights enforcement. Included among them were putting a one-year freeze on new commission guidelines; appointing an individual "steadfastly opposed" to "reverse discrimination" created by, conservatives argue, Title VII of the Civil Rights Act of 1964; reorganizing agency components so that they are in line with Reagan's civil rights program; and more aggressively seeking input from the private sector regarding agency enforcement activities.[9] A subsequent plan was drafted that would have abolished regulations requiring numerical goals for women and minorities.

President Reagan installed Clarence Thomas to lead the agency. Thomas, like those installed at the Civil Rights Commission, had an entirely different view of racism, discrimination, and the need for strong enforcement of equal employment laws. In justifying the discontinuance of collecting and using certain data to determine discrimination, Thomas contended that "statistics have been misused to charge discrimination against employers."[10] Thomas also cut staff: EEOC staff was reduced by 10 percent from 1983 to 1984, from 3,316 to 2,980, a reduction of 336 staffers.

The dismantling of federal civil rights enforcement was multifaceted. One seldom identified factor is the Paperwork Reduction Act of 1980 (PRA). Originally conceived as a tool to help administer government more efficiently, the law came to be used as a cover for Reagan administration efforts to deregulate civil rights enforcement by ceasing data collection in areas that shed light on the extent to which civil rights violations may or may not have occurred. Under the act, the Office of Management and Budget (OMB) "stopped certain agencies like HUD and the Veterans Administration from collecting racial and ethnic data altogether."[11] Also, OMB "abolished its statistical branch and informed the various state governments that unless there was a specific 'federal' need, the government would no longer collect statistics that were useful to the states, even if these did assist them in carrying out their civil rights functions."[12]

The Reagan dismantling of civil rights enforcement mechanisms was in line with his other funding cuts for programs that assisted the poor, particularly poor African Americans. According to the Center on Budget and Policy Priorities, President Reagan cut billions from these types of programs. Table 5.2 compares the funding for selected social programs from 1981, Reagan's first year as president, to 1988, the last year of his presidency.

The Reagan approach to civil rights enforcement continues currently under President George W. Bush. According to a report that contrasted Bush's enforcement to Clinton's, although the rate of civil rights complaints has remained steady since 1999—at about 12,000 per year—Justice Department referrals for prosecution in civil rights cases and civil sanctions against civil rights violators have declined.[13] The number of referrals declined from 3,053 in 1999 to 1,903 in 2003, and the number of civil sanctions declined from 740 in 2001 to 576 in 2003.[14]

Opposition to Affirmative Action Legislation

Affirmative action policies refer to "any measure, beyond simple termination of a discriminatory practice, adopted to correct or compensate for past

Table 5.2 Reagan Administration Cuts in Social Programs, FY1981 and FY1988 (dollars)

	1981	1988
Training and employment	9,106,000	2,887,000
Energy assistance	1,850,000	1,162,000
Health services, including community health centers and care for the homeless	856,000	814,000
Legal services	312,000	232,000
Compensatory education	3,545,000	3,291,000
Housing assistance for the elderly	797,000	422,000
Community services block grant (funding local antipoverty agencies)	525,000	290,000

Source: Joe Davidson, "Reagan: A Contrary View," www.msnbc.msn.com/id/5158315.

or present discrimination or to prevent discrimination from recurring in the future."[15] These programs have focused on four areas that have, historically, been venues of substantial racial discrimination: employment, public contracting, education, and housing. Affirmative action programs date to the 1960s and can be traced to legal rulings calling for an "affirmative duty" of local school boards to desegregate public schools and requiring ederal government contractors to take affirmative action toward employees and applicants for employment in areas such as recruitment, employment, and promotion (Executive Order 11246).[16] The order also requires that all employers with fifty or more employees and federal contracts in excess of $50,000 file written affirmative action plans with the government. Subsequent executive orders expanded or contracted the range of affirmative action, depending on the ideology of the particular president.

Affirmative action has played a large role in black economic and educational enhancement. The growth of the black middle class that began in the 1970s is largely attributable to increased access to higher educational and economic opportunities brought about by these compensatory programs. Over time, there has been "considerable convergence between Black and White workers at the high end of the occupational scale."[17] The growth in the number of black professionals, particularly lawyers and doctors, can be traced to increased access to higher education during the 1970s and since.

Affirmative action policies have long been a target of conservative Republican criticism. The consensus Republican position regarding affirmative action, particularly since the 1980s, has been to consistently oppose it and seek its demise. Republicans often argue that affirmative action has been anticompetitive, that it results in reverse discrimination, and that it holds whites responsible for racial wrongs in which they, individually, may have had no involvement. Consequently, Republican activists in Congress and throughout the country have used the courts, state and local referenda and initiatives, and legislation to end or restrict affirmative action. In 1995, California governor Pete Wilson signed an executive order abolishing a wide range of affirmative action programs affecting hiring and contracting in state agencies.

The Republicans' 1994 seizure of the House and Senate worried supporters of affirmative action who feared that the shift in congressional control marked the beginning of the GOP's effort to end affirmative action, particularly as it related to small disadvantaged businesses. Important efforts that took place then to reduce the reach and benefit of affirmative action continue. Republican senator Mitch McConnell proposed legislation that would end affirmative action, and the Senate Republican Policy Committee submitted a brief in a Piscataway, New Jersey, case that opposed an affirmative action policy that sought to facilitate faculty diversity.[18] Republican efforts to end, or substantially undermine, affirmative action were fueled in part by increased conservative activism in the states against these policies. This activism during the 1990s led to a number of notable events, including federal courts voiding preferential admissions of minority students to colleges and universities in certain states, invalidating minority preferences in public and private employment, and nullifying state and local efforts to increase minority group participation as contractors and subcontractors on publicly financed construction projects.[19] All of these occurrences came at the initiative of conservative activists who filed the lawsuits and complaints.

Two legislative actions in early 1995 also restricted affirmative action. The first was a move by the Republican-controlled Congress to repeal a Federal Communications Commission policy requiring radio licensees to adopt affirmative minority recruitment and outreach measures. The policy was created to encourage minority ownership of broadcast companies. The second eliminated an established and long-standing contracting goal for the US Agency for International Development (USAID). The goal, known as the Gray Amendment after former representative William Gray and first enacted in 1983, directed USAID to award at least 10 percent of its development assistance funding to businesses owned and controlled by socially and economically disadvantaged individuals or other disadvantaged entities.

Not all legislative efforts to end or curb affirmative action were successful. Republican senator Phil Gramm offered an amendment to the FY1996 legislative branch appropriations bill to prohibit agencies funded by the bill from awarding federal contracts on the basis of race, color, national origin, or gender.[20] Another FY1996 appropriations bill, for the Commerce, Justice, and State departments, initially contained a provision that would have barred agencies covered by the measure from using appropriated funds for certain types of affirmative action programs.[21] Republican representative Jan Meyers introduced a bill that would have eliminated the 8(a) program, a Small Business Administration program to facilitate the development and growth of minority small businesses.

The most notable legislative threat to affirmative action came from Republican senator Bob Dole and Republican representative Charles Canady. They introduced legislation in 1995 to bar the federal government from intentionally discriminating against, or granting a preference to, any individual or group based on race, color, national origin, or sex, in federal contracting, federal employment, or federally conducted programs. The bill would also have prohibited the government from requiring or encouraging federal contractors to grant such preferences, which were defined as quotas, set-asides, numerical goals, timetables, and other numerical objectives. The bill was a frontal attack on affirmative action and all data used to facilitate programs to that end.

Dole, who was preparing for a 1996 presidential bid, supported the

California Civil Rights Initiative (also known as Proposition 209), a conservative-backed plan that called on voters to decide whether to ban affirmative action in state government and state universities. Proposition 209 was the result of efforts of groups such as the American Civil Rights Institute, an interest group dedicated to ending affirmative action and led by a prominent black conservative, Ward Connerly.

While most of the legislative attempts to end or curtail affirmative action were unsuccessful, the point here is that they were all introduced by Republicans. The partisan push to end these programs resulted in constant criticism of the party by affirmative action supporters, which only perpetuated the belief that the GOP was anti-black.

Reagan's Opposition to Strengthening Voting Rights

The 1965 Voting Rights Act (VRA) is considered by many to be the most important and significant civil rights legislation ever. It was crafted to respond to the various instruments developed throughout the South to keep African Americans from voting. These instruments were created to avoid compliance with the Fifteenth Amendment, which granted male suffrage "without regard to race, color, or previous condition of servitude." This amendment, and others, were part of the congressionally mandated Reconstruction, which dramatically remade southern society and ushered in a period of unprecedented black political, social, and economic development. Conservative opposition to Reconstruction eventually led to its demise, and new laws and changes to state constitutions were initiated that rendered black politics as impotent as it was prior to Reconstruction.

By the end of the nineteenth century, most southern states had held constitutional conventions to permanently disenfranchise African Americans. It all began in Mississippi, which lengthened residency requirements; imposed literacy tests, property requirements, and poll taxes; and disqualified convicts. Other states built on what Mississippi had done. Virginia required voters to bring paperwork with them to prove their compliance with new laws and instituted a two and a half minute time limit for voting if others were waiting in line, which effectively made it impossible for illiterate residents to cast a completed ballot. Louisiana instituted a "grandfather clause," which allowed permanent registration if one's father and grandfathers were qualified to vote on January 1, 1867; blacks did not qualify under this provision, because they were prohibited from voting in 1867.[22] These and other disenfranchisement mechanisms drove virtually every African American from the southern political process. The 1867 black registration rate in Mississippi was 70 percent; by 1889, that number fell to 9 percent. Louisiana's black registration fell from 130,334 to 5,320 in a four-year period. Alabama's 1900 constitutional change drove down black registration totals from 181,471, prior to the change, to 3,000, just after.[23]

The 1965 passage of the VRA changed the landscape of black political participation, particularly in the South, by outlawing these mechanisms, which had effectively locked African Americans out of the voting process for generations. Also, the VRA literally changed the face of the US government by transforming the political landscape from a closed society to one more culturally, racially, and economically representative of the nation than ever before. It created an environment whereby white America became accustomed to seeing black candidates on ballots around the nation and, in some cases, whites even voted for those candidates. While the VRA primarily targeted African Americans, the entire nation benefited from it, and the country is better for the diversity it engendered.

The VRA has been an unparalleled success: 1.3 million new black voters were registered in the South in the first two years of its existence, and continued efforts since have left African Americans near parity with whites in terms of voter registration rates.[24] The new voters led to more black elected officials. In 1965, approximately seventy African Americans held elected office in the eleven southern states; that number grew to 248 by 1968, to 1,397 by 1974, and to 2,535 by 1981.[25] But the VRA's success is not limited to the South. Now, more than 9,000 African Americans serve as elected officials around the nation. While African Americans are still underrepresented among the nation's elected officials, this incredible growth could not have happened without the Voting Rights Act.

As a consequence of the VRA's success, African Americans hold dear the act and consistently support its renewal by high margins. To oppose the renewal or strengthening of the VRA is seen in much of the African American community as an assault on black voting rights. But President Reagan opposed the extension of the act and supported a substitute measure that would have weakened it by raising the burden of proof for voting rights violations. After intense lobbying, however, Reagan signed an extension with four major components:

> The bill extended the preclearance provision for 25 years; it provided a bail out mechanism for the preclearance provision; it allowed private parties to prove voting rights violations by showing that an election law or procedure "results" in discrimination; and, finally, it extended provisions requiring areas of the country to provide bilingual election materials.[26]

The 1982 fight to renew the VRA was one that pitted President Reagan and his conservative supporters against African Americans and their liberal supporters.

In 1985, the second Reagan administration "developed new rules for enforcing the Voting Rights Act that would make it more difficult for Black and Hispanic people and other minority groups to challenge state and local election laws as discriminatory."[27] Viewed by critics as an attempt to weaken the 1982 extension of the VRA, the Reagan administration contended that the then-proposed changes reflected an effort to conform with the amendments to the 1982 act. The net effect of the ruling was to reverse the burden of proof by placing it on the victims of discrimination. In so doing, "the new rules narrow the way the law is enforced as it applies to special elections to fill vacant offices and to redistricting plans prepared by local officials in response to court orders."[28] The change would have allowed for some reduction as it related to minority voting strength in a particular voting district—as long as that reduction did not constitute a major reduction of that strength, though what constitutes a major reduction was not spelled out in the new rules.

Opposition to the
Rev. Dr. Martin Luther King Jr. Holiday Bill

Rev. Dr. Martin Luther King Jr. is the world's most revered African American. His contribution to the United States through his leadership of the civil rights movement elevated him to mythic status in black households around the nation. He was the face of the civil rights movement, and his emphasis on nonviolent civil disobedience became a strategy that has been emulated throughout the world. King's leadership helped change public policy and led to the passage of landmark legislation such as the Civil Rights Act of 1964 and the Voting Rights Act of 1965. His leadership helped pave the way for wholesale changes in US race relations and led to what some scholars refer to as America's second Reconstruction.[29]

King's April 1968 assassination created anguish and anger throughout the African American community and sparked riots in numerous US cities. Shortly after the assassination in 1968, Representative John Conyers introduced the first bill calling for a federal holiday to commemorate King's life. The bill was blocked in the House, a move that led to the submission to Congress of petitions containing more than 6 million names supporting the holiday. In each congressional session thereafter until the bill was passed, legislation was submitted to institute a federal holiday to honor King. The fifteen-year period from initial introduction to passage of the bill through Congress is a study in perseverance over conservative opposition.

Although history shows that a Republican (Maryland's Charles McC. Mathias Jr.) introduced the bill in the Senate, a Republican (Kansas's Robert Dole) managed the bill on the Senate floor, a Republican leader (Tennessee's Howard Baker) ensured its quick consideration, and a Republican president (Ronald Reagan) signed the Martin Luther King Jr.

holiday bill into law (on November 2, 1983), the primary opposition to the holiday also came from Republicans. For example, Republican senator Jesse Helms attacked the proposal, saying King espoused "action-oriented Marxism."[30] Another Republican senator, John East, sought to water down the King proposal by creating, instead, a "National Civil Rights Day." Republican senator Gordon Humphrey proposed renaming the day to honor Abraham Lincoln instead of King. One other former elected official, also Republican, referred to King as a "reprehensible individual" and lamented the fact that it is "very unfortunate that we have a national holiday for King . . . [and] that we in fact place his holiday in more esteem than any other American."[31]

President Reagan initially opposed legislation commemorating King's life with a federal holiday and was highly critical of him. Reagan signed the bill into law only after it became clear that Congress would vote to override his veto; in other words, he had no real alternative. He could have allowed the bill to go into law without his signature, but that would have been mean-spirited and politically gratuitous and would have represented one additional example of what many believed to be Reagan's antipathy toward blacks. He would have gained nothing by allowing the bill to go into law without his signature, and it cost him nothing to sign the legislation. Indeed, his signing of the bill into law is held up by conservatives who defend his record on racial issues as evidence of his support for civil rights.

Reagan stated a number of reasons for his opposition to the bill. He believed that the holiday would be too costly to the federal treasury. He shared conservative concerns that King was linked to communist elements—a charge that critics have leveled against King since his rise to prominence. When asked by a reporter following the ceremony in which he signed the bill into law if he believed King had communist connections, Reagan replied, "Well, we'll know in about 35 years won't we," a reference to FBI wiretaps that will be unsealed in 2017. That remark set off a controversy, and he telephoned King's widow, Coretta Scott King, to apologize and put the issue to rest.

Reagan's Opposition to
Economic Sanctions in South Africa

The international struggle to end apartheid began shortly after the minority South African government in 1948 officially sanctioned and enforced racial segregation. The policies were implemented by the National Party, which won the 1948 elections on the apartheid platform it had built on recommendations of the party-created Sauer Commission. The commission recommended the continuance and strengthening of racial segregation. That platform resonated with a sufficient number of white South Africans and led to the National Party's takeover of the country's government. Apartheid more stringently codified South Africa's previous racist political regimes.

Apartheid policies separated South Africans into three categories: white, black, and coloured and created a framework that dictated where nonwhites could live and work and the extent to which they could be educated.[32] Apartheid prohibited black political participation and choked the political and economic life out of black South Africans. They were forced to live in separate townships, attend overcrowded and underfunded schools— if they could go at all—and carry "pass cards" at all times to verify their identity. The Separate Amenities Act erected race-based barriers to beaches, buses, hospitals, and schools, with blacks always getting the poorest quality amenity. Decades of apartheid resulted in the oppression, murder, and exploitation of millions of black South Africans as the system used racial segregation and classification to serve as the enforcement mechanism for its white supremacist ideology. The system controlled every aspect of black life in South Africa, including requiring blacks to live in certain areas. It also did away with any pretense of freedom and equality, which had been at least spoken of in the United States. It was a dehumanizing policy that became the scourge of the international community.

US opponents of apartheid always pushed for a strong government stance and called for an end to this brutal segregation policy. These calls for official confrontation with the South African government were in stark contrast to President Reagan's policy toward that government. Reagan utilized a policy of "constructive engagement" with South Africa, a policy that failed to aggressively confront the country's repressive apartheid regime. Constructive engagement was a tentative, ineffective US policy of quiet diplomacy and negotiation with the South African government over its apartheid policies.[33] Critics of the policy charged that its implementation gave tacit support for the repressive regime. According to one former member of the House of Representatives who was a prominent player in the congressional movement toward sanctions, Republican policy had been that of constructive engagement with South Africa merely out of sympathy for the minority in South Africa and in the interests of US businesses that benefited from the relationship through the political and economic suppression of black South Africans.[34]

Chester Crocker, assistant secretary of state for African affairs, defended the policy, noting that it was "aimed at encouraging reform in South Africa by working with the government there, rather than by bluntly attacking it."[35] The lack of forthrightness in the Reagan policy was seen as tacit acceptance of apartheid and drew condemnation in the African American community. Constructive engagement, as a policy, revealed a fundamental misunderstanding of the realities of apartheid and the position of the United

States in the world. In one statement, Reagan expressed the view that "South Africa is not a totalitarian society; there is a vigorous opposition press" and that "our influence over South African society is limited."[36]

Also drawing fire in the black community was the fact that Reagan sided with conservative critics of the African National Congress (ANC), the leading black South African organization dedicated to ending apartheid. Reagan and his GOP allies charged that the ANC was a terrorist group, with Communist Party ties and refused to recognize the organization. Also, the Reagan administration chose to support Mangosuthu Buthelezi, the prominent black South African Zulu leader and head of the Inkatha Freedom Party, the ANC's chief black rival. Buthelezi was a prominent critic of the ANC and was seen in many circles as a leader propped up by conservative Western support in an attempt to undermine the ANC. Because Buthelezi was viewed suspiciously by most antiapartheid groups, support of him further contributed to the belief that Reagan was not as interested in freedom for black South Africans as in protecting the interests of multinational corporations with US ties. The move also was seen as a political slap at Nelson Mandela, whose incarceration symbolized the struggle to end apartheid and elevated him to near mythic status in South Africa.

African Americans, along with people of all races around the world, vigorously opposed apartheid and sought legislation that would place the US government on record as a proponent of ending the system. Legislation began to emerge in US state and local legislatures, as well as in the US Congress, that condemned apartheid and contained provisions to help end it. Economic sanctions were seen as a potentially important option that could have been used to turn up the political heat on the South African government. The District of Columbia municipal government, for example, passed a law that barred the local government from doing business in or with the Republic of South Africa, a move that was resisted by congressional Republicans who tried to overturn the local law.[37]

The Congressional Black Caucus and leaders of black civil rights organizations led federal efforts in this regard. Caucus members and others introduced legislation to impose economic sanctions on South Africa. Many African Americans saw the similarities between South African apartheid and "Jim Crow" laws in the United States and sought to help their continental "brothers and sisters." In 1984, Washington, DC, congressman Walter E. Fauntroy helped spark congressional efforts to pass legislation to impose economic sanctions against the South African government for its racial policies. Fauntroy—along with civil rights activists Randall Robinson and Mary Frances Berry—was arrested at the South African embassy on Thanksgiving eve 1984. Reports of the arrests, which were broadcast worldwide throughout the Thanksgiving holiday, raised the consciousness of Americans regarding the apartheid regime in South Africa and "catalyzed" and "gave focus" to the efforts of outside groups dedicated to ending apartheid.[38] The publicity also raised questions about the legitimacy of a government that purported to represent a nation in which 80 percent of its populace was unable to participate in the political process.

The Thanksgiving eve arrests triggered thousands of concerned citizens to protest in front of the South African embassy during the months that followed and led to the arrest of many protesters. Among the protesters were elected officials, political activists, athletes, and entertainers, all of whose efforts increased pressure on Congress and the Reagan administration to change US policy toward South Africa. The attention given to the protests created the climate necessary to pass an aggressive sanctions bill, and supporters and opponents spent all of 1985 trying to bend the issue to their advantage.

Reagan and other Republican opponents of sanctions contended that the punishment would open South Africa's white minority government to takeover by the most radical elements of black South Africa, namely the ANC. Reagan stated that South African sanctions were unjustified and were not backed by most South Africans.[39] Reagan previously made statements sympathetic to the white minority rulers of South Africa, once asking rhetorically, "Isn't it time we laid off South Africa for a while . . . [and let] South Africans work at solving their problems while we solve our own?"[40] His views on South Africa were in stark contrast to those of black civil rights organizations and a growing number of international organizations.

Some Republicans sought to shift sanctions pressure from South Africa to other regimes, such as the Soviet Union and China, and preferred to support President Reagan's policy of constructive engagement. This was a difficult political time for Republicans, who controlled the Senate and were heading into the fall elections with an issue that was dividing their caucus in the upper chamber of Congress. The electoral environment led some Republicans to support sanctions legislation, which put the Reagan administration in a difficult position.

To cut off additional GOP support, prevent the passage of sanctions legislation, and preserve constructive engagement, President Reagan invoked, among other laws, the International Emergency Economic Powers Act (IEEPA), also known as the "Trading with the Enemy Act," as the impetus for issuing Executive Order 12532.[41] The use of the legislation was a political reach for the president because it required him to declare apartheid a threat to the national security of the United States in order to invoke the new regulations called for in the executive order. The order "appeared to call for sanctions, but only on the thinnest of grounds."[42] The actual purpose of the executive order was to give Senate Republicans cover to vote against the bill that imposed strict sanctions. These Senate Republicans could take the position that since the president had already initiated sanctions, there was no reason to vote for the bill. Reagan hoped this would open the door for a divide-and-conquer strategy by engaging in a political "end run" around Congress to keep it from doing what many antiapartheid groups wanted: to impose strict sanctions against the South African regime.

The protests and negotiations resulted in success when, on September 15, 1986, Congress passed and presented for approval to President Reagan the Comprehensive Anti-Apartheid Act of 1986.[43] President Reagan vetoed the measure on September 26, 1986, prompting both houses of Congress to override his action. The act became law on October 2, 1986, and helped create an international environment of condemnation of the government in South Africa.

The heightened international economic and political condemnation of apartheid joined with continued internal protests to topple apartheid. By 1990, Nelson Mandela, the long-imprisoned leader of the antiapartheid movement in South Africa, was released from prison and by 1994 was elected the nation's president. One can argue that apartheid's fall could have been hastened had the Reagan administration supported as aggressive a political tact as it did in trying to end communism in the Soviet Union.

Even after the sanctions legislation was put in place, the Reagan administration tried to avoid full enforcement. According to a General Accounting Office investigation, the administration "failed to carry out certain provisions of antiapartheid legislation passed by Congress last year against South Africa and ignored or dragged its feet on others."[44] South African exports of strategic materials made their way into the country through a loophole in the 1986 Comprehensive Anti-Apartheid Act and reached the United States through foreign intermediaries.[45] The report also revealed that the administration failed to convene a conference of industrial nations to consider further sanctions, as the act required.[46]

Bush's Veto of the Civil Rights Act of 1990

President George H. W. Bush opposed the Civil Rights Act of 1990, charging that it was a "quota bill" that would foster divisiveness and litigation rather than conciliation and do more to promote legal fees than civil rights.[47] President Bush's decision may have been driven by politics—more specifically, a need to shore up his support from conservatives who became disenchanted after he reversed his "no new taxes" pledge. The bill was also controversial because it sought to address a number of recent Supreme Court decisions that were seen as narrowing civil rights protections and also because it sought to strengthen enforcement of Title VII of the Civil Rights Act of 1964. Consequently, the debate surrounding the 1990 civil rights bill was particularly partisan. According to one account of House debate of the bill, "Republicans called the legislation 'a fraud' and 'a charade' that would turn employers against employees. Democrats, meanwhile, suggested that Republicans were really against equal opportunity."[48] The antagonism on both sides of the debate was driven in part by Republican political strategy, which sought to paint every Democratic-sponsored civil rights act as a "quota bill" in an effort to force the majority in both houses to defend what, at that time, was seen and argued to be "reverse discrimination."

The term *quota* has clear racial implications. It infers that whites will be displaced from their jobs in favor of less-qualified blacks. Its use fans the political flames of racial anxiety, leaving those who feel jeopardized more receptive to campaigns that exploit fear. The term was used by Republicans throughout the 1990 campaign season, most notably and to great effect by Jesse Helms in his reelection campaign against former Charlotte mayor Harvey Gantt. It was also seen as a potentially important tactic leading up to the 1992 elections. The Republican emphasis on quotas was seen as an attempt to put the Democrats in an untenable position and force them to weaken a bill that was designed to correct past wrongs. Following President Bush's veto, Democrats were forced to rewrite the bill in a way that stripped out some important provisions that were popular in the black community. Sponsors of the 1991 bill specifically prohibited hiring quotas, "a move aimed almost exclusively at giving political cover to those who want to vote for the job rights bill but face constituent complaints about 'reverse discrimination.'"[49]

President Bush's veto of the Civil Rights Act of 1990, even if it was seen as a function of legitimate political concerns, was destined to be viewed negatively in the African American community. That a "civil rights bill" was vetoed by a Republican only confirmed in the eyes of some that the GOP was anti-black, particularly since it was so strongly supported by African American members of Congress and their organizational supporters throughout the nation. And though an admittedly weaker civil rights bill passed in 1991, the damage to President Bush and Republicans generally had been done. Their inaction on the bill, other than to oppose it, was seen as part of an unwillingness to foster racial fairness.

Opposition to Minimum Wage Increases

The Fair Labor Standards Act (FLSA) requires companies with revenues of at least $500,000 to comply with federal minimum wage standards. Smaller firms also must comply with the standards if they are engaged in interstate commerce or in the production of goods for commerce.[50] The FLSA contains a number of exemptions from the minimum wage standard that may apply to some workers, including a youth subminimum wage of $4.25 that employers can pay employees under twenty years of age during their first ninety consecutive calendar days of employment. The Department of Labor can also certify eligibility for a subminimum wage for selected full-time students, apprentices, and workers with disabilities.

Conservatives and liberals have battled over the utility of the federal minimum wage since the salary floor was established in 1938, and their positions closely track those of their major supporters.[51] Conservatives are consistently critical of the minimum wage and want to keep the wage as low as possible. The traditional conservative argument against raising the minimum wage reflects that of the business community, which contends that increasing the wage has a chilling effect on small businesses and prevents them from taking on new workers, and that a lower minimum wage would spur hiring and result in lower unemployment rates around the country. Conservatives also argue that a low minimum wage is acceptable because the wage applies primarily to teenagers and other young workers who are in school or live with parents. Some opponents of minimum wage increases prefer the abolition of the income guarantee altogether, while others have supported the institution of a subminimum wage for teenagers.

The traditional liberal argument, which is backed by labor unions around the country, is that a high minimum wage is the best way to lift the working poor out of poverty, or near poverty, and give them an opportunity to live a better life. Liberals see it as an issue of fundamental fairness and economic justice that gives those at the lowest wage levels a better opportunity to meet their financial needs. A low minimum wage helps consign too many Americans to the status of the "working poor," those workers around the nation who are full-time employees and earn an annual income that is just above the federal poverty threshold. Supporters also contend that an increase in the minimum wage would result in a pay increase for some who make just above the minimum wage. They also reject the argument that increasing the minimum wage is a job killer. Well-regarded studies exist that argue that the minimum wage has had little or no effect on job levels; some even contend that minimum wage increases actually boost employment.

Data regarding the minimum wage show that those who earn at that level are not just teenagers who receive additional support from their families. According to 2005 US Department of Labor data, 40 percent of minimum wage earners are the sole wage earners in their households. There are more than 2 million people in the United States who earn at or below the minimum wage. Forty-nine percent of minimum wage earners are adults over the age of twenty-five. According to the Bureau of Labor Statistics, nearly 75 percent of all minimum wage or below earners work in the service industry, nearly 60 percent of whom work in food preparation and serving-related jobs. The 2005 minimum wage of $5.15 equates to an annual income of $10,712 for someone who works forty hours per week. That annual salary is just $1,142 above the 2005 poverty level of $9,570 for a single person, and a husband and wife who both earn the minimum wage will take in $21,424, which is $2,074 above the poverty level of $19,350 for a family of four. It is important to note, however, that the poverty level, when geographically based cost of living differences around the nation are considered, should be seen as a minimal indicator of poverty. Given that, those who live just above the poverty level are not substantially better off than those at or just below the poverty level, and someone earning just above the minimum wage in an expensive locale might actually be worse off than a minimum wage earner in an inexpensive area.

The GOPs stance in opposing minimum wage puts it into direct conflict with African American interests. African Americans constitute 19 percent of all workers who make the minimum wage and are therefore disproportionately positioned to benefit from any increases in the wage rate. Nearly six in ten African American minimum wage earners are women, so resisting increases in the minimum wage extends beyond just those who earn that income. As nearly half of minimum wage workers are adults and nearly 60 percent of African American minimum wage earners are women, holding the line on the wage floor impacts children as well. Given that minimum wage earners are barely above the poverty level, the GOP's position on the minimum wage can be seen as a desire to keep cheap labor available without regard to the fiscal consequences of those low earners.

Crime Control Policy: Mandatory
Minimums, Three Strikes, and the Death Penalty

The Grand Old Party has built much of its post–civil rights–era political success on aggressive crime control proposals. Beginning with Barry Goldwater's 1964 presidential campaign, Republican politicians successfully promoted criminal justice policies that are more punitive. Richard Nixon's call for "law and order" during his 1968 campaign was particularly effective in this regard. By the mid-1970s, Republicans, backed by like-minded scholars and policy analysts, advocated crime control policies that are more punitive and turned away from the notion of rehabilitation.[52] That this was a significant political development is an understatement. It opened a door to electoral victory that Republican candidates successfully exploited. They played on growing white racial anxiety that came with the African American civil rights movement and, later, the black power movement, which challenged and overturned the racial status quo. As Republicans saw "law and order" and punishment over rehabilitation as political winners, a race emerged to see who could propose the most aggressive crime control policies. This race fueled the movement for crime control policies such as mandatory minimums for drug offenders, "three strikes," and the accelerated use of the death penalty.

In the 1980s, the GOP increased its crime control rhetoric in two notable ways. First, they blamed Democrats and liberalism for the growing crime rates and lawlessness and charged Democratic elected officials, particularly mayors of large cities, with "coddling" criminals and being "soft on crime." Republicans did this, in part, by always talking about it as an issue, heightening its significance in the eyes of voters while, at the same time, creating anxiety among many of those same voters. This strategy put Democrats in a defensive position on a powerful issue. Second, the GOP led the fight for stiffer penalties for those convicted of crimes, creating laws that called for increased use of mandatory minimum sentences, lifetime imprisonment for those convicted of a third crime (three strikes), and increased use of the death penalty. Each of these penalty changes disproportionately affected African Americans, further clouding their relationship with the GOP, which developed and advocated the policy changes. The Republican strategy here was so strong that, in some cases, it required Democrats with substantial numbers of moderate or conservative voters to support policy changes that they might not have supported otherwise in order to preserve their electoral viability.

Mandatory minimums require those convicted of a nonviolent drug offense, for example, to serve a mandated prison term before they can be eligible for parole without regard to the amount of drugs involved or the defendant's role in the offense. Federal mandatory minimum sentences were not widely implemented until the Narcotics Control Act of 1956 required such penalties "for most offenses involving the distribution and importation of drugs."[53] Within a decade and a half, however, nearly all such penalties were abolished by the Comprehensive Drug Abuse Prevention and Control Act. Federal mandatory minimums returned in the mid-1980s when Republicans controlled the White House and the Senate. By 1994, more than sixty federal offenses carried mandatory minimum sentences.[54]

Particularly cited by African American critics of mandatory minimums are the sentencing disparities that exist within the system with regard to certain crimes, especially cocaine possession. The sentencing disparities, as well as the larger issue of mandatory minimums, are seen as reflective of racial unfairness, since African Americans are disproportionately affected by the sentences. According to the US Sentencing Commission, the debate surrounding cocaine sentencing lies in "the 100-to-1 quantity ratio between powder and crack cocaine."[55] The commission also notes that "depending on the exact quantity, the mandatory minimum penalties and sentencing guidelines prescribe prison terms for crack defendants that generally range from three to almost eight times longer than for defendants with equivalent amounts of powder cocaine."[56] This is a significant distinction, because African Americans are more likely than whites to be convicted of crack cocaine possession. Further, by the 1990s, African Americans made up 14 percent of illegal drug users, but 35 percent of those arrested for drug possession, 55 percent of those convicted, and 74 percent of those sentenced to prison for drug possession.[57]

Many in the African American community criticize mandatory minimums for four primary reasons. First, some opponents say they remove the rehabilitation function of incarceration because, by requiring inmates to serve such a significant portion of their sentences before they are eligible for parole, they remove any incentives for good behavior. Second, some black opponents see them as an attempt to target African Americans for imprisonment, which would increase the well-established disparities in the criminal justice system. Third, mandatory minimums are exorbitantly costly, particularly in the absence of diversion, job training, and other programs that could turn potential criminals away from acts that will land them in prison. The irony here is that conservatives who have been traditionally portrayed as fiscally prudent have advocated and passed into law policies that cost more money that the liberal-supported alternative programs. Last, mandatory minimums do not deter the crime they were ostensibly created to deter. According to one study, mandatory minimums "reduce defendants' incentives to plead guilty, reduce guilty pleas, and lengthen case processing time. They sometimes result in imposition of penalties more severe than anyone immediately involved believes appropriate."[58]

Mandatory minimums have led to substantial increases in US incarceration rates. This is particularly problematic in the African American community. According to Justice Department statistics, African Americans make up nearly half of all those incarcerated in the United States. Further, African American women now make up the fastest-growing population of those incarcerated.

The Supreme Court, in 2005, overturned laws requiring mandatory minimums, telling judges to treat those guidelines only as recommendations and formulas for crimes like drug dealing or repeat offenses. However, the Supreme Court has never questioned the power of Congress to pass legislation requiring minimum sentences for given crimes, and that is what conservatives in the House are now trying to do. This has created a movement to revive mandatory minimums, an effort that is currently being driven by Republicans. In 2005, Republican representative James Sensenbrenner introduced legislation that creates a new group of mandatory minimum penalties for nonviolent drug offenses, including a five-year penalty for passing a marijuana cigarette to someone who has been in drug treatment.[59]

Three strikes policies came to the forefront of US crime control policy in the 1990s during an era in which Republicans were pushing for tougher responses to the perceived increase in violent crime. The policies, which mandate life imprisonment for someone convicted of a third crime, are based on the belief that someone who commits three crimes is a career criminal who cannot be rehabilitated. The push for these laws was used as a technique to distinguish the GOP from the Democrats and continued a tradition of playing on white racial anxiety. That anxiety was fueled in part by increased media attention to homicides. According to one study, despite a 33 percent decline in homicides from 1990 to 1998, coverage of homicides on the ABC, NBC, and CBS evening newscasts increased by 473 percent during that period. The first modern three strikes law dates to 1993, when Washington state voters approved a referendum mandating life imprisonment with no parole for those convicted of a third felony.

These laws have been criticized as being draconian and sending people to prison for life when the third "strike" is relatively minor. Under these statutes, felons' third strikes have included stealing videotapes, golf clubs, and a slice of pizza. According to 2003 California Department of Corrections data, 65 percent—nearly two-thirds—of those sentenced under that state's three strikes laws are imprisoned for nonviolent offenses.[60] Some argue that three strikes laws have a perverse unintended consequence in that they may actually increase homicide rates.[61] According to one study, cities in states with three strikes laws experienced short-term increases in homicide rates of 13–14 percent and long-term increases of 16–24 percent compared to cities in states without the laws.[62] The thinking here is that those criminals with two felony convictions who are engaged in activity that could lead to their being arrested, prosecuted, and sentenced to life imprisonment—for the possession of a small amount of illegal drugs, for example—have nothing to lose if they kill their victims, witnesses, or anyone else who could contribute to their potential third conviction, because they will get the same sentence for the homicide as they would for the drug possession.

The use of the death penalty has been a particularly thorny issue in the relationship between African Americans and the GOP. Republicans have used their support for the death penalty as a campaign issue, something through which they seek to demonstrate their toughness on crime and distinguish them from Democrats. African Americans are disproportionately sentenced to the death penalty. According to the Death Penalty Information Center, African Americans constitute 34 percent of all those executed in the United States since the death penalty was reinstated in 1976, nearly three times their proportion in the nation's populace.[63] African Americans made up 42 percent of all those on death row in 2004.[64] There is a well-established perception of racial bias in the application of the death penalty, so the application of the death penalty means more to African Americans than to whites, given the disparate use of the punishment.[65] Republicans' aggressive support for the death penalty has been a consistent staple in their efforts to undermine Democratic candidates in political campaigns. As Table 5.3 shows, eight of the ten states that have instituted the death penalty most frequently since 1976 were in the former Confederacy, and all have as high a percentage of African Americans as any state in the nation.

The effects of these policies on African Americans have been substantial and call into question the GOP's commitment to racial fairness. In 2005, nearly half of America's prison inmates were African American, and black women constitute the fastest growing population of those incarcerated. Moreover, black men have a 32 percent chance of serving time in prison at some point in their lives. That Republicans have been at the forefront of the movement to stiffen crime control policies and to oppose efforts to balance sentencing disparities is seen in some segments of the black community as an attempt to "warehouse" African American men in prison and "destroy" the black community. Despite these misgivings and evidence that the policies reinforce a structural unfairness that disproportionately impacts African Americans, Republicans have been the staunchest defenders and advocates of these crime control policies.

Felon Disenfranchisement

The success of conservative crime control policy not only resulted in a substantial increase in felony convictions and incarceration, but also increased the rates of felon disenfranchisement. Between 1970 and 2000, the number of state and federal prisoners has grown by over 600 percent, from fewer than 200,000 to nearly 1.4 million.[66] Nearly 5 million Americans, 2 percent

Table 5.3   Executions Since 1976, by Jurisdiction

Jurisdiction	Executions Since 1976
Texas	336
Virginia	94
Oklahoma	75
Missouri	61
Florida	59
Georgia	36
North Carolina	34
South Carolina	32
Alabama	30
Louisiana	27

Source: Department of Justice, Office of Justice Programs, Bureau of Justice Statistics, *Capital Punishment, 2004* (Washington, DC: Department of Justice, 2005), p. 9.

of the voting-age population, are prohibited from voting because of previous felony convictions. The laws that created these barriers are controversial, particularly in the case of those who have completed their sentences, parole, or both, and have thus completely "paid their debt to society."

The history of felon disenfranchisement laws has racial roots. Conservatives created these laws in the post-Reconstruction era in an effort to keep African Americans out of the political process, even using minor offenses "as part of a larger strategy to disenfranchise African Americans."[67] Over time, forty-eight states and the District of Columbia have prohibited inmates from voting while incarcerated for a felony offense, thirty-six states have prohibited felons from voting while they are on parole (with thirty-one of these states excluding felony probationers as well), and three states have denied the right to vote to all ex-offenders who have completed their sentences.[68] These policies conflict with public opinion. More than 75 percent of African Americans and nearly 60 percent of whites polled accepted the legitimacy of felon voting rights.[69] The Joint Center for Political and Economic Studies found in 1999 that 70 percent of whites and 85 percent of African Americans opposed lifetime disenfranchisement.[70] In addition, "a 2001 study found that about 15 percent of respondents supported lifetime disenfranchisement of felons and a 2002 survey found that 80 percent believed that all ex-felons should have the right to vote."[71] Critics of felon disenfranchisement laws object to the fact that those disenfranchised are US citizens who should not have to forfeit their right to vote. Critics also cite the racial implications of these laws, given their overall impact on African American political participation.

This impact is measurable: More than 13 percent of African American men (1.4 million) are disenfranchised, a rate seven times the national average; in six states that deny the vote to ex-offenders, one in four black men is permanently disenfranchised.[72] Given current incarceration rates, three in ten of the next generation of black men can expect to be disenfranchised at some point in their lifetime. In states that disenfranchise ex-offenders, as many as 40 percent of black men may permanently lose their right to vote. Ex-offenders who have completed their sentences make up approximately 1.7 million disenfranchised people in the United States.[73] The state of Florida had an estimated 827,000 ex-felons who were unable to vote in the 2000 presidential election. According to one national study, estimates of felon turnout range from a low of 20.5 percent (for the 1974 congressional elections) to a high of 39 percent (for the 1992 presidential election), with an average estimated felon turnout of about 24 percent in nonpresidential-year Senate elections and about 35 percent in presidential election years.

While well below general turnout rates, these estimates are significant in that they could change electoral outcomes. According to one analysis, the outcome of the 2000 presidential election "would almost certainly have been reversed had voting rights been extended to any category of disenfranchised felons."[74] This analysis argues that Democratic nominee Al Gore would have won the popular vote by more than 1 million votes. The disputed election in Florida reveals the impact felon disenfranchisement had on the 2000 contest. The analysis argues that given estimated rates of turnout (27.2 percent) and preference (68.9 percent) for Florida incarcerates, Gore would have carried the state by 80,000 votes and thereby gained the presidency.[75]

The political implications of felon disenfranchisement on the result of the 2000 presidential election were not limited to Florida. According to one study, researchers found that in nine swing states—Arizona, Florida, Iowa, Missouri, Nevada, New Mexico, Oregon, Washington, and Wisconsin—the number of disenfranchised felons exceeded the margin of victory.[76] Given the demography of the US felon population, it is not unreasonable to assert that in those states where Democrats won, their margins would have been larger were it not for felon disenfranchisement; also, Republican margins would have been smaller, including some Republican defeats, if this disenfranchisement had not occurred. A total of 846,486 felons were disenfranchised in Democratic states (those won by Democratic nominee Al Gore), which represented 1.2 percent of all voters; just over 2 million were disenfranchised in Republican states (those won by Republican nominee George W. Bush), representing 3 percent of all voters.[77]

These laws have definitive political implications for African Americans and the Republican Party. Criminology demography tells us that those incarcerated in US prisons tend to be economically poor and disproportionately minority. This is significant, because the poor and minorities tend to vote Democratic. Disenfranchising voters, particularly in closely contested southern states, can remove critical masses of potential Democratic voters from election rolls, thereby making Republicans better positioned to win elections in jurisdictions in which they are not demographically well suited to succeed. Given that African Americans are charged with crimes and convicted at disproportionately high rates, and given the concentration of African Americans in southern states, this disenfranchisement, if overturned, would shift the balance of voters in southern states more toward the Democratic Party and away from the GOP.

As a result of these political realities, Republicans have no political incentive to overturn these laws and have been the most vocal opponents of laws that would ease restrictions on felon participation in the electoral process. They benefit more than Democrats from the current disenfranchisement laws. Indeed, some Republican officials see politics in the efforts by Democrats to allow felons to have their voting privileges reinstated. As one Maryland Republican Party official stated, "I see things like that coming up so that a Democratic governor or whomever is really just trying to gain votes, votes that they know they could pretty well count on."[78] While the historical genesis of these kinds of laws can be found in the actions of anti-Reconstruction conservative Democrats, it is notable that Republicans have not taken proactive steps to reverse the status quo on felon disenfranchisement.

The 2000 Election and Aftermath

Elections are the foundation of democracy, and nations around the world are judged as more or less democratic by the legitimacy of their electoral processes. Elections that proceed without, or with few, irregularities are judged as legitimate and as the exemplification of the people's will. Elections that proceed with numerous and significant irregularities are viewed as contrary to the democratic process. The United States, as the world's leading democracy, is often seen as the epitome of electoral efficiency. Elections are held on one day, and more than 100 million votes are quickly counted to name the victors. Indeed, prominent Americans are often on the scene in nations around the world to observe and certify the legitimacy of elections. So it is notable when there are electoral disparities in the United States. However, given US voting history, it is not unusual for there to be problems in US elections. Many of these problems go unnoticed or underreported, in large part because it is believed that they do not make a substantial difference in outcome. As elections have become more closely contested, particularly in recent years, they are given heightened attention because a few votes could decide a contest.

The 2000 presidential election was the most controversial election since the 1876 contest between Rutherford B. Hayes and Samuel Tilden. The contest between Texas governor George W. Bush and Vice-President Al Gore revealed a number of flaws in the US electoral process. Presidential elections are actually a collection of state contests, not the single national election many believe. As a consequence of this fact, and the reality of varying degrees of competence and administrative discretion, there are differences in how elections are run. States run elections through the various counties, and those counties run their elections on the resources they have. Wealthier counties are more likely to have greater quantities of the latest technology than poorer counties. These variables are complicated by generations-long desires to control the process to ensure that particular candidates, parties, or both, are able to maintain control of a particular jurisdiction. These desires have racial and class overtones, which helps explain why electoral management decisions sometimes focus on race and class.

The US Commission on Civil Rights conducted an investigation that revealed a number of voting irregularities, all of which adversely affected African American voters. The commission found that "Black voters were

disproportionately the victims of faulty voting equipment, erroneous purging of voter lists, switching of polling places at the last minute, and potential intimidation by the presence of police at heavily Black voting
precincts."[79] Further, in Florida, 54 percent of the votes rejected during the
2000 general election were those of African Americans, who make up 11
percent of Florida voters; blacks were nearly ten times as likely as whites
to have their ballots rejected.[80] The overwhelming disparity in black disqualified votes contributed to the comprehensive anger in the African
American community over the administration of the election. This was particularly notable in light of the closeness of the election. Given African
American voting patterns, it is not unreasonable to assume that better and
fairer election administration could have brought about a different electoral
result.

The problems appear to stem from a 1998 law passed by the Florida
legislature designed in the wake of corrupt elections in Miami the previous
year. The goal of the measure was to remove ineligible voters from the registration rolls: felons with unrestored voting rights (including those who
were convicted of crimes in other states—but not in Florida—and should be
eligible to vote in Florida), those who died, and those who moved.
According to one report, however, the law's implementation took on a partisan edge: "Passed by the Republican legislature's majority, the new code
included an extraordinary provision to turn over the initial creation of
'scrub' lists to a private firm; no other state, either before or since, has pri-
vatized this key step in the elimination of citizens' civil rights."[81] This law
set the stage for the removal of thousands of Floridians, disproportionately
black, from the state's registration rolls, precluding them from voting in the
2000 presidential election. While the total number was never verified, at
least one expert estimated that those with felony convictions in other states,
but not Florida, who were improperly removed from Florida's registration
rolls exceeded 100,000.[82] That number, added to those improperly purged
for other reasons, easily exceeded Bush's margin of victory.

The 2000 election was marked by voting irregularities throughout the
state that contributed to the election of Republican governor George W.
Bush as president. The irregularities diluted the black vote as well as, to
some extent, the Hispanic vote in the state. African American votes were
uncounted at higher rates than those of other voters around the state. The
2000 Florida election notably influenced the relationship between African
Americans and the Republican Party, because GOP representatives, nationally and in the state, were especially aggressive in opposing efforts by
African American leaders to call attention to, and seek remedy for, the overwhelmingly disproportionate rate of uncounted votes cast by African
Americans. Republicans resisted efforts to reinstate erroneously purged
black voters.

Conclusion

A review of these public policy issues and battles reveals that the Republican Party has consistently opposed positions on those legislative issues of particular importance and interest to African Americans. Opposing such efforts as to honor Rev. Dr. Martin Luther King Jr. with a holiday, to end apartheid in South Africa, and to extend voting and civil rights protections could not be further from black policy preferences. These positions take the GOP and African Americans in opposite directions and both contribute to and frame the hostility that exists between the two entities. On every important policy issue discussed in this chapter, the GOP has forcefully advocated positions that adversely affect African Americans. Some of the opposition has been driven by sincere differences of opinion on these issues, while some has been driven by a need to satiate the GOP's social conservative base by appealing to white America's worst racial anxieties. Any future efforts by the Republican Party to win more African American support must operate against and overcome this record.

Notes

1. Hanes Walton, *When the Marching Stopped: The Politics of Civil Rights Regulatory Agencies* (Albany: State University of New York Press, 1988), p. 148, quoting US Congress, House of Representatives, Committee on Education and Labor, *A Report on the Investigation of Civil Rights Enforcement by the Equal Employment Opportunity Commission*, Serial No. 99-0 (Washington, DC: Government Printing Office, 1986), p. 2

2. Kenneth O'Reilly, *Nixon's Piano: Presidents and Racial Politics from Washington to Clinton* (New York: Free Press, 1995), pp. 369–370, quoting Douglas Massey and Nancy Denton, *American Apartheid: Segregation and the Making of the Underclass* (Cambridge: Harvard University Press, 1993), p. 207.

3. Nadine Cohodas, "Compromise in the Works: Judiciary Deadlock Continues on Civil Rights Commission," *CQ Weekly*, October 1, 1983, p. 2028.

4. Mary Frances Berry, interview by author, tape recorded, November 2, 2005.

5. I served as a civil rights analyst at the US Commission on Civil Rights from June 1993 to January 1996. During my time at the commission, I had numerous conversations with veteran staff members who noted the changes in the organization pre- and post-Reagan. They often noted the lack of funding and the problems it caused. Particularly notable was the inability to conduct research and the requirement that the commission purge and destroy certain historical documents.

6. General Accounting Office, *U.S. Commission on Civil Rights: Agency Lacks Basic Management Control* (Washington, DC: General Accounting Office, 1997), p. 6.

7. Ibid., p. 49.

8. Ronald Walters, *White Nationalism, Black Interests: Conservative Public Policy and the Black Community* (Detroit: Wayne State University Press, 2003), p.

71, quoting "Excerpts from Final Report on EEOC Prepared by Transition Team of Reagan Administration," Development Group Report, 15, E-1, January 23, 1981.

9. Ibid.

10. Walton, *When the Marching Stopped*, p. 133, quoting "OMB Issues Paperwork Requirements," *Civil Rights Forum Newsletter*, September 1984, pp. 6, 8, 12. See also Juan Williams, "Chairman of EEOC Tells Panel Statistics Misused to Prove Bias," *Washington Post*, December 15, 1984, p. A4. According to Williams, Thomas urged the government to stop using statistics as an indicator of possible discrimination.

11. Walton, *When the Marching Stopped*, p. 192, quoting Ann Mariano, "OMB Doesn't Want Forms to Ask Race Questions," *Washington Post*, June 17, 1985 (national weekly edition), p. 32.

12. Walton, *When the Marching Stopped*, p. 192, quoting US Congress, House, *Federal Government Statistics and Statistical Policy Hearing Before the Committee on Government Operations*, 97th Cong., 2nd sess. (June 3, 1982), pp. 222–223.

13. Eunice Moscoso, "Civil Rights Enforcement Falls in Bush Term, Study Says," *Seattle Post-Intelligencer*, November 22, 2004, quoting report by the Transactional Records Access Clearinghouse, nonpartisan research center at Syracuse University.

14. Ibid.

15. US Commission on Civil Rights, *Statement on Affirmative Action* (Washington, DC: US Commission on Civil Rights, 1977), p. 2.

16. See, for example, *Green v. County Board*, 391 U.S. 430 (1968); *Swann v. Board of Education*, 402 U.S. 1 (1971); *Keyes v. Denver School District*, 413 U.S. 189 (1973). See also US President (L. Johnson), Executive Order 11246, Reassignment of Civil Rights Functions, September 24, 1965, *Weekly Compilation of Presidential Documents*, vol. 1, September 27, 1965, p. 305.

17. Stephen Carter, *Reflections of an Affirmative Action Baby* (New York: Basic Books, 1991), p. 71, citing Reynolds Farley and Walter Allen, *The Color Line and the Quality of Life in America* (New York: Russell Sage, 1987). While it is clear that affirmative action has been a factor in creating a larger black middle class, many black critics of the policies point out that income stratification in the African American community has grown concomitantly with the expanded black middle class. The growth in the black middle class through affirmative action has also contributed to the closing of the gap between white middle-class and African American middle-class incomes. This fact, no doubt, is problematic for white racial conservatives who want to reduce to the best extent possible competition for their sons, daughters, nieces, and nephews.

18. 91 F.3d 147 (3d Cir. 1996), appeal dismissed sub nom. *U.S. v. Board of Education of the Township of Piscataway*, 522 U.S. 1010 (1998).

19. Charles Dale, *Affirmative Action Revisited: A Legal History and Prospectus* (Washington, DC: Congressional Research Service, 2001), p. 1.

20. Gramm's amendment was S. Amdt. 1825 to the bill HR 1854.

21. The provision to the bill, HR 2076, was eliminated on the Senate floor by unanimous consent.

22. For a discussion of state-level attempts to disenfranchise black voters, see John Hope Franklin and Alfred Moss, *From Slavery to Freedom: A History of Negro Americans* (New York: McGraw-Hill, 1988), pp. 231–235.

23. Jack Greenberg, *Race Relations and American Law* (New York: Columbia University Press, 1959), p. 139.

24. Charles Bullock and Charles Lamb, *Implementation of Civil Rights Policy* (Monterey, CA: Brooks/Cole Publishing, 1984), p. 39.

25. Ibid., p. 44.

26. Ibid., p. 29.

27. Robert Pear, "Rules to Enforce Voting Rights Due," *New York Times*, September 1, 1985, p. 1.

28. Ibid., p. 11.

29. See Manning Marable, *Race, Reform, and Rebellion: The Second Reconstruction in Black America, 1945–1990* (Jackson: University Press of Mississippi, 1991).

30. Robert Rothman, "Helms Ends King Filibuster—Vote Set October 19," *CQ Weekly*, October 8, 1983, p. 2084.

31. Carol Swain and Russ Nieli, eds., *Contemporary Views of White Nationalism in America* (Cambridge: Cambridge University Press, 2003), p. 182.

32. At a subsequent point, Asians, or Indians and Pakistanis, were added as a fourth category.

33. Constructive engagement had numerous critics. See also Michael Clough, "Beyond Constructive Engagement," *Foreign Policy*, no. 61 (Winter 1985): 3–24; Deborah Toler, "Constructive Engagement: Reactionary Pragmatism at Its Best," *Issue: A Journal of Opinion* 12, no. 3/4 (Autumn 1982): 11–18; Sam C. Nolutshungu, "Skeptical Notes on 'Constructive Engagement,'" *Issue: A Journal of Opinion* 12, no. 3/4 (Autumn 1982): 3–7; Alex Thompson, "Incomplete Engagement: Reagan's South Africa Policy Revisited," *Journal of Modern African Studies* 33, no. 1 (March 1995): 83–101; Bernard Magumbane, "Constructive Engagement or Disingeneous Support for Apartheid," *Issue: A Journal of Opinion* 12, no. 3/4 (Autumn 1982): 8–10.

34. Walter E. Fauntroy, interview with author, tape recorded, December 5, 2005.

35. John Felton, "South Africa Warned of Sanctions: Conservatives in Congress Join in Campaign Against Apartheid," *CQ Weekly*, December 8, 1984, p. 3072.

36. "South Africa: Presidential Actions—Transcript," *U.S. State Department Bulletin*, October 1985.

37. Robert Rothman, "'Disinvestment' Allowed to Stand: District's South Africa Law Ignites Battle," *CQ Weekly*, February 18, 1984. Republican representative Philip Crane introduced two resolutions (H. Con. Res. 216 and H. Res. 372) to overturn the District's law.

38. Henry Richardson, interview by author, Washington, DC, October 24, 2005.

39. David Hoffman and Lou Cannon, "Reagan Pledges Resistance to New Sanctions," *Washington Post*, August 12, 1986, p. A1.

40. Jeremy Mayer, *Running on Race: Racial Politics in Presidential Campaigns, 1960–2000* (New York: Random House, 2002), p. 169.

41. 50 FR 36861, 3 CFR, 1985 Comp., p. 387.

42. Richardson interview.

43. Representative William H. Gray introduced this bill as HR 4868 on May 21, 1986. Many similar bills were introduced throughout 1984, 1985, and 1986. Fauntroy's bill, HR 1098, introduced on February 2, 1985, sought to prohibit new loans by United States persons to the Government of South Africa, to prohibit new investments in business enterprises in South Africa, to prohibit the importation of South African krugerrands or other gold or silver coins, to prohibit the importation

of coal and uranium from South Africa, to prohibit exports to South Africa of nuclear items, and to prohibit exports of goods or technology to or for use by the South African government. Many elements of the Fauntroy bill were included in the Gray bill, which became law.

44. Claire Robertson, "GAO Faults Administration on South Africa Sanctions," *Washington Post*, October 24, 1987, p. A5.

45. See General Accounting Office, *Status Report on Implementation of the Comprehensive Anti-Apartheid Act* (Washington, DC: General Accounting Office, 1987).

46. Robertson, "GAO Faults Administration."

47. "House Joins in the Standoff Over Civil Rights Measure," *CQ Weekly*, August 4, 1990, p. 2517.

48. Ibid.

49. Joan Biskupic, "Democrats Scramble for Cover Under GOP 'Quota' Attacks," *CQ Weekly*, May 25, 1991, p. 1378.

50. Federal, state, or local government agencies, hospitals, and school employees are also covered.

51. See John Kennan, "The Elusive Effects of Minimum Wages," *Journal of Economic Literature* 33 (December 1995): 1949–1965.

52. Christopher Uggen and Jeff Manza, "Democratic Contraction? Political Consequences of Felon Disenfranchisement in the United States," *American Sociological Review* 67 (December 2002): 781.

53. Marvin Free, "The Impact of Federal Sentencing Reforms on African Americans," *Journal of Black Studies* 28, no. 2 (1997): 269.

54. Ibid.

55. US Sentencing Commission, *Report to Congress—Cocaine and Federal Sentencing Policy*, February 1995, chap. 7.

56. Ibid.

57. US Bureau of the Census, *Statistical Abstract of the United States,* 1999; Bureau of Justice Statistics, *Sourcebook of Criminal Justice Statistics,* 1998; National Household Survey on Drug Abuse, 1998; Bureau of Justice Statistics, *Prison and Jail Inmates at Midyear,* 1999.

58. See Michael Tonry, "Mandatory Penalties," *Crime and Justice* 16 (1992): 243.

59. HR 152.

60. Vincent Schiraldi, Jason Colburn, and Eric Lotke, *Three Strikes and You're Out: An Examination of the Impact of 3-Strikes Laws 10 Years After Their Enactment* (Washington, DC: Justice Policy Institute, 2004), p. 4.

61. Tomislav Kovandzic, John Sloan, and Lynne Vieraitis, "Unintended Consequences of Politically Popular Sentencing Policy: The Homicide-Promoting Effects of 'Three Strikes' in U.S. Cities (1980–1999)," *Criminology and Public Policy* 1, no. 3 (2002): 399–424; Thomas B. Marvell and Carlisle E. Moody, "The Lethal Effects of Three-Strikes Laws," *Journal of Legal Studies* (January 2001).

62. Kovandzic, Sloan, and Vieraitis, "Unintended Consequences," p. 420.

63. Death Penalty Information Center, "Race of Death Row Inmates Executed Since 1976," available at www.deathpenaltyinfo.org/article.php?scid=5&did=184 (accessed December 8, 2005).

64. Department of Justice, Office of Justice Programs, Bureau of Justice Statistics, *Capital Punishment, 2004* (Washington, DC: Department of Justice, 2005), p. 1.

65. See *Callins v. Collins*, 114 S. Ct. 1127, 1135 (1994); J. Blackmun, dissenting from denial of certiorari.

66. Uggen and Manza, "Democratic Contraction?" p. 781.

67. Ibid. It should be noted that the conservatives of that era were Democrats, and it is ironic that laws created by conservatives solely to keep African Americans out of the political process are, in some measure, responsible for keeping Democrats from winning elections throughout the nation.

68. The Sentencing Project, "Felony Disenfranchisement Laws in the United States," September 2005, p. 1, available online at www.sentencingproject.org/pdfs/1046.pdf.

69. *Washington Post*/Kaiser Family Foundation/Harvard University poll, released July 11, 2001.

70. Alec Ewald, *Punishing at the Polls: The Case Against Disenfranchising Citizens with Felony Convictions* (New York: Demos, 2003), p. 54.

71. Ibid.

72. Ibid., p. 1.

73. The Sentencing Project, "Felony Disenfranchisement Laws."

74. Uggen and Manza, "Democratic Contraction?" p. 792.

75. Ibid.

76. See Justice Policy Institute, "Swing States: Crime, Prisons, and the Future of the Nation," August 2004, p. 14.

77. Ibid.

78. Audra Miller, interview by author, tape recorded, Annapolis, Maryland, July 12, 2005.

79. Garrine Laney, *The Voting Rights Act of 1965, as Amended: Its History and Current Issues* (Washington, DC: Congressional Research Service, 2001), p. 46.

80. Ibid. See also Robert Pierre and Peter Slevin, "Fla. Vote Rife with Disparities, Study Says Rights Panel Finds Blacks Penalized," *Washington Post*, June 5, 2001, p. A1. See also Gregory Palast, "Florida's 'Disappeared Voters': Disenfranchised by the GOP," *The Nation*, February 5, 2001, which noted that the Hillsborough County elections supervisor found that 54 percent of the voters targeted by the "scrub" are African American, in a county where blacks make up 11 percent of the voting population.

81. Palast, "Florida's 'Disappeared Voters.'"

82. Ibid.

6

GOP Political Symbolism
Angers African Americans

POLITICAL SYMBOLISM IS AN IMPORTANT, BUT OFTEN UNDER-appreciated, aspect of US politics. When adroitly and negatively used, political symbolism enables a candidate, or party, to undermine an opponent by transmitting images and messages to the public that move voters away from that opponent. It can hurt support for a given candidate and is also useful in conveying controversial positions on issues, such as race, with limited negative political implications. The Republican Party has used political symbols to gain white conservative votes and to undercut Democrats. This use of carefully selected symbols has become an impediment to attracting African American support for Republican candidates. This chapter surveys and analyzes GOP use of political symbolism and its effect on the party's African American support.

By the late 1960s, thanks to civil rights laws that were created to address and protect the rights of aggrieved citizens, overt racism was outside the norm of acceptable political behavior. Racial conservatives who resisted this changing order thus had to find new ways—covert and symbolic—to communicate their racial positions. Certain words that had not previously been associated with race—*crime, poverty, welfare*—became "regarded by some as code words with which whites could communicate, in socially acceptable language, their anxiety, concerns, and stereotypes about race."[1] Taking a tough stance on criminals, for example, "can be a signal that a candidate endorses the stereotypes of blacks held by many white voters and shares their resentment over government intervention on behalf of blacks."[2] These code words became part of a new symbolic racial language that Republicans effectively used to court white racial conservatives:

> Republicans generally and Ronald Reagan in particular discovered a vocabulary for articulating the racial hostility of white Americans without speaking of race specifically. This coded language—a language of

"groups," "taxes," "big government," "quotas," "reverse discrimination," "welfare," and "special interests"—became critical to the maintenance of the conservative presidential majority in the latter half of the 1980s.[3]

This new symbolic racial language also allowed Republican politicians and activists to oppose progressive policies aggressively without overtly revealing hostility toward minority interests, particularly African Americans. The language can be understood as carrying two messages—one acknowledged by the candidate and socially acceptable and "plausibly denied," and the other taboo.[4] In so doing, this new language proved an able cover that allowed racial conservatives the opportunity to play on white racial anxiety for the purpose of securing their support.

As the 1960s continued, many of these conservatives became disenchanted with the Democratic Party and its embrace of civil rights and, as was noted in Chapter 3, found a new home in the Republican Party. It was during this period that the increasingly conservative GOP began to utilize implicit and racial symbolism to secure the support of conservative whites. These efforts have worked in tandem with public policy positions to create an environment that is viewed by many as hostile to African Americans. The covert use of political symbolism is a response to the change in the societal norm of racial equality that began to emerge in the 1950s and 1960s. According to Tali Mendelberg, professor and author of *The Race Card: Campaign Strategy, Implicit Messages, and the Norm of Equality*, overt racial appeals can hurt white candidates—hence the need for using symbols to communicate racial messages.[5] The message from the GOP to African Americans has often been that the party embodies a racial conservatism and behavioral norms that oppose black progress and equality. While these messages are often conveyed without whites clearly noticing, African Americans are acutely aware of the negative imagery included in these symbols and what they represent.

Republican use of political symbolism has generally fallen into two categories: electoral campaigning; and political strategy and public statements. Political symbolism in electoral campaigning refers to those actions taken by candidates and their operatives to negatively use race and racial stereotypes to prime voters to move toward that candidate. Racial priming is a long-standing technique in politics and, as it pertains to race, generally requires the demonization of an individual or group; it has been repeatedly used by GOP candidates. Symbolism in political strategy and public statements has the same effect but takes place in noncampaign settings. Moreover, this form of political symbolism has important legislative and judicial implications and reflects ideological positions on issues, such as civil rights enforcement, that run counter to those of the majority in the African American community. Both categories of political symbolism play on the fears of racial conservatives that their favored status in the racial order is in jeopardy and can only be resisted by supporting the candidate who promises to protect their position without regard to the political consequences, the racial consequences, or both.

Electoral Campaigning

The Republican Party's historical use of racial stereotyping has repelled black voters and has damaged the GOP's relationship with the African American community. As Mendelberg notes, overt racism lies outside the current cultural norm; consequently, it is infrequently used and is largely denounced when tried. Noteworthy examples of both the covert and overt elements of political symbolism in electoral campaigning can be found in the Southern Strategy of Richard Nixon's 1968 presidential campaign; Ronald Reagan's 1980 presidential general election campaign kickoff in Philadelphia, Mississippi; Vice-President Bush's 1988 Willie Horton campaign ads; former Ku Klux Klan member David Duke's election to the Louisiana legislature as a Republican; Senator Jesse Helms's 1990 "quota" ad in his reelection campaign against African American challenger Harvey Gantt; Governor George W. Bush's 2000 Republican presidential primary campaign speech at Bob Jones University and his position on the Confederate flag debate in South Carolina; and Republican efforts to purge African American voters from election rolls throughout the South.

The Southern Strategy

Generally, the Southern Strategy refers to Republicans' efforts to win conservative white support by distancing themselves from progressive and moderate positions on racial issues of importance to African Americans. The use of this strategy dates to the end of Reconstruction, when Republicans began to retreat on their promises to support and fight for African American freedom. However, the strategy became widely known during the 1960s when Barry Goldwater and Richard Nixon sought the presidency.

The 1964 presidential election was thought by many observers of the day to be a colossal disaster for the Republican Party, as Senator Barry Goldwater's presidential campaign moved the party further to the right than it had ever been before. Goldwater, who opposed the 1964 Civil Rights Act, led a party whose civil rights platform planks were weaker than those in the 1960 platform. Goldwater's only chance to win the presidency required a sweep of the South, which would not be possible with a moderate civil rights position. The Goldwater camp concluded that the downside of losing black votes by opposing civil rights and other black interests would be over-come by the upside of enormous gains in the white South.

The US electorate responded to the Republican Party's new direction by giving President Lyndon Johnson one of the most lopsided victories in presidential election history. Many of the contributors to Goldwater's resounding defeat were moderate and liberal Republicans who became dis-affected by their party's right turn. The defections left conservatives in charge of the party's decisionmaking apparatus. While Johnson won a resounding victory, Goldwater dominated the South, winning in Alabama, Georgia, Mississippi, and South Carolina and doing well despite losing in Arkansas, Florida, Kentucky, North Carolina, and Tennessee. It was from the wreckage of the 1964 election, and Goldwater's performance in the South, that Richard Nixon's Southern Strategy emerged.[6]

Nixon's claim to represent the "silent majority" and "the nonshouters and nondemonstrators" was an important symbolic statement to those who grew weary of the protests and demonstrations of the 1960s. Nixon's words were also reassuring to those with negative views of the racial unrest of the era, such as the 1965 riots in Watts and Detroit and similar unrest following the 1968 assassination of Rev. Dr. Martin Luther King Jr., and viewed civil rights demands as the cause of the unrest. Nixon's strategy centered on try-ing to win over conservative southerners who had not previously voted for Republicans. It did so by using terms such as *law and order*, which played on white fears and stereotypes of African American community disorder. The implication of the strategy was that African American lawlessness would run rampant in white neighborhoods if Hubert Humphrey were elect-ed president. It played on white economic fears by charging that "reverse discrimination" was rampant in the US workplace and confirmed to some that African American progress could come only at the expense of whites, an inference that was plumbed by the Southern Strategy.

The strategy was also important for the legacy it left in US politics. Its success made it attractive to office seekers throughout the nation, and it became more entrenched as a campaign strategy, particularly in the South. Over time, the strategy evolved in such a way that it became possible to play on the racial animus in southern white society through the use of code words such as *states' rights* and *reverse discrimination* that conveyed the same sen-timents as more overt racial language had in previous generations. In that way, it became a roadmap that the GOP used to traffic in racial stereotypes and play on the latent (and not so latent) racism that exists in people. As Lee Atwater once noted in discussing the evolution of the strategy:

> You start out in 1954 saying "Nigger, nigger, nigger." By 1968 you can't say "nigger"—that hurts you. Backfires. So you say stuff like forced bus-ing, states' rights, and all that stuff. You're getting so abstract now [that]

you're talking about cutting taxes, and all these things you're talking about are totally economic things and a by-product of them is [that] blacks get hurt worse than whites. And subconsciously maybe that is part of it. I'm not saying that. But I'm saying that if it is getting that abstract, and that coded, that we are doing away with the racial problem one way or the other. You follow me—because obviously sitting around saying, "we want to cut this" is much more abstract than even the busing thing *and* a hell of a lot more abstract than "Nigger, nigger."[7]

The strategy also helped the Reagan campaign win support from so-called Reagan Democrats in 1980; using imagery of the "welfare queen" and referring to affirmative action as "anti-white" proved to be quite effective.

Reagan's 1980 General Election Kickoff

Ronald Reagan, in the postmortem following his defeat for the 1976 Republican presidential nomination, concluded that the road to the presidency ran through the South. Successfully navigating this political roadmap would require him to convince southern voters he could and would represent their interests. It was through the use of political symbolism that he was able to convey this message. The most notable step in this regard centered on the start of his 1980 general election campaign following that year's Republican national convention.

Reagan launched his postconvention campaign at the state fair in Philadelphia, Mississippi. This may be viewed as an unusual move, given that Mississippi was already strongly trending toward the Republican Party column for the November election. He likely did not have to campaign there to win the state; President Carter, a southerner from nearby Georgia, had carried the state by just 14,000 votes in 1976. However, Philadelphia, Mississippi, was a symbolically important place in the civil rights movement, the place where three civil rights workers—James Chaney, Michael Schwerner, and Andrew Goodman—were murdered after being released by local police who held them while they were in town investigating the burning of a black church. When they were released in the middle of the night, they were confronted by angry racists who beat and murdered them and left them in a ditch. Philadelphia, Mississippi, is thus a sore spot for many African Americans, since it represents the worst of the white supremacy movement.

Reagan sent a powerful signal when he spoke at the state fair. He underscored a number of conservative themes in his speech, while emphasizing and lauding the virtue and necessity of states' rights. He played on many of the sentiments that had won the state for Barry Goldwater sixteen years earlier. States' rights has a particular two-sided resonance in the American South that does not exist in the same way in much of the nation.

For African Americans, states' rights has been linked to the concept of white supremacy and the right of states to engage in any activity required to maintain that status quo—be it racial discrimination, segregation, or worse. States' rights was the basis of the Civil War, which is inextricably linked to US slavery. So, in the eyes of many—black and white alike—states' rights is a very controversial concept. By using Philadelphia, Mississippi, to take a stand for states' rights, "Reagan had calculated (correctly on both fronts) that the symbolism would be understood in the South and ignored in the North."[8] In other words, Reagan could play the "race card" with few non-southerners noticing, or caring.

Reagan so embodied racially conservative sentiments that he was endorsed by the Ku Klux Klan.[9] He was widely criticized for not immediately rejecting the endorsement, and it would be three weeks before his campaign issued a press release repudiating the Klan's support.[10] The fact that the Klan felt comfortable enough with Reagan to make such a public statement of support can be seen as a response to the adroit use of political symbolism throughout Reagan's campaign. That it took him so long to denounce the group suggests that he initially welcomed the endorsement or, minimally, did not reflexively understand why such support was symbolically offensive.

Ronald Reagan's campaign kickoff in Philadelphia was important for two reasons. First, it angered African Americans, particularly in the civil rights establishment, and it was considered disrespectful to the memory of the civil rights movement and three murdered civil rights workers. Second, it called attention to Reagan's social conservatism. The result of the controversy surrounding Reagan's appearance was that white conservatives found a measure of comfort in the fact that he was willing to incur the wrath of the civil rights establishment by showing that his racial views were similar to their own. Many who voted for President Gerald Ford in 1976 gave Reagan a second look, perhaps believing the old adage "the enemy of my enemy is my friend."

Reagan's success with conservative Democrats was not limited to the South. He also did well in the industrial Midwest, capitalizing on the economic uncertainty that gripped the region. Due to growing white economic concerns, a growing white backlash emerged toward compensatory policies for African Americans. Reagan and the GOP played on this environmental development to win races throughout the Midwest. According to Stanley Greenberg,

> These white Democratic defectors express a profound distaste for blacks, a sentiment that pervades almost everything they think about government and politics. . . . Blacks constitute the explanation for [white defectors'] vulnerability and for almost everything that has gone wrong in their lives; not being black is what constitutes being middle class; not living with

blacks is what makes a neighborhood a decent place to live. These senti- ments have important implications for Democrats, as virtually all progres- sive symbols and themes have been redefined in racial and pejorative terms.[11]

Reagan, and many Republicans since, have done a good job convincing conservatives that affirmative action and racial liberalism are why they were losing their jobs or having their wages cut instead of the real reason: economic policy decisions that effectively encouraged US industry to move to cheaper labor markets abroad and push down domestic wages for the jobs that remained.

Reagan's 1980 campaign was not his first experience in trafficking in blatant racial symbolism for electoral purposes. In his 1976 bid for the GOP nomination against incumbent president Gerald Ford, Reagan's North Carolina campaign distributed a flyer that alleged that Ford was going to name Massachusetts senator Edward Brooke, an African American, as his running mate.[12] The implication of the flyer was clear: if you wanted a white vice-president, then vote for Reagan, a message that particularly res- onated with white racial conservatives throughout the state.

Vice-President Bush and Willie Horton

George H. W. Bush was known as a political moderate prior to his selection as Ronald Reagan's running mate in 1980. Bush campaigned aggressively against Reagan for the 1980 GOP nomination, famously referring to Reagan's supply-side economic proposals as "voodoo economics." He was pro-choice and had a relatively good relationship with African Americans. Bush was also a member of the Eastern Establishment, New England patri- cians for whom moderation was a key character trait. As Kenneth O'Reilly, author of *Nixon's Piano: Presidents and Racial Politics from Washington to Clinton,* noted,

> His maturation as a practitioner of racial politics represented the last flop in a series of flip-flops dating to his senior year at Yale (1948) when he chaired the campus drive for the United Negro College Fund. Bush came out of the Republican Party's wing of racial liberalism embodied by his father, [Connecticut] Senator Prescott Bush, Jr., who served, three years after his son's Yale duties, as Connecticut chair for the Negro College Fund. When Bush moved to Texas . . . he stuck with the Yankee Republicans and otherwise challenged the Sun Belt's conventional racial wisdom—telling a Houston newspaper reporter in 1963 that he did "not think the Republican Party should be a rallying place for segregationists." In June of that year, as chair of the Harris County Republican party, he established an organization of black Republicans (the Republican Alliance), opened an office near an all-black college (Texas Southern), placed party funds in a black-owned bank, and sponsored "a black girls' softball team."[13]

Bush's racial progressivism was out of line with the prevailing conservative winds that controlled the Republican Party during the 1980s.

Bush, no doubt, understood the electoral mathematics confronting his 1988 presidential bid. After serving eight years as President Reagan's vice-president, Bush had to defend policies far more conservative than he probably would have liked. However, he understood that embracing those policies would be necessary to secure his election against Democratic nominee Michael Dukakis. Reagan's presidency demonstrated the utility of political symbolism and implicit appeals. Trailing by 18 percentage points in major polls as the 1988 election drew closer, the Bush campaign ran an advertisement that was construed in many circles as playing on racial stereotypes and white fears of black criminals; a black man raping a white woman represents, perhaps, the most egregious possible example in that regard.[14] The political potential of using Willie Horton and his story as a wedge issue for the GOP was made plain when Bush media director Roger Ailes bluntly told a reporter, "The only question is whether we depict Willie Horton with a knife in his hand or without it."[15] Lee Atwater reportedly said, "If I can make Willie Horton a household name, we'll win the election."[16]

William J. Horton Jr., renamed Willie Horton by Bush campaign manager Lee Atwater (Horton never went by "Willie"), came to represent those fears. Horton was convicted of murder during a 1974 robbery in which either Horton or an accomplice—it was never proven which one pulled the trigger—killed someone. Massachusetts, like many US states and the federal penal system, made some prisoners eligible for a weekend furlough program. Horton took nine such passes without incident. During a 1987 furlough, Horton kidnapped a man and raped his fiancée. There was a particular irony in Bush's ad and his taking aim at Dukakis in that way, since furloughed convicts murdered a police officer and a schoolteacher while Ronald Reagan was governor of California. Reagan had continued the program; Bush ignored the contrast.

Campaign efforts were supported by actions of technically independent political action committees that spent millions of dollars to buy television advertising time to run a commercial supporting the Bush campaign that featured Horton's mug shot and that charged Dukakis with being weak on crime and criminals. The inference was: vote for Dukakis if you want more "Willie Hortons"; vote for Bush if you don't. The African American community found the ad and its inference particularly negative toward blacks. The feeling was that the ad had implications, reaching beyond Dukakis and Horton, that reflected negatively on African Americans. The Maryland Republican Party sent a fundraising letter that stated, in part, "You, your spouse, your children and your friends can have a visit from someone like Willie Horton if Mike Dukakis becomes president."[17] The fact that the Bush campaign so aggressively focused on Horton was seen as an attempt to play on racial fears and stereotypes. What was particularly inflammatory to African Americans was that there were other felons furloughed under the program who also committed crimes. One such case involved a "White police officer who had gone bad and killed a friend over insurance money."[18] In focusing on Horton and not the police officer, Bush over-looked the white killer in favor of the black rapist.

David Duke

David Duke, who came to fame as a white supremacist who espouses antiminority rhetoric, is viewed by many as an extreme racist. He became the national director of the Knights of the Ku Klux Klan in 1974, shortly after graduating from Louisiana State University (LSU). Duke developed his racist reputation while at LSU, where he wore a Nazi uniform and swastika paraphernalia and held birthday parties celebrating Adolf Hitler. Duke was largely considered a peripheral, insignificant, though incendiary, figure until he entered politics. His emergence placed him in league with a long line of southern demagogues—racial conservatives who used a unique blend of racial populism leavened with racial anxiety to win elections. While this electoral strategy—using overt racial appeals—now falls outside the norm of acceptable political behavior, its progeny—using covert racial appeals tempered by code words—is now the preferred method for playing on race to win elections.

Republicans have repeatedly made the point that Duke wasn't a true Republican, noting that he campaigned for political office under different party labels in 1988. He entered the 1988 Democratic primaries in the spring, then ran as the nominee of the conservative Populist Party that fall. In 1989, he ran for—and won—a seat in the Louisiana House as a Republican (he ran for the US Senate and for governor as a Republican). Republican activists cited his party shifting as evidence that he was "a pretender, a charlatan, and a political opportunist."[19] The Republican criticism of Duke was understandable, because his victory as a Republican created an image problem for the party, particularly in its stated attempts to attract black voters. They could not afford to be linked to his kind of racial demagoguery, for fear that other like-minded electoral aspirants would try to take the Duke approach to victory in their states. It would have been a political killer for the party, as it is difficult to see a scenario in which a critical mass of African Americans would support a party under whose banner an overt racist won elected office.

These observations, along with the fact that Presidents Reagan and Bush endorsed Duke's opponent John Treen in the state House Republican primary, are irrelevant. The point is that Duke felt that his views would be most attractive to Republican voters and that the GOP was closer to him philosophically than any other party. Duke, as Wayne Greenshaw, author of *Elephants in the Cottonfields: Ronald Reagan and the New Republican South*, argued, "was very much a part of modern day Republicanism [in the Deep South] in his view on the issues."[20] Duke was vindicated in this regard by his election to the Louisiana legislature and his large, but losing, vote total in subsequent gubernatorial and US Senate elections. Duke won 60 percent of the white vote in the 1990 US Senate election against incumbent J. Bennett Johnston. His 44 percent of the total vote exceeded expectations. Duke also won 700,000 votes in the 1991 gubernatorial race.

That Duke's campaigns as a Republican hurt the party vis-à-vis African Americans is irrefutable. An analysis of his impact on African American politics in Louisiana demonstrated that his candidacies increased African American registration, turnout, and support for the Democratic candidate.[21] As political scientists Hanes Walton and Maxie Foster noted in their study of David Duke's political impact on African American voters, "Overall, this meant greater mobilization of voters to register and vote Democratic, in line with what African American voters did in Georgia in the 1940s and 1950s, when they were confronted with the political demagogue [Herman] Talmadge and others of his stripe."[22]

David Duke's relative, albeit short, rise to prominence confirms that there is a critical mass of voters who respond to the rhetoric presented by Duke and others. These racially conservative voters tend to be Republican, making the party less hospitable to racial moderates and liberals. It was a powerful symbol to African Americans that someone with Duke's background and beliefs could run for office as a Republican and win. To some, his victory is the reflection of years of Republican appeals to white racial resentment.

Jesse Helms vs. Harvey Gantt

North Carolina senator Jesse Helms made a name for himself by being very conservative—often obstructionist—on social issues, particularly race. He built his career on an "appeal to a nativist, even racist element in the state that has always been there."[23] He switched to the Republican Party in 1971, concluding that the Democrats no longer reflected his style of conservatism. Over the years, Helms came to represent those in the party who opposed anything that could be construed as racially moderate or liberal. He opposed the King holiday bill, affirmative action, sanctions against the apartheid government in South Africa, and immigration. Helms never supported civil rights legislation. A consistent Reagan ally, Helms became so widely known for his obstinacy that he earned the nickname "Senator No."

North Carolina, like much of the country, began to see significant demographic changes during the 1970s and 1980s. The Research Triangle area of Raleigh-Durham–Chapel Hill, in particular, became an attractive place for people moving to the state, and many of them did not share Helms's views on a range of issues. Consequently, the senator's brand of racial demagoguery began to show some weakness. He overcame the demographic changes by increasingly playing on the racial anxiety of many North Carolinians by injecting race into his campaigns and legislative activities. Because of this approach, Helms often entered his election campaigns with almost no support from African Americans—who are more than 20 percent of the statewide electorate—which required him to win an overwhelming majority of white votes to win reelection. According to political scientists Earl Black and Merle Black, authors of *The Rise of Southern Republicans*, "His campaign appeared to calculate the share of the White vote they needed for victory and then worked White Carolinians with divisive and emotionally charged television and radio ads, direct mail, and phone banks until their tracking polls showed they were comfortably exceeding their target."[24]

Two-term Charlotte mayor Harvey Gantt challenged Helms in 1990. Gantt hoped to represent a change for North Carolina, away from its racially divisive politics. Gantt led in the polls leading up to the election until Helms aired an ad that injected race into the campaign in a particularly hard-hitting and controversial way that crossed the line from aggressive, "hardball" politics. He ran ads accusing Gantt of using his racial minority status to get, and immediately sell, a license to start a television station.[25] Playing on the controversy over affirmative action, Helms's ad showed a white man's hands crumpling a job rejection letter. The announcer in the ad said, "You needed that job and you were the best qualified, but they had to give it to a minority because of a racial quota. Is that really fair? Harvey Gantt says it is. Gantt supports Ted Kennedy's racial quota law that makes the color of your skin more important than your qualifications."

The implications of the ad were clear and profound: electing Harvey Gantt to the US Senate would make it more difficult for whites to find work. This was particularly inflammatory in the eastern part of North Carolina, where many textile mills were in the forefront of the phenomenon of "outsourcing"—closing plants in the United States and sending the jobs to cheaper labor markets abroad. Helms used race to play on the economic uncertainty created by the job losses. He was able to convince many voters that affirmative action and liberal civil rights policies, not economic policies favorable to such job movement, were the reason they could not find work. The ad was the next step in racial-electoral politics, coming two years after the infamous Willie Horton ads.

The quota advertisement was not the only way Helms trafficked in racial hostility for electoral purposes during his campaign against Gantt. He also attacked Gantt for receiving racial preferences, charging that Gantt used them improperly. The announcer in the advertisement asked, "How did Harvey Gantt become a millionaire? He used his position as mayor and his minority status to get himself and his friends a free TV station license from the government. Only weeks later, they sold out—to a white-owned corporation for $3.5 million." The claim was not entirely true. While the Gantt group did make the quick sell, the Federal Communications Commission said that race was not a factor in their decision.[26] The advertisement played on white racial hostility by suggesting that Gantt's financial success was due solely to his using his race to "game the system" for his own benefit.

Governor Bush in South Carolina, at Bob Jones University, and the South Carolina Confederate Flag Debate

The 2000 Republican presidential nomination fight was particularly nasty in the wake of the Iowa caucus and New Hampshire primary. Governor George W. Bush and Senator John McCain were vying to become the clear frontrunner and solidify a hold on the Republican nomination. Bush and McCain understood that the South Carolina primary shaped up to be a make-or-break contest and were aggressively seeking as many votes as possible. Bush sought to win the primary by capturing the support of conservative South Carolinians, who make up the majority of the state's electorate.

In so doing, Bush made two important symbolic statements that used race and black people as a whipping post to generate conservative support. First, he chose to make a campaign speech at Bob Jones University, an institution that had a history of supporting segregation and was viewed by some as the embodiment of white supremacy. Until 1975, the university restricted student admission to whites. The change was sparked by political pressure and an Internal Revenue Service decision to rescind its tax-exempt status because of its discriminatory policies. When the change was made, the university instituted a policy prohibiting interracial dating. The policy was modified in 2000 to allow interracial dating, but it encouraged parental notification by students. The university also opposed racial intermarriage. In June 1998, Jonathan Pait, a public relations spokesperson for the university, explained the school's prohibition against interracial dating: "God has separated people for His own purposes. He has erected barriers between the nations, not only land and sea barriers, but also ethnic, cultural, and language barriers. God has made people different from one another and intends those differences to remain. Bob Jones University is opposed to intermarriage of the races because it breaks down the barriers God has established."[27]

Bush could have addressed and wooed conservative South Carolinians without appearing at Bob Jones University, an institution whose racial history was well known. Choosing to speak there was unnecessary to win conservative support and, as a consequence, was a gratuitous and incendiary slap at racial moderation.

Second, he refused to speak out on the debate taking place in the state at the time regarding the placement of the Confederate flag on top of the South Carolina statehouse. Bush called it an issue for the state to decide and declined to give his opinion on the controversy (African Americans wanted it removed; conservatives did not, calling it an important historical symbol). This was a disappointing stance in the eyes of many African Americans, who viewed the Confederate flag debate as an attempt by racial conservatives in the state to give state sanction to the symbolism of white supremacy. According to professor David Lublin, author of *The Republican South: Democratization and Partisan Change*, "Some whites want to maintain the Confederate flag as an expression of white political power or, as one southerner put it, 'It's our way of telling them who's on top.'"[28] There is an irony here with regard to Bush's silence. While citing "state sovereignty" as his reason for not addressing the controversy in South Carolina, he did not hesitate to speak out on a state issue in Massachusetts: a decision by its Supreme Court to allow gay and lesbian marriages. This can be seen as an example of political expediency, in that the marriage issue was a political winner for him, whereas the flag issue could have been a political lóser. This was particularly transparent to African American Democrats, who have usually led the fight to remove the flag from public schools and buildings.[29]

Governor Bush's South Carolina primary supporters also used race in a telephone campaign against Senator John McCain. McCain and his wife are parents of an adopted child from Bangladesh. The campaign told selected South Carolinians that McCain had a "black child," which had the potential to trigger a range of negative racial connotations and which suggested that McCain was too liberal on race relations. It was irrelevant that the child was not black. The dark-skinned child served the purpose of Bush's supporters who wanted to exploit a part of McCain's family life negatively and play on racism for political gain.

The fight over the Confederate flag, in South Carolina and other southern states, is an appropriate metaphor for the relationship between African Americans and the Republican Party. As John Judis and Ruy Teixera, authors of *The Emerging Democratic Majority,* note, "Republicans are strongest in some of [the] same states, such as Mississippi, Alabama, and South Carolina, with the largest percentage of Black voters."[30] Race in these states is still the most important political issue—more significant than education, transportation, and the economy in the minds of many southern voters. Race is so strong that voters will even punish a Republican who takes a position on an issue that can be seen as capitulating to black demands. South Carolina governor David Beasley lost his 1998 reelection bid in large part because he favored taking down the flag.[31]

GOP Purge and Ballot Security Programs

While the GOP's founding principles were liberal and progressive, the party—both in an officially organized fashion and in more localized, individual ways—has an established history of voter suppression and intimidation that has greatly contributed to its deteriorated relationship with African Americans. Since the emergence of the civil rights movement, the GOP's drive to win elections has been complicated by large turnouts of African American voters. Republicans understand the electoral implications of this all too clearly, as one Republican state representative in Michigan noted in the period just before the 2004 elections about Detroit, a city with an 83 percent African American population: "If we do not suppress the Detroit vote, we're going to have a tough time in this election."[32] This comment, and countless others like it, reflect Republican acceptance of the emergence since the 1960s of a new political truism: the GOP is more likely to win elections when black turnout is low. In response to this truism, the GOP has had to actively seek to "keep the lid" on the black vote in closely contested races. To that end, the party has employed numerous "voter purge" and "ballot security" programs that have intimidated black voters and reduced black voter turnout.

Voter purges and ballot security programs are not inherently illegitimate, since voter fraud does exist and should be rooted out of elections. The problem with these particular ballot security programs is that they target minority voters and remove legally registered voters from registration rolls with the effect being reductions in minority participation. Given the available evidence, voter fraud, to the extent that it exists, is a multiracial phenomenon; the GOP, however, treats it as a minority one. As Laughlin McDonald, one of the foremost voting rights scholars in the United States has noted, these purge programs "are invariably presented as good government measures necessary to prevent voter fraud, but far too often they are actually designed to suppress minority voting—and for nakedly partisan purposes."[33]

The controversy surrounding the purging process has numerous components. First, many of the purged voters do not know they are ineligible to vote until they arrive at the polling place to cast their ballots. Second, purged voters are disproportionately poor and minority, which raises the potential specter of political targeting to keep certain individuals from voting. Third, purged voters who want to challenge their removal are faced with the burden of proof that they were unfairly removed, as opposed to the burden being on the jurisdiction that engaged in the purge. Voters in these circumstances are often prevented from casting provisional ballots, which can be counted upon a decision reversal, thereby rendering them voteless for that election. This presents an onerous barrier for someone to overcome to exercise the most fundamental element of democracy. The examples cited here are part of the story. Similar examples can be found in a number of other cities and states across the country.[34]

Republican "purge program" initiatives have been undertaken in a number of states, virtually all of which disproportionately target African American voters. The lineage of contemporary purge programs can be traced to the Chicago-based Operation Double Check (ODC). The program was created in the run-up to the 1964 presidential election to canvass voters to verify voter registration addresses. Republicans concluded that such a program was necessary, because the feeling around the country among them was that Mayor Richard Daley and his political machine stole the 1960 election in favor of Senator John Kennedy, and they wanted to prevent a repeat in 1964. That concern, coupled with Chicago's reputation for crooked elections, suggested that there was an argument to be made that closer scrutiny of the voting process was warranted there, and Republicans were able to strike nearly 3,000 voters from the city's registration rolls.

Some purge programs have become the subject of litigation. In one case, Republican National Committee documents revealed official support for such activities. One document was a 1986 memorandum from Kris Wolfe, the RNC's Midwest political director, to Lanny Griffith, the party's southern political director. Wolfe advised Griffith that a well-orchestrated purge program "will eliminate 60–80,000 folks from the rolls" and "could keep the black vote down considerably."[35] According to a state district court judge who presided over a lawsuit by local voters over the action, the plan "was an insidious scheme by the Republican Party to remove Blacks from the voting rolls" and that "the only reasonable conclusion is that they initiated this purge with the specific intent of disfranchising these Blacks of their right to vote."[36]

It is impossible to know precisely how many African Americans have been purged from voter rolls and, of that number, how many would have actually voted but for this bar. However, the fact that there have been systematic efforts by the GOP in states across the country to target African American voters for the express purpose of preventing them from voting is a substantial black mark against the party in its efforts to win black votes. It should also be noted that, on occasion, the controversy around these efforts angers the black community so much that it mobilizes more blacks to vote than would otherwise be expected. These purge programs create a backlash among black voters.

Republican use of ballot security programs also has a sordid history and has been a prominent feature of GOP political strategy for decades. These programs are supported by a number of measures, including posting at the polls uniformed men who sometimes wear badges or guns so that they look like law enforcement officers; posting off-duty police officers at the polls;

photographing or videotaping voters; questioning potential voters or poll officials, often in aggressive and hostile ways that can embarrass or humiliate; spreading false information about voting requirements, candidates, and the election date in the days before the election; and challenging voters on the basis of inaccurate registration lists that disproportionately winnow out low-income people. These tactics, which are often used in combination to heighten the impact, are a form of vote suppression—a polite term for the disenfranchisement of eligible minority voters.[37] Further, they rely on the amorphous notion of "reasonable cause" and raise questions about how a poll watcher can make the determination to challenge a voter on anything beyond race, ethnicity, or economics if the poll watcher has no specific information on an individual voter.

Many ballot security programs have their genesis in Operation Eagle Eye (OEE), a program created by the Republican National Committee that dates back to 1962. The program, designed to watch for fraud in large cities, surpassed all previous attempts to organize and coordinate Republican efforts to monitor and win elections.[38] While the party always contended that the program was designed to prevent voter fraud, OEE's national director, Charles Barr, said in 1964 that he expected "1.25 million voters to be either successfully challenged or discouraged from going to the polls."[39] Since the creation of OEE, Republican ballot security programs have been implemented throughout the country, virtually all of which have been located in black and minority precincts.

New Jersey was one of six states that were part of "Commitment '81," an RNC program that was created to elect state and local candidates in those states; and a National Ballot Security Force was created to support those efforts. The US District Court in New Jersey and an investigation conducted by the New Jersey attorney general revealed that the security force "dispatched armed off-duty police officers and sheriffs wearing official-looking armbands to heavily Black and Democratic precincts in Newark, Camden, and Trenton."[40] The party spent nearly $80,000 on the program, which included mailings and the posting of signs at polling places in these precincts warning that they were being patrolled by security force members and offering a $1,000 reward for anyone giving information leading to the arrest and conviction of election law violators.[41] The point man for the state's operations was a Republican assemblyman from Newark who "once publicly referred to Martin Luther King as 'Martin Luther Coon' [and] began his demagogic political career as a preacher of armed white self-defense following the 1967 Newark riots."[42] The state also received national attention in 1993 when some black ministers "reported receiving offers of cash from people identifying themselves as Republicans" in exchange for not endorsing New Jersey governor Jim Florio's reelection campaign or for not mentioning the election on the Sunday before it was to be held.[43]

In 1990, a coalition of North Carolina Republican groups and the Jesse Helms reelection committee "sent postcards to 125,000 voters, 97 percent of whom were African American, giving them false information about voter eligibility."[44] The postcards stated that voters would be asked to give their name, residence, and period of residence in that precinct and, also, that knowingly giving false information in response to those questions was a federal crime.[45] In fact, asking for the information was illegal.

South Carolina has a particularly formidable history in these programs and other forms of racial discrimination. Charleston County Republicans formed the Ballot Security Group (BSG), which had a two-decade record of targeting black Democratic voters. Republican-nominated poll watchers and managers denied blacks assistance at the polls and they "intimidated and harassed African-American voters."[46] According to a former state magistrate judge, the denial of assistance frustrated some black voters to the extent that they said, "'Oh, never mind,' and just turned around and walked out the door."[47] Whites who requested assistance were allowed to take a person of their own choosing into the booth as a matter of course. A judge who presided over litigation concerning the BSG noted that there were links between its members and the official Election Commission and that one "particularly problematic" poll manager assigned by the commission was removed from a black precinct "because of his efforts to deny African American voters their right to have assistance from the person of their choice."[48]

In a 1998 South Carolina election, white Republican state representative Son Kinon mailed over 3,000 brochures to African American voters warning them to be careful on election day:

> You have always been my friend, so don't chance GOING TO JAIL on Election Day! . . . SLED [South Carolina Law Enforcement Division] agents, FBI agents, people from the Justice Department and undercover agents will be in Dillon County working this election. People who you think are your friends, and even your neighbors, could be the very ones that turn you in. THIS ELECTION IS NOT WORTH GOING TO JAIL!!!!!![49]

These and other instances (e.g., flyers listing the wrong election date and claiming that parking tickets and overdue rent should be paid before election day) can only be construed as race-driven efforts designed to stifle black turnout.

The 1985 creation of the Republican National Lawyers Association (RNLA) put at the disposal of the party a new tool to enable it to challenge laws or to decipher what can and cannot be done regarding these types of activities. The RNLA could also be counted on to defend the national party and its state, county, and local affiliates against legal challenges to party purge and security programs as well as any other activities that could bring litigation. The presence of the RNLA has served to professionalize and make more sophisticated party efforts in this regard.[50]

While the GOP has strenuously denied charges that its purge and ballot security programs are racially driven, there is virtually no evidence in the record that demonstrates otherwise. As this review shows, Republicans have repeatedly implemented these kinds of programs in minority precincts, though the party calls these same districts "heavily Democratic" in an attempt to downplay the racial implications of their actions. Indeed, the GOP has not announced ballot security programs targeting predominantly white, middle-class precincts. Moreover, these programs traffic in "language and metaphors that trade on stereotypes of minority voters as venal and credulous."[51]

Political Strategy and Public Statements

Republican use of political symbolism—whether planned or inadvertent—extends to noncampaign venues as well. In any case, the strategic decisions and political statements indicate, minimally, a misunderstanding of the role racism has played in African American society or, more substantially, a deliberate attempt to use African Americans and issues of importance to them as a turning point to rally white conservative voters. Among the noteworthy noncampaign uses of political symbolism that have repelled African American support for the Republican Party are Republican efforts in the early 1980s to develop "alternative" black leadership to counter the traditional civil rights establishment; President Bush's 1991 nomination of Clarence Thomas to the US Supreme Court; Reagan administration support for tax-exempt status for Bob Jones University; Republican resistance to integrate the Fourth Circuit Court; Trent Lott's comments lauding Strom Thurmond's Dixiecrat presidential campaign; and President Reagan's "welfare queen" code language regarding African American women.

Efforts to Develop "Alternative" Black Leadership

President Ronald Reagan's political advisers, along with party officials and activists, concluded that the president and the party could not build a useful relationship with established African American leaders. The Congressional Black Caucus, the National Association for the Advancement of Colored People, the Urban League, and other such groups took a negative view of Reagan and his conservative policies and politics.

Rather than seek to improve its relationship with these groups and, by extension, African Americans, Republican activists began to attack the credibility of the civil rights establishment. They also began to identify, recruit, and promote a new cadre of black leaders to serve as an alternative to the traditional establishment. As Representative Newt Gingrich noted, "It is in the interest of the Republican party and Ronald Reagan to invent new Black leaders, so to speak."[52] The hope behind the effort was that these newly developed leaders would vie for leadership in the black community and be seen as legitimate leaders and opinion makers. This would make it easier to marginalize the traditional establishment. The additional hope was that these new leaders could be enlisted to make heretofore unpopular conservative Republican policies more palatable to the mass of African Americans.

This effort began in the immediate pre-Reagan era, as conservative foundations began to support black conservative intellectuals and activists. The new organizations that began to form were able to obtain foundation support to facilitate their activities. With Ronald Reagan's ascension to the White House, however, these efforts took on added significance. With party backing, individuals such as Clarence Thomas, Thomas Sowell, Robert Woodson, Glenn Loury, Walter Williams, and Clarence Pendleton, among others, were promoted by conservative groups as challengers to established African American leadership. These individuals were academics, government officials, and activists who, since the early 1980s, have sought to provide, as Clarence Thomas once said, "an alternative to the consistently leftist thinking of the civil rights leadership and the general black leadership."[53]

These individuals were also provided with access to the media to promote their ideas and denounce traditional African American leadership. Throughout it all, an ironic rhetorical circle developed: the more they denounced African American leadership, the more they became controversial; the more controversial they became, the more they were able to access the media; the more they were able to access the media, the more they were seen to be tools of the conservative movement rather than as legitimate alternatives to the traditional civil rights establishment. Throughout the 1980s, headlines citing the "rise" of black conservatives trumpeted the arrival of this "alternative" to the traditional civil rights establishment.

Ultimately, though, the attempts to create an alternative black leadership structure failed, in large part because the alternative leaders had no constituencies. They were simply created and offered to the public with no real records of community service. While there is evidence of conservatism in the African American community on selected issues—for example, school voucher programs and abortion—there has yet to be the full-scale movement of significant numbers of African Americans toward political conservatism, even after a generation of priming. Republican activists often cite this selected-issue conservatism as proof that African Americans are ready to embrace the GOP. It appears, though, that the GOP has confused selected-issue conservatism with acceptance of all aspects of the GOP's brand of contemporary conservatism.

Bush's 1991 Nomination of
Clarence Thomas to the Supreme Court

Thurgood Marshall stepped down from the US Supreme Court in 1991. Marshall built a legendary career as a civil rights lawyer who, as an NAACP litigator, helped use the law to end official segregation in the United States. President Kennedy named Marshall to the US Court of Appeals for the Second Circuit in 1961. Four years later, President Johnson named Marshall as solicitor general of the United States and, in 1967, associate justice of the US Supreme Court, the first African American to serve on the Court. It is not possible to overstate Marshall's contribution to American law and society.

Republicans saw his decision to step down from the Court as an opportunity to make it more conservative. That could have been done with any conservative nominee. However, the Bush political operation and Republican operatives saw an opportunity to score points with the African American community by selecting an African American (pressure was mounting in the African American community to name a black person to replace Marshall) to fill the post while putting the seat in conservative hands. Thomas's nomination could have been seen as a political "double whammy" in that it served two purposes: for Republicans, making the seat conservative; for African Americans, naming a black person to the seat.

Bush, in announcing his nominee in a White House rose garden ceremony, called Thomas "the best qualified candidate" to serve on the Court. That was a largely derided comment, particularly given Thomas's relative inexperience. His judicial career began the previous year, when President Bush appointed him to the US Court of Appeals in Washington, DC. He served as head of the Equal Employment Opportunity Commission, where he oversaw federal enforcement of Title VII of the 1964 Civil Rights Act, which prohibited racial employment discrimination. Prior to that appointment, Thomas served as assistant secretary for civil rights in the Department of Education.

The problem for many African Americans in all this was Thomas's conservative ideology and politics. He was among the early blacks identified and sponsored by white conservatives, which placed him in the crosshairs of many long-standing black leaders. He was widely quoted as opposing affirmative action and other social policies that were popular in the black community. He has been derisive of the traditional civil rights leadership and hostile to black interests. Bush's nomination of Thomas was therefore seen as further proof in the minds of black leaders that the president and the party were more interested in using race for political gain than in trying to reconcile racial division. The nomination put some black leaders in a racial box and challenged their commitment to focusing on a black nominee.

The overwhelming majority of black organizations opposed Thomas's Supreme Court nomination. Many charged Thomas with being an apologist for conservative policies that have hurt African American progress. Some black organizations supported Thomas, arguing that, given his background, it was unlikely he would forget where he came from. During this period, a Trojan horse theory began to emerge in some quarters of the black community that contended Thomas would "do the right thing" once he took a seat on the Supreme Court. Some of those supporters, such as the Southern Christian Leadership Conference, have since criticized Thomas for being hostile to black interests and racial fairness. The consensus that has congealed among many in the black community is that Thomas, perhaps the most conservative member of the Court, is supporting efforts to roll back the clock on many important civil rights issues facing black America.

Reagan Administration Support for
Tax-Exempt Status for Racially Discriminating Schools

Bob Jones University (BJU) was founded in 1927 on fundamentalist Christian teachings. Among the pillars of the institution was a policy prohibiting African Americans from admission to the university. This policy existed without federal sanction until 1970, when the Internal Revenue Service (IRS) ruled that educational institutions with discriminatory policies would have their federal tax exemption revoked. This policy change was implemented to discourage the growth of segregated private academies, which began to emerge following court-ordered desegregation.[54]

The Department of Justice reversed the IRS policy revoking the tax exemptions for such schools in 1982. The move caused a wave of controversy and bad publicity in the country, with Reagan accused of supporting racial segregation. Reagan responded to the criticism by saying he personally opposed using tax policy to subsidize segregated schools but contended that there was no basis in existing law for denying tax breaks, suggesting that Congress should pass legislation to make its intention clear.[55] The litigation that started with BJU and Goldsboro (North Carolina) Christian Schools (GCS) suing the IRS eventually reached the US Supreme Court. In an unusual move, the Court appointed an attorney to argue in favor of the abandoned IRS policy. The Department of Justice joined with attorneys for BJU and GCS in arguing that the IRS was never authorized to deny tax-exempt status to schools that practiced racial discrimination. The Reagan administration argued that the reversal decision was based on the preservation of religious freedom, not support for racial segregation. William T.

Coleman Jr., an African American Republican attorney and former secretary of transportation in the Ford administration, defended the IRS policy, saying, "The argument is that because their racism is religiously based, they have a right to tax benefits denied to all others who cannot defend their policy on religious grounds."[56]

Supporting religious freedom in this case required the Reagan administration to take the position that institutions such as BJU and GCS should be able to continue their racial discrimination and receive tax exemptions. The Reagan position, supported by conservatives nationally, was untenable and indefensible in the eyes of black America. It showed once again that Reagan was not supportive of racial reconciliation and would use the power of government to facilitate racial intolerance. The case also proved to be one of a number of instances where Reagan aggressively took positions that were in direct conflict with the majority of African Americans.

Resistance to Integrate the Fourth Circuit Court

The Fourth US Circuit Court of Appeals is one of the busiest courts in the country on racial issues. The states it oversees—Maryland, North Carolina, South Carolina, Virginia, and West Virginia—have the highest proportion of African American residents (22 percent) of any multistate circuit in the nation. The Fourth Circuit has been criticized for its case disposition, and Congress has been criticized for failing to fill its vacancies. The Fourth Circuit disposes of cases faster than any other circuit, and its pending caseload dropped 22 percent between 1996 and 1999, while the national average rose 9 percent. The circuit also hears oral argument in a smaller percentage of cases than any other circuit court and dismisses 87 percent of appeals.

As a consequence of these and other data, concern began to arise in the 1990s that the circuit was too expedient in administering justice and that the judicial process was unfair to defendants. This had particular resonance for African Americans, given the high percentage of blacks engaged in court action in the Fourth Circuit. Part of the concern centered on the credibility of an all-white bench presiding in such a diverse circuit; some maintained that the status quo undermined the circuit's credibility. Another practical concern arose as well. Fewer judges handling more cases in less time than the national average suggests that more of the work of the circuit is being done by staffers who had never faced Senate confirmation.

Compelling arguments have been advanced that Republican reticence to fill seats on the Fourth Circuit was part of a larger ideological dispute between Senate Republicans and the Clinton administration. GOP senators disapproved of Clinton and his nominees and wanted to restrict as much as possible the long-term influence of Clinton over the federal judiciary; this could best be done by blocking as many of his nominees as possible. This was particularly important in the Fourth Circuit, where Republican appointees held six of the eleven seats (there were four vacancies).

The case of the Fourth Circuit, however, took on a racial dimension that was difficult to ignore: the circuit with the highest percentage of African Americans in the country under its jurisdiction did not have a black judge. In September 1999, President Clinton nominated James A. Wynn Jr., a moderate African American North Carolina state judge, to fill a vacancy on the circuit, but Senator Jesse Helms blocked the nomination. It is unusual for a senator to block the nomination of a circuit court judge from his own state, particularly when that state is not represented on the bench; North Carolina was not during this period. He used judicial administration as a cover for his preference to not integrate the Fourth Circuit bench. He cited the cost of taking on a new judge—$1 million for the judge, staff, and associated costs—as prohibitive and relied on the advice of the circuit's chief judge, who testified before the Senate that they did not need any new judges.[57] His testimony and writings were in contrast to that of his predecessor, who testified that new judges were needed to handle the large caseload.

Helms's position forced Clinton to replace the Wynn nomination with that of Roger Gregory, an African American lawyer from Virginia with bipartisan backing from both of his US senators. Gregory received a "recess" appointment, good for one year. President Bush nominated Gregory to a permanent seat on the circuit in 2001, with the backing of both Virginia senators. Gregory won appointment by a 99 to 1 vote; Trent Lott of Mississippi cast the lone dissenting vote, one he stated was a protest of recess appointments of judges.

Republican resistance to integrating the court reverberated throughout the black community. The episode reflected negatively on the party among African Americans. The thought that the circuit representing the largest number of African Americans of any circuit in the nation did not have a black judge grated on many. It did not help Republicans in the black community that a member of the party actively opposed the integration of the bench. It should be noted that Republican opposition to black judicial nominees is not limited to the Fourth Circuit. John Ashcroft, then a senator, blocked the federal judicial nomination of black Missouri Supreme Court judge Ronnie White. White was widely viewed as well qualified for the appointment, and Ashcroft's opposition was viewed as racially motivated.

Trent Lott and Strom Thurmond

Trent Lott, at a December 2002 celebration commemorating Senator Strom Thurmond's 100th birthday, praised the retiring senator for an unprecedented congressional career. He reflected on Thurmond's accomplishments and, in the course of his remarks, made a statement that proved quite controversial: "I want to say this about my state. When Strom Thurmond ran for president, we voted for him. We're proud of it. And if the rest of the country had followed our lead, we wouldn't have had all these problems over all these years, either."[58]

Thurmond ran for president in 1948 as a Dixiecrat, a faction of prosegregationist racists who opposed desegregation and other efforts to prevent discrimination against African Americans. His candidacy was based solely on the defense and preservation of segregation. The Dixiecrats walked out of the 1948 Democratic convention to protest the inclusion of a pro–civil rights plank in the party's platform. Thurmond, representing the newly formed States' Rights Democratic Party, won four states, all southern.

Lott initially denied any malicious intent in his comments, and his spokesperson said it was "wrong" to read anything into what was characterized as remarks "intended to pay tribute to a remarkable man who led a remarkable life."[59] Lott's statement caused a tremendous uproar in US politics at the end of 2002. A Gallup poll conducted during the weekend after the controversy erupted revealed a tremendous gap in perceptions of the Republican Party. Gallup asked African Americans which party best reflects "your values," and blacks chose the Democrats over the Republicans by a 74 percent to 6 percent margin.[60] Gallup data also revealed that 65 percent of African Americans polled believed that Lott was prejudiced against African Americans and that 63 percent felt that Lott genuinely believed that the country would have been better off had Thurmond been elected president in 1948.

Lott also reminded people of Thurmond's racist past. That past, and its racial implications, rub raw the political and social wounds felt by many African Americans all over the country. This complicates, and makes more difficult, GOP outreach efforts to African Americans, because it is another in a long line of episodes involving white Republicans who have used negative racial symbolism to make a point. It also calls into question the GOP's sincerity when it claims to want to turn the page of racial animosity and start a new chapter in its relations with the black community.

Upon winning a seat in Congress in 1972 (after leaving the Democratic Party), Lott built a reputation as a consistent opponent of African American civil rights and as someone who traded in racial symbolism. Lott has opposed extension of the Voting Rights Act, expansion of fair housing laws, and establishment of the Martin Luther King Jr. holiday, among other bills. He opposed allowing judges to award payments covering lawyers' fees to plaintiffs who brought successful civil rights suits and allowing the government to impose administrative penalties against people who practiced racial discrimination in the sale or rental of housing.[61] He supported measures that outlaw busing for school desegregation and that forbid affirmative action in federal contracting; he also supported tax exemptions for Bob Jones University and the extension of a design patent owned by the United Daughters of the Confederacy.[62]

Lott's controversial statement regarding Thurmond's 1948 campaign was not an isolated event. Lott has a history of such statements and connections to racist organizations. He lauded Confederate general Jefferson Davis, noting that the "fundamental principles" in which he believed "are very important to people across the country, and they apply to the Republican Party."[63] He filed an amicus curiae brief in a 1983 Supreme Court case urging reversal of an Internal Revenue Service ruling that discontinued Bob Jones University's tax-exempt status because of its racially discriminatory policies.[64] He spoke to meetings of the Council of Conservative Citizens (CCC), a white supremacist organization based in Mississippi, and hosted its officers in his Senate office; he once stated that the CCC stands "for the right principles and the right philosophy."[65] He has publicly stated that he sometimes feels "closer to [Confederate president] Jefferson Davis than any other man in America," and that the Civil War was the "war of aggression."[66] In a speech to the Sons of Confederate Veterans, Lott said, "The spirit of Jefferson Davis lives in the 1984 Republican platform."[67] Lott refused to cosponsor a 1989 congressional resolution designating June 21 as Chaney, Goodman, and Schwerner Day to acknowledge the contributions of the three civil rights workers who were murdered in 1964 in Mississippi.[68]

One of the underexamined problems for the GOP in the Lott-Thurmond controversy was what resulted from it all. The party accepted Lott's decision to step down (albeit unwillingly) as Senate majority leader, but he remained in the Senate. The troubling point from the perspective of African Americans could be that it is apparently acceptable for a person who is nostalgic for segregation to remain a Republican senator, as long as that person is not in the party leadership. Republicans may have underestimated how extensively the decision to allow Lott to remain in the Senate has damaged their reputation in the black community.

The Welfare Queen

President Reagan campaigned for the presidency in 1980 on a platform that called in part for a reduction in funding for social programs. The campaign promises were in keeping with conservative orthodoxy, which has argued that too much welfare makes a society weak and lazy and turns it into a "welfare state." This orthodoxy facilitates a type of social Darwinism in that it believes that the government should not be in the business of supporting individuals who can't "get it together" and take care of themselves. Further, the belief is that people should rise and fall on their own merits, and the competition fostered by that philosophy will bring out the best in them all and that they can thus live a more productive life.

The fulfillment of this orthodoxy required defunding, to the greatest extent possible, a wide range of social welfare programs. Since the New Deal, however, these programs had been widely accepted as necessary to protect those individuals who were in need and who were seen as part of the social contract. Consequently, these programs were sufficiently popular that eliminating them was long seen as mean-spirited. Defunding the programs would be easier in an environment in which support for them was destabilized. The most effective tactic used to this end was to change the rhetoric used to describe these programs in such a way as to make those who benefited from them less popular in the eyes of the public at large.

President Reagan was in the forefront of this effort as it related to welfare, consistently referring to female recipients of assistance as "welfare queens"; he talked often of the welfare queen who drove a Cadillac to pick up her welfare check. According to one member of the House of Representatives who chaired the Congressional Black Caucus during Reagan's first year in office and led the group into its first, and only, meeting with Reagan during his presidency, Reagan's view of African Americans appeared to be formed largely on the basis of welfare queen symbolism.[69]

Professor Ange-Marie Hancock notes that the targeted use of the term helped create a "politics of disgust" that forged an environment in which cutting welfare programs would be viewed as acceptable.[70] According to Hancock, the term and the racial symbolism surrounding it "is a construct designed to justify ideologically specific forms of public policy."[71] Reagan spoke often of the welfare queen living off the taxes collected from hard-working Americans, but he rarely spoke of this woman's race. By letting the inherent stereotypes of black single mothers do the work for him, he could make his point without using the words. He was also assisted by a news media that "fanned the flames of political disgust" by almost always using footage of only black women in their stories on welfare and social programs (in the case of television news media), or (in the case of print media) they discussed welfare mothers in the context of women who don't work, are teen mothers, or are drug users.[72] This merely reinforced or validated what some already had in mind regarding welfare and black people.

According to Professor Ronald Walters, the impact of the Republican drumbeat of the welfare queen was substantial in that it congealed the notion of race and welfare dependency in the minds of many white conservatives.[73] Once that juxtaposition "solidified in the public imagination, there was a return to the [Jim Crow–era] concept of the 'undeserving poor' and to images of laggard, lazy, dull welfare recipients on the 'dole' who deserve the punishment visited upon them because they constitute a drag upon the economy and a blot upon the moral image of the nation."[74] The GOP attack on social welfare generally triggered "citizens' predisposed moral judgments of single, poor Black mothers" and became a debate framed by "values and individual behavior" rather than need.[75]

No other GOP use of political symbolism has had as deep an impact on the interaction between African Americans and the Republican Party than the consistent, derogatory, and inflammatory use of the welfare queen as the reason why the social welfare system needed reform and retrenchment. The welfare queen helped make African American women targets of a new generation of racial stereotyping and set the stage for a significant change in the way the US government operated on social issues. The New Deal and the Great Society helped stitch together a significant safety net for all Americans in need. The use of the welfare queen helped make it socially acceptable to snip away at that net and made it easier for conservatives to challenge other social programs they found distasteful—like affirmative action. The welfare queen also introduced a new thesis into the political dialogue: that the poor had too much money, the rich had too little money, and the way to deal with this problem was to cut human needs programs for the needy and cut taxes for the wealthy.

Links to Racist and White Supremacist Organizations

Prominent Republicans have had or currently have links to racist and white supremacist organizations. Some of the links are direct, though most are indirect. This complicates the party's standing in the African American community, because the connections give the impression that these prominent Republicans—be they elected officials, prominent activists, or commentators—are sympathetic to racists' beliefs and the inclinations of these groups. Senator Trent Lott, Representatives Bob Barr and Tom Tancredo, and Mississippi governor Haley Barbour are among the most notable Republicans to be associated with racist groups. The significance of these connections lies in the comfort with which Republicans are involved in the groups and the extent to which these organizations take very prominent anti-black positions.

Charles Martel Society

The Charles Martel Society (CMS) was founded in 2001 by William Regnery II. Regnery is part of the Regnery publishing family and has been known to be a major fundraiser for "radical right" causes. The society is named after the French military leader who defeated Moorish armies at Tours, France, in 732. Martel's name has appeared in the title of other clubs and groups that have espoused anti-Arab or anti-immigrant views. CMS publishes *The Occidental Quarterly: A Journal of Western Thought and Opinion*. The journal has been described as "a magazine that espouses white nationalism and whose statement of principles calls for limiting immigration to selected people of European ancestry."[76]

Philosophy. According to a November 11, 2003, statement of principles issued by the editors and publisher of *The Occidental Quarterly*, the organization supports the continued prominence of Western culture. It laments the current demographic trends that show that whites will become a minority in the United States and sees limiting immigration as the only solution to the problem. Federal decentralization and territorial separation should be used to prevent and resolve social, ethnic, and racial conflicts. Quality of life should be the emphasis of social and economic policy; not increases in the material standard of living. Efforts to promote global democracy and human rights should be rejected. A great many of the articles in the journal discuss the importance of saving and reviving the white race, especially in the United States. Many theories by scientists are put forth in the magazine to show why races should be separated and why the white race is superior in most aspects to other races.

Political connections. The CMS has been involved with conservative opinion makers through Regnery Publishing, a prominent publisher of books written by such authors as Ann Coulter and G. Gordon Liddy. John O'Neill, a former FBI expert on Al-Qaida, is an author frequently published under Regnery. Regnery Publishing, however, was bought in 1993 by Eagle Publishing, which is owned by Tom Phillips. The Phillips publishing family seems to have more direct political ties than the Charles Martel Society. According to the Center for Responsive Politics, "Phillips International (then called Phillips Publishing International) gave $125,150 in soft money to the Republican National Committee (RNC) in 1997–1998, while Eagle Publishing gave the RNC another $19,500 (the RNC, not incidentally, was chaired by Regnery author Haley Barbour until January 1997)."[77] Also, "the Phillips Publishing PAC has contributed $64,450 to various Republican officeholders and seekers during the same period, while Phillips himself gave $1,000 in contributions to 15 different Republican candidates in 1998."[78]

William Regnery, CMS founder, is a cousin of Alfred Regnery, who served as deputy assistant attorney general during the period 1981–1986 and as administrator of the Office of Juvenile Justice and Delinquency Prevention. Colorado representative Tom Tancredo has received support from *The Occidental Quarterly*. Representative Tancredo endorsed Kris Kobach, a former US Justice Department official who ran for Kansas's 3rd Congressional District. Kobach, who spoke at the 2004 Republican

National Convention, was endorsed by Vice-President Dick Cheney and Representative Tancredo.

Council of Conservative Citizens

The CCC was founded in 1985 by veterans of the White Citizens' Council, a prosegregation organization formed in Mississippi in the 1950s. The founders of the CCC wanted to establish a new organization that would satisfy their frustrations with the way they saw the country going. They used the old White Citizens' Council mailing lists to establish the new organization and named Gordon Lee Baum as chief executive. Baum was a personal injury lawyer from St. Louis who was a member of the old White Citizens' Council. By the late 1990s, the CCC had 15,000 members in more than twenty states, but most heavily in Mississippi, Alabama, and Georgia.[79] The organization opposes affirmative action, quotas, and integration when it is forced upon people by the government. Most recognizably, they oppose third world immigration.

The CCC is often described as a racist organization bent on a white-only United States. The CCC has a number of philosophical beliefs that place it at odds with African Americans, including the belief that the United States is a European country, that states' rights is a fundamental tenet, and that white European national heritage should be protected.[80] Although the focus is not exclusively on racial issues, the articles, links, press releases, and items for sale mostly have to do with race and expressly how to preserve the white race. Its "Statement of Principles" notes, "We oppose the massive immigration of non-European and non-Western peoples into the United States that threatens to transform our nation into a non-European majority in our lifetime."

The CCC publishes its own monthly paper called the *Citizens Informer*. The paper is also available to any nonmember who wants to go to the website and pay for a subscription. One article in the paper referred to the date of the US Supreme Court's decision in *Brown v. Board of Education* as "Black Monday" and called for the repeal the Civil Rights Act of 1964 and the Voting Rights Act of 1965.[81] The CCC also publishes a series of booklets, including one entitled *The King Holiday and Its Meaning*, intended to provide a "critical analysis" of that day of honor.[82] It has expressed concerns about the declining white population in South Africa, noting that "since the African National Conference took power in South Africa, crime and violence have run rampant" and that "cannibalism is on the rise."[83]

Most political ties to the CCC are local in nature, but there are some officials with national name recognition who participate at one level or another. Mississippi governor Haley Barbour attended a fundraiser sponsored by the council.[84] Kirk Fordice, Mississippi governor from 1992 to 2000, was a featured speaker at council meetings. In fact, twenty-six of the twenty-eight national and state politicians linked to the CCC come from Mississippi.[85]

To these Republicans can be added others, such as Buddy Witherspoon, an RNC committeeman from South Carolina. Witherspoon is a CCC member and refused to revoke his membership in the group because of its radical nature. Then-representative Robert L. Barr, who served on the House Judiciary Committee, has also addressed the organization, as has then-senator Jesse Helms. Senator Trent Lott has been connected to the council in many instances. Lott noted in a 1992 address to the council that "the people in this room stand for the right principles."[86] Trent Lott's uncle, Arnie Watson, says that Lott was an honorary member when he was in the House, although Lott denies accepting any membership. Lott also appears in photos with council leaders.

The work of groups like the Charles Martel Society and the Council of Conservative Citizens and their close proximity to the Republican Party only augment the view that members of the GOP support racists. However, some conservative Republicans believe that these organizations hurt their movement and seek to disavow themselves from them. As David Keene, head of the American Conservative Union, told the *Washington Post*, his group barred the CCC from their annual Conservative Political Action Conference because they "are racists."[87]

Analysis

These examples of political symbolism demonstrate that the Republican Party, in order to reinforce racial conservatives' attraction to the party, willingly engages in negative racial imagery toward African Americans, preying on and validating racial and economic fears that conservatives have regarding African Americans. Such behavior incurs the ire of African Americans, thereby undermining any Republican outreach efforts. The irony here is that "standing up" to black people makes the party even more attractive to racial conservatives. Such activities also demonstrate that there is still an element in the US electorate that can be primed through racial imagery and that these voters generally tend to support Republican candidates. Some of these examples provide some level of "plausible deniability" to Republicans and can be viewed as something other than racial. This is because the charge of racism can be defended by showing that the action in question was less about race and more about policy—for example, affirmative action in the case of the Jesse Helms ad. However, while such attempts at deniability can be attempted, the fact is that the racial dimension outweighs the policy defense in the minds of the public. Also, an argument can be made that the action in question was gratuitous and that the point could have been made without injecting race. For example, Helms *could have* contrasted his position against Gantt's without using racial imagery. He simply chose not to.

These examples, which show a willingness on the part of the GOP to play on negative racial stereotypes of African Americans to gain white votes, have occurred at sufficiently regular intervals over the last few decades to indicate a pattern of appearing in the news just as the previous controversy is fading from US political consciousness. They have remained in the consciousness of many African Americans and thus play a role in their electoral decisionmaking.

The use of race as a tool for political symbolism dates back to the abolition movement and is unlikely to ever pass from the US electoral scene. As these examples demonstrate, the Republican Party has a substantial history of using political symbolism—symbolism that has been generally a political plus for the party but that is becoming increasingly imperiled. Demographic changes throughout the nation that make the country more "minority" will make it increasingly difficult for the GOP to play on racial anxiety to win elections. The California Republican Party is having a difficult time now because of its inability to attract minority voters when many white Californians are leaving and moving to nearby states such as Oregon, Nevada, and Arizona.

Notes

1. Michael Hagen, "References to Racial Issues," *Political Behavior* 17, no. 1 (1995): 49.
2. Ibid., p. 66, quoting Donald Kinder, Tali Mendelberg, Michael C. Dawson, Lynn M. Sanders, Steven Rosenstone, Jocelyn Sargent, and Cathy Cohen, "Race and the 1988 American Presidential Election," paper presented at the annual meeting of the American Political Science Association, Atlanta, Georgia, September 1989.
3. Ibid., p. 50, quoting Thomas Byrne Edsall and Mary D. Edsall, *Chain Reaction: The Impact of Race, Rights, and Taxes on American Politics* (New York: W. W. Norton, 1991), p. 214.
4. Ibid., p. 64, quoting Kathleen Hall Jamieson, *Dirty Politics: Deception, Distraction, and Democracy* (New York: Oxford University Press, 1993), p. 84.
5. Tali Mendelberg, *The Race Card: Campaign Strategy, Implicit Messages, and the Norm of Equality* (Princeton: Princeton University Press, 2001), p. 7.
6. The 1966 elections proved to be an important milepost in the Republican revival. The GOP gained forty-seven seats in the House of Representatives, elected three new senators, and won eight gubernatorial races.
7. Alexander Lamis, "The Two-Party South: From the 1960s to the 1990s," in Alexander Lamis, ed., *Southern Politics in the 1990s* (Baton Rouge: Louisiana State University Press, 1999), p. 8.
8. Kenneth O'Reilly, *Nixon's Piano: Presidents and Racial Politics from Washington to Clinton* (New York: Free Press, 1995), p. 350.
9. Martin Schram, "Reagan Beats a Retreat on Klan Remark," *Washington Post*, September 3, 1980, p. A1.
10. O'Reilly, *Nixon's Piano*, p. 350.

11. Hagen, "References to Racial Issues," p. 50, quoting Edsall and Edsall, *Chain Reaction*, p. 182.

12. Jeremy Mayer, *Running on Race: Racial Politics in Presidential Campaigns, 1960–2000* (New York: Random House, 2002), pp. 135–136, quoting *Wichita Eagle*, April 15, 1976.

13. O'Reilly, *Nixon's Piano*, pp. 378–379.

14. Mayer, *Running on Race*, pp. 211–214.

15. Ibid., pp. 218–219.

16. Eric Alterman, "G.O.P. Chairman Lee Atwater: Playing Hardball," *New York Times Magazine*, April 30, 1989, p. 30.

17. O'Reilly, *Nixon's Piano*, p. 385.

18. Ibid., p. 383.

19. Rhodes Cook, "GOP Planning to Woo Blacks to Widen Its Local Base," *CQ* 47, no. 9 (March 4, 1989): 477.

20. Wayne Greenshaw, *Elephants in the Cottonfields: Ronald Reagan and the New Republican South* (New York: Macmillan, 1982), p. 184, quoted in Hanes Walton, ed., *African American Power and Politics: The Political Context Variable* (New York: Columbia University Press, 1997), p. 243.

21. Hanes Walton and Maxie Foster, "Southern Comfort: The Impact of David Duke's Campaigns on African American Politics," in Walton, *African American Power and Politics*, pp. 238–251.

22. Ibid., p. 248, quoting Hanes Walton, *The Native Son Presidential Candidate: The Carter Vote in Georgia* (New York: Praeger, 1992), pp. 1–34.

23. Rob Christensen and Jack Fleer, "North Carolina: Between Helms and Hunt No Majority Emerges," in Lamis, *Southern Politics in the 1990s,* p. 85.

24. Earl Black and Merle Black, *The Rise of Southern Republicans* (Cambridge: Belknap/Harvard University Press, 2002), p. 105.

25. Christensen and Fleer, "North Carolina," p. 84.

26. Chandler Davison, Tanya Dunlop, Gale Kenny, and Benjamin Wise, *Republican Ballot Security Programs: Vote Protection or Minority Vote Suppression—Or Both?* (Washington, DC: Center for Voting Rights and Protection, 2004), p. 73; Thomas Edsall, "Helms Makes Race an Issue: Carolina GOP Also Pushes 'Ballot Security,'" *Washington Post*, November 1, 1990, p. A1; William Douglas, "Campaign 96, The Race for Congress, North Carolina: Same Race, Different Tack, Helms, Gantt Seek the Middle," *Newsday*, October 24, 1996, p. A49.

27. "Bob Jones University: A Boot Camp for Bigots," *Journal of Blacks in Higher Education*, no. 27 (Spring 2000): 16.

28. David Lublin, *The Republican South: Democratization and Partisan Change* (Princeton: Princeton University Press, 2004), p. 144.

29. Ibid.

30. John Judis and Ruy Teixera, *The Emerging Democratic Majority* (New York: Scribners, 2002), p. 113.

31. Governor Beasley was also undone by an aggressive campaign by Jim Hodges in which he criticized Beasley's opposition to a state lottery that was proposed to help improve funding for state public schools.

32. *Detroit Free Press*, July 16, 2004.

33. Laughlin McDonald, "The New Poll Tax," *American Prospect,* December 23, 2002, p. 27.

34. Davidson et al., *Republican Ballot,* pp. 48–96.

35. Thomas Edsall, "Ballot Security Effects Calculated: GOP Aide Said Louisiana Effort 'Could Keep the Black Vote Down,'" *Washington Post*, October 24, 1986, p. A1.

36. McDonald, "New Poll Tax," p. 27.

37. Davidson et al., *Republican Ballot*, p. 7.

38. Ibid., p. 25, citing Harlington Wood, *Ballot Security: "Why Not Victory?"* for . . . *the Republican Party in 1964*, "Republican National Committee–Special Projects 1964: Operation 'Eagle Eye' (copy of kit given key party workers)," papers of the Democratic National Committee, Series I, Box 55, LBJ Library.

39. Davidson et al., *Republican Ballot,* p. 32, citing "GOP's 'Operation Eagle Eye' at Polls Stirs Democrats," *Washington Evening Star*, November 2, 1964, p. A4.

40. Ibid., p. 52; McDonald, "New Poll Tax."

41. Richard J. Meislin, "Jersey Controversy Widens over G.O.P. Patrols at Polls," *New York Times*, November 7, 1981; Adam Clymer, "G.O.P. to Expand to Other States 'Ballot Security' It Used in Jersey," *New York Times*, November 9, 1981, p. B6.

42. Editorial, "Indelicate Delegate," *New York Times*, June 18, 1984, p. A18.

43. Walter Fauntroy, interview by author, tape recorded, December 5, 2005; Rachel Berry, "Democratic National Committee v. Edward J. Rollins: Politics as Usual or Unusual Politics?" *Race and Ethnic Ancestry Law Digest* 2 (Spring 1996): 46.

44. People for the American Way Foundation/National Association for the Advancement of Colored People (PFAWF/NAACP), *The Long Shadow of Jim Crow: Voter Intimidation and Suppression in America Today* (Washington, DC: PFAWF/NAACP, 2004), p. 3.

45. Edsall, "Helms Makes Race an Issue."

46. *United States of America, et al. v. Charleston County, S.C., et al.*, C.A. No. 2L01-0155-23, 32.

47. McDonald, "New Poll Tax."

48. Davidson et al., *Republican Ballot,* p. 77, quoting *United States of America, et al. v. Charleston County, S.C., et al.*

49. John Monk, "In Dillon County, GOP Effort on Black Vote Backfires," *The State*, November 20, 1998; PFAWF/NAACP, pp. 9–10.

50. Davidson et al, *Republican Ballot*, p. 47.

51. Ibid., p. 97.

52. Ronald Walters, *White Nationalism, Black Interests: Conservative Public Policy and the Black Community* (Detroit: Wayne State University Press, 2003), p. 224, quoting Jack Anderson and Michael Binstein, "The Republicans' Racial Rhetoric," *Washington Post*, January 16, 1995, p. D9.

53. Ibid., p. 224, quoting Stan Faryna, Brad Stetson, and Joseph Conti, eds., *Black and Right: The Bold New Voice of Black Conservatives in America* (Westport, CT: Praeger, 1997), p. 5.

54. Goldsboro Christian Schools (GCS) was a coplaintiff with BJU in suing the IRS to reverse the 1970 rule change.

55. Phil Gailey, "Bob Jones, in Sermon, Assails Supreme Court," *New York Times*, May 25, 1983, p. A23.

56. Linda Greenhouse, "Rights Official Defends Tax Break for Racially Biased Schools," *New York Times*, October 13, 1982, p. A19.

57. Brooke Masters, "Virginian May End the Impasse Over Integrating Court: Warner Backs Clinton Nominee," *Washington Post*, July 30, 2000, p. C1.

58. Stephen Hayes, "A Very Sorry Majority Leader: Trent Lott Apologizes, Over and Over," *Weekly Standard*, December 23, 2002.

59. Ibid.

60. Gallup Poll/Frank Newport, "Trent Lott, Blacks' Views on the Republican

Party, Bush Approval, Al Gore, the Economy, Iraq, Religion in America," December 24, 2002, available at http://poll.gallup.com/content/default.aspx?ci=7483 (accessed June 23, 2006).

61. David Rosenbaum, "Divisive Words, Voting Record: Lott Opposed Many Bills with Links to Civil Rights, *New York Times*, December 14, 2002, p. A19.

62. Ibid.

63. Trent Lott interview in *Southern Partisan* 4 (Fall 1984).

64. Jim Abrams, "Lott Hangs on as Bush Assails His Comments on Thurmond," Associated Press State and Local Wire, December 13, 2002.

65. Thomas Edsall, "Controversial Group Has Strong Ties to Both Parties in the South," *Washington Post*, January 13, 1999, p. A2; Jason Zengerie, "Bob Barr's Credibility Gap," *New Republic*, January 4, 1999, p. 13.

66. David Brooks, "We Don't Talk This Way," *Newsweek*, December 23, 2002, p. 31.

67. Robert George, "Vacant Lott," *National Review*, December 10, 2002.

68. Kevin Merida, "3 Consonants and a Disavowal: The More You Ask Trent Lott About His Ties to the White-Supremacist CCC, the Less He Has to Say," *Washington Post*, March 29, 1999, p. C1.

69. Walter Fauntroy, interview by author, tape recorded, Washington, DC, December 5, 2005.

70. Ange-Marie Hancock, *The Politics of Disgust: The Public Identity of the Welfare Queen* (New York: New York University Press, 2004). See also Martin Gillens, *Why Americans Hate Welfare: Race, Media, and the Politics of Anti-Poverty Policies* (Chicago: University of Chicago Press, 2001).

71. Hancock, *Politics of Disgust*, p. 57.

72. See ibid., pp. 65–87.

73. Ronald Walters, *White Nationalism, Black Interests: Conservative Public Policy and the Black Community* (Detroit: Wayne State University Press, 2003), p. 154.

74. Ibid.

75. Hancock, *Politics of Disgust*, p. 51, citing Daniel Patrick Moynihan, *Miles to Go: A Personal History of Social Policy* (Cambridge: Harvard University Press, 1996), p. 229.

76. Andrew Murr, "Sites, Dating the White Way," *Newsweek*, August 9, 2004, p. 9.

77. Nicholas Confessore, "Hilary Was Right," *American Prospect Online,* January 17, 2000.

78. Ibid.

79. Anti-Defamation League, *Extremism in America: Council of Conservative Citizens*, April 23, 2005, available at www.adl.org/learn/ext_us?CCCitizens.asp?xpicked=3&item=12 (accessed December 7, 2005).

80. Council of Conservative Citizens, www.cofcc.org/manifest.htm (accessed December 7, 2005).

81. Robert Patterson, "Black Monday After 50 Years," *Citizens Informer* 36, no. 1 (January–March 2005), p. 9.

82. Ibid.

83. Council of Conservative Citizens (Shelby County Tennessee Chapter), http://cofcc.org/shelby.htm (accessed December 7, 2005).

84. Matt Bai, "Pulling Back the Curtain," *Newsweek*, February 1, 1999, p. 28; Nicholas Dowidoff, "Mr. Washington Goes to Mississippi," *Newsweek*, October 19, 2003, p. 48.

85. Patrick Jonsson, "The Klan's Diminishing Shadow," *Christian Science Monitor*, January 2005, p. 1.

86. Howard Fineman, Eleanor Clift, and Martha Brant, "Ghosts of the Past," *Newsweek,*. December 23, 2002, p. 22.

87. Thomas Edsall, "Lott Renounces White 'Racialist' Group He Praised in 1992," *Washington Post,* December 16, 1998, p. A2.

7

An Ongoing Quest for Black Votes?

THE NATIONAL LEADERSHIP OF THE REPUBLICAN PARTY, MOST notably its national party chairs, has publicly voiced the need for the party to reach out more proactively to the African American community and win their votes. These leaders and others associated with the party in one way or another have spoken of the need to reclaim the party's historical position in the black community and overcome its "anti-black" reputation. They position their desire for black votes in the context of "doing the right thing" and "not leaving anyone out" of the Republican "big tent." It is also certain that some party leaders are uncomfortable with the fact that the party's rise in recent decades has been built on a conservative overt resistance to black interests.

While these are all valid and legitimate factors spurring the GOP into action, this redoubled interest in winning black votes is driven by the cold political realities that come with the changing demography of the United States. Minorities are becoming an increasing percentage of the US population, and presidential elections are becoming more closely contested. The fact that the country is becoming "browner" does not bode well for a party that has built much of its recent success on resisting change in the status quo for minorities. Consequently, the party cannot maintain its political dominance without winning a greater share of black votes than it currently enjoys. As the group of voters that form the largest voting bloc of minority Americans—and the largest percentage of voters who do not support the party—the Republicans have a bigger political upside in the African American community than in any other group of voters. After all, there really is nowhere else to go but up for the GOP in the black community; it couldn't really get much worse.

Over the past few decades, each Republican national chair has, with increasing sincerity and effort, spoken of the need to win black votes. Current national party chair Ken Mehlman has earned praise throughout the party for his efforts in this regard. Leaders in African American Republican circles have singled out Mehlman for praise, believing that he, more than any previous chair, not only "talks the talk" of the party's need to do better with African Americans, but will do what is necessary to improve the party's standing in the black community.[1] They view this as a stark change from previous chairs, some of whom have said the right thing but have rarely followed their words with the actions necessary to make significant change.

To date, these efforts have borne virtually no political fruit. A minuscule number of US elected officials are African American Republicans. There are no African American Republicans in the US Congress, despite more than a decade of GOP dominance of both chambers. That the party has been unable to cultivate winning black candidates in an environment in which virtually all of the benefits that come with congressional dominance, most notably fundraising, accrue to the party can be seen as an organization failure, on the one hand, or a policy failure—adopting policies that do not resonate with the black community—on the other.

History, Ideology, Paradox

In preparing this book, I relied on a careful review of the historical record and on interviews with political elites—virtually all of whom are African American Republicans—to examine the events, policies, and political strategies that have shaped the relationship between the GOP and the black community. Three important conclusions can be drawn from this research.

First, the historical relationship between the party and the black community, while significant, important, notable, and critical to African American political, social, and economic development during the Reconstruction era, is often overstated. Republican activists and others who laud the GOP's early support for African American interests are correct in noting the role of the "party of Lincoln" in black political development. These same activists and others are mistaken when they try to portray this effort as unanimous within the party and long lasting. A review of the historical record shows that the party began retreating from its commitments to African Americans within a generation of the party's founding, particularly with the Hayes-Tilden Compromise of 1877. From that point, over the objections of a small but important faction of Radical Republicans, the party began to compete with the Democratic Party for the southern conservative and racist vote. These efforts set in motion a multigenerational period in which the party, in some parts of the country, marginalized and demonized black America to win elections. The lily white movement is one of the darkest and underexamined eras of US Republicanism. That a party would systematically purge voters, particularly those as loyal to the GOP as post-Reconstruction–era blacks, can only be seen as an attempt to repudiate the liberal social policy positions on which the Republican Party was founded. That repudiation, with decreasing amounts of opposition, continues to this day.

Second, many African American GOP activists do not understand the link between ideology and voter support. If they did, then perhaps they would call for the party to moderate some of its policy positions to win black votes. Republicans want African American votes; they just do not want to moderate their positions to achieve them. Every black Republican interviewed for this project rejected the notion that the party needs to moderate its positions to win more black votes. This reflects a fundamental misunderstanding of the black vote. African Americans, when taken in total, vote and support policies that are left of center; in fact, their support for the GOP has been strongest when the party was to the left of the Democrats. The party lost support as it moved right ideologically. Given the position of the black community on the full range of public policy issues, it's difficult to see how the GOP can win more black votes without moderating its positions; indeed, the GOP has moved away from black people.

Third, the political paradox in which the GOP still finds itself calls into question just how far it will go to win more black support. The overreliance of the Republican Party on white voters is still required, given the inability of the party to make significant inroads in the black and Hispanic communities. This paradox, coupled with contemporary dominance of national politics, may make it irresistible for some Republican activists to change their strategic focus by seeking more black voters, particularly if this shift alienates white voters who respond favorably to racial stereotyping and symbolism that denigrates African Americans and their policy interests.

Why can't the GOP win a substantial amount of black support nationally? African American Republican activists characterize the issue as one of public relations, political marketing, and the need to overcome the "liberal media" and traditional black leadership. Many of these activists see the problems the Republicans have in the black community as one of communication. This thesis suggests that the party has not done a good enough job of explaining the value of its policy positions to African Americans. Once the message is improved, the thesis suggests, African Americans will see that the Republican Party best represents its political, social, and economic interests and will respond favorably with their votes. African American Republicans also feel strongly that their attempts to break through in the black community are hampered by a media that does not provide a balanced view of Republicanism and does not afford black Republicans with very much air time to present their arguments. Last, the role of the traditional black leadership is consistently cited by African American Republican activists as a barrier for the party in trying to reach the masses of black voters. Jesse Jackson and Al Sharpton, in particular, were consistently cited by interviewees as standing between the Republican Party and the African American public. These and other prominent black Democrats, according to some of these activists, want to keep the black community dependent on the Democratic Party for their own personal gain.

Others see the issue differently and focus on Republican policy positions and the base on which their electoral success is grounded. According to Professor Ronald Walters, the main reason why Republicans have a problem in the African American community is "that the GOP at this point in history seems to be using a racial animus that black people instinctively understand."[2] The policy positions of the GOP, which are often resistant to change in the social and economic status quo, coupled with their upsurge of conservatism, has been "frightening to the black people and scared the hell out of black people and it's going to be very difficult to win black votes unless that changes, I mean very substantial black votes across the board."[3] Even if the party were to offer candidates that are attractive to African Americans, they would have to walk a fine political line between policy and politics.

Another problem facing Republicans is that most black leaders are "overtly black" in terms of their policy advocacy. The color-blind approach taken by many Republicans does not match the reality on the ground for many African Americans. Most black Republican leaders were silent in the mid-1990s when Charles Murray and Dinesh D'Souza both published books that contended that blacks are intellectually and culturally inferior. The controversy surrounding these books and the publicity they received would have been a good time for black Republicans to step up and defend black America. Two prominent black Republicans, Robert Woodson and Glenn Loury, did take exception and resigned their positions at the American Enterprise Institute (AEI) in protest (Murray and D'Souza were both fellows at AEI when their books were published).

This points to an inherent contradiction in the relationship between African Americans and the Republican Party. African Americans live with the reality of race every day, and their leaders and their organizational affiliations should be concerned about their welfare. Republicans, particularly conservative Republicans, want to act as if race no longer plays a role in the lives of African Americans or the larger society and, therefore, want to ignore it completely. The color blindness they seek is seen by many in the African American community as a euphemism for indifference to the fate of African Americans or an attempt to ignore issues of importance to them.[4] So when Republicans push for cuts to human needs programs in the name of balancing the budget or creating more social discipline, African Americans understand that they will be disproportionately affected. When Republicans push for more prison construction and stiffer incarceration policies in the name of safer streets, African Americans understand that it is going to be blacks who will fill the new facilities. When Republicans push for increased use of the death penalty to deter crime, particularly in the face of data that show that capital punishment does not prevent crime, African Americans understand that it is blacks who will be executed at disproportionately higher numbers than whites. So there is an inherent conflict of interest between the GOP and African Americans on a number of issues that must be overcome if the party hopes to win substantial portions of the black vote.

Some black Republican elites emphasize the party's initial history as a supporter of black equality as a reason for contemporary African Americans to support the party now.[5] That view overstates the length and significance of the relationship between African Americans and the GOP. While it is unquestionable that the party was founded, in large measure, as a mechanism to fight human slavery and promote political equality for African Americans, it is also unassailable that the party quickly backpedaled from its historic commitment to African Americans when it became politically unpopular to maintain that commitment.

The Republican Party and the Black Community: Future Prospects

The future relationship between the GOP and the black community is unclear. On the one hand, the party is a political loser in the African American community. On the other hand, the party appears to be in the early stages of a serious push to win more black votes. However, while the party has begun to say the right things in terms of winning more African American support, significant policy changes have yet to occur. And years of anti-black public policy cannot be overcome in short order. Be that as it may, everything about GOP future efforts to win black votes will be viewed through a Hurricane Katrina–influenced prism. That prism includes visuals of tens of thousands of African Americans being stranded, black bodies floating on flooded streets, and a Republican-led federal government being universally criticized as incompetent and unable to manage its response to a huge crisis. While there is no doubt that the governmental failures were comprehensive and existed at all levels, the federal government, with more resources and power at its disposal, has rightly received the bulk of the criticism.

African Americans, like everyone else, define their interests in five categories: income, housing, education, health care, and justice. Republican policy and politics, particularly since the conservatives' rise to power within the party, too often have worked against black interests in those categories. African Americans have seen this and have consequently largely rejected Republican courting.

A party's future is often formed by its past. The more recent the past, the more relevant it is in determining where a party is heading. The Democratic Party was able to overcome its racist past characterized by southern conservatism. Its opposition to civil rights during the Civil War and Reconstruction ultimately gave way to a more enlightened and progressive approach to black America. It took time. It wasn't easy. But the party ultimately went from near unanimous opposition in the African American community during the 1870s to near unanimous support more than a century later. There are some who would argue that passage of the Civil Rights Act of 1964 and the Voting Rights Act of 1965—two important steps in garnering black support—actually opened the door for southern conservatives to march out and join the GOP and led to the diminution of the Democrats' political dominance.

In the case of the Republican Party, the multigenerational history of purging, demonizing, and opposing African American political empowerment, coupled with the use of negative political symbolism, covert racism, and public policy—which some African Americans believe have been aimed at the black community—represent bricks in a political wall between the Republican Party and African Americans that may take as long to destroy as it did to build.

Notes

1. Tape recorded interviews by author: Renee Amoore, August 4, 2005; Andre Cadogen, May 3, 2005; Niger Innis, March 18, 2005; Michael Steele, December 9, 2005; Phyllis Berry Myers, July 25, 2005; Bill Calhoun, June 23, 2005.

2. Ronald Walters, interview by author, tape recorded, July 26, 2005.

3. Ibid.

4. Adam Shatz, "Glenn Loury's About Face," *New York Times Magazine*, January 20, 2002.

5. Cadogen interview.

Selected Bibliography

Alterman, Eric. "G.O.P. Chairman Lee Atwater: Playing Hardball," *New York Times Magazine*, April 30, 1989.

Black, Earl, and Merle Black. *The Rise of Southern Republicans* (Cambridge: Belknap/ Harvard University Press, 2002).

Brennan, Mary. *Turning Right in the Sixties: The Conservative Capture of the GOP* (Chapel Hill: University of North Carolina Press, 1995).

Clay, William L. *Just Permanent Interests: Black Americans in Congress, 1870–1991* (New York: Amistad Press, 1992).

Cook, Rhodes. "GOP Planning to Woo Blacks to Widen Its Local Base," *CQ* 47, no. 9 (March 4, 1989): 474–477.

Crabtree, Susan. "Watts Plans Bus Trips, Reorganizes PAC to Attract Minorities, Money to GOP," *Roll Call*, November 12, 2001, p. 3.

Davidson, Joe. "GOP Seeks Ways to Draw Blacks," *Wall Street Journal*, November 28, 1984, p. 64.

Dawson, Michael. *Behind the Mule: Race and Class in African-American Politics* (Princeton: Princeton University Press, 1994).

DeSantis, Vincent P. "The Republican Party and the Southern Negro, 1877–1897," *Journal of Negro History* 45, no. 2 (April 1960).

DuBois, W. E .B. *Black Reconstruction in America, 1860–1880* (New York: Free Press, 1992).

Eldersveld, Samuel, and Hanes Walton. *Political Parties in American Society*, 2nd ed. (Boston: Bedford/St. Martin's Press, 2000).

Fears, Darryl. "GOP Makes 'Top Priority' of Converting Black Voters," *Washington Post*, December 25, 2003, p. A3.

Fletcher, Michael. "GOP Plans More Outreach to Blacks, Mehlman Says: Goal Is to Broaden Party Base, Help Swing Future Races," *Washington Post*, August 7, 2005, p. A5.

Foner, Eric. *Free Soil, Free Labor, Free Men: The Ideology of the Republican Party Before the Civil War* (New York: John Wiley, 1978).

———. *Reconstruction: America's Unfinished Revolution, 1863–1877* (New York: Harper & Row, 1988).

Free, Marvin. "The Impact of Federal Sentencing Reforms on African Americans," *Journal of Black Studies* 28, no. 2 (1997).

Friedman, Rachel Zabarkes. "Southern Conservative Comfort: Will Georgia Voters

Embrace GOP Rising Star Dylan Glenn?" *National Review Online*, July 14, 2004.

General Accounting Office. *Status Report on Implementation of the Comprehensive Anti-Apartheid Act* (Washington, DC: General Accounting Office, 1987).

George, Robert. "Vacant Lott," *National Review*, December 10, 2002.

Gillens, Martin. *Why Americans Hate Welfare: Race, Media, and the Politics of Anti-Poverty Policies* (Chicago: University of Chicago Press, 2001).

Gould, Louis. *Grand Old Party: A History of the Republicans* (New York: Random House, 2003).

Graham, Hugh Davis. "The Origins of Affirmative Action: Civil Rights and the Regulatory State," *Annals of the American Society of Political and Social Science* 523 (September 1992).

Greenberg, Stanley B. *The Two Americas: Our Current Political Deadlock and How to Break It* (New York: Thomas Dunne Books/St. Martin's Press, 2004).

Greenshaw, Wayne. *Elephants in the Cottonfields: Ronald Reagan and the New Republican South* (New York: Macmillan, 1982).

Hagen, Michael. "References to Racial Issues," *Political Behavior* 17, no. 1 (1995).

Hancock, Ange-Marie. *The Politics of Disgust: The Public Identity of the Welfare Queen* (New York: New York University Press, 2004).

Huckfeldt, Robert, and Carol Weitzel Kohfeld. *Race and the Decline of Class in American Politics* (Urbana: University of Illinois Press, 1989).

Judis, John, and Ruy Teixera. *The Emerging Democratic Majority* (New York: Scribners, 2002).

Kidder, Louise, and Charles Judd. *Research Methods in Social Relations*, 5th ed. (Fort Worth: Holt, Rinehart & Winston, 1986).

Klingman, Peter, and David Geithman. "Negro Dissidence and the Republican Party, 1864– 1872, " *Phylon* 40, no. 2 (June 1979).

Kotlowski, Dean. *Nixon's Civil Rights: Politics, Principle, and Policy* (Cambridge: Harvard University Press, 2001).

Lamis, Alexander. *Southern Politics in the 1990s* (Baton Rouge: Louisiana State University Press, 1999).

Lublin, David. *The Republican South: Democratization and Partisan Change* (Princeton: Princeton University Press, 2004).

Marable, Manning. *Race, Reform, and Rebellion: The Second Reconstruction in Black America, 1945–1990* (Jackson: University Press of Mississippi, 1991).

Mayer, Jeremy. *Running on Race: Racial Politics in Presidential Campaigns, 1960–2000* (New York: Random House, 2002).

Mendelberg, Tali. *The Race Card: Campaign Strategy, Implicit Messages, and the Norm of Equality* (Princeton: Princeton University Press, 2001).

Miller, Steve. "GOP Plots Tactics to Lure Black Voters: Bush Netted Only 9% in 2000 Election," *Washington Times*, April 12, 2001, p. A6.

Miner, Barbara. "Why the Right Hates Public Education," *The Progressive* 68, no. 1 (January 2004).

Nokken, Timothy, and Keith Poole. "Congressional Party Defection in American History," paper prepared for the annual meeting of the American Political Science Association, San Francisco, August 29–September 2, 2001.

O'Reilly, Kenneth. *Nixon's Piano: Presidents and Racial Politics from Washington to Clinton* (New York: Free Press, 1995).

People for the American Way. *Buying a Movement: Right-Wing Foundations and American Politics* (Washington, DC: People for the American Way, 1996).

———. *Community Voice or Captive of the Right? The Black Alliance for Educational Options* (Washington, DC: People for the American Way, 2003).

Phillips, Kevin. *Post-Conservative America: People, Politics, and Ideology in a Time of Crisis* (New York: Vintage Books, 1983).

Quarles, Benjamin. *Black Abolitionists* (New York: Oxford University Press, 1969).

Schatz, Adam. "Glenn Loury's About-Face," *New York Times Magazine*, January 20, 2002.

Schemo, Diana Jean. "Graduation Study Suggests That Some States Sharply Understate High School Dropout Rates," *New York Times*, September 17, 2003.

Schram, Martin. "Reagan Beats a Retreat on Klan Remark," *Washington Post*, September 3, 1980, p. A1.

Seltzer, Richard, and Robert C. Smith. "Race and Ideology: A Research Note Measuring Liberalism and Conservatism in Black America," *Phylon* 46 (Summer 1985).

Sherman, Richard B. *The Republican Party and Black America from McKinley to Hoover, 1896–1933* (Charlottesville: University of Virginia Press, 1973).

Sitkoff, Harvard. *A New Deal for Blacks: The Emergence of Civil Rights as a National Issue: The Depression Decade* (Oxford: Oxford University Press, 1981).

Smith, Robert C. *Encyclopedia of African-American Politics* (New York: Facts on File, 2003).

Sneider, Daniel. "Powell, Kemp Polish GOP Appeal to Blacks," *Christian Science Monitor*, August 13, 1996, p. 6.

Stampp, Kenneth, and Leon Litwack. *Reconstruction: An Anthology of Revisionist Writings* (Baton Rouge: Louisiana State University Press, 1969).

Swain, Carol. *The New White Nationalism in America: Its Challenge to Integration* (Cambridge: Cambridge University Press, 2002).

Swain, Carol, and Russ Nieli, eds. *Contemporary Views of White Nationalism in America* (Cambridge: Cambridge University Press, 2003).

Van Dongen, Rachel. "GOP Steps Up Minority Outreach Efforts," *Roll Call*, September 11, 1997, p. 1.

Walton, Hanes. *African American Power and Politics: The Political Context Variable* (New York: Columbia University Press, 1997).

———. *Black Political Parties: An Historical and Political Analysis* (New York: Free Press, 1972).

———. *Black Politics: A Theoretical and Structural Analysis* (Philadelphia: J. B. Lippincott, 1972).

———. *Black Republicans: The Politics of the Black and Tans* (Metuchen, NJ: Scarecrow Press, 1975).

———. *The Native Son Presidential Candidate: The Carter Vote in Georgia* (New York: Praeger, 1992).

———. *When the Marching Stopped: The Politics of Civil Rights Regulatory Agencies* (Albany: State University of New York Press, 1988).

Walters, Ronald. *White Nationalism, Black Interests: Conservative Public Policy and the Black Community* (Detroit: Wayne State University Press, 2003).

Weems, Robert, and Lewis Randolph. "The National Response to Richard M. Nixon's Black Capitalism Initiative: The Success of Domestic Detente," *Journal of Black Studies* 32, no. 1 (September 2001).

Weiss, Nancy. *Farewell to the Party of Lincoln: Black Politics in the Age of FDR* (Princeton: Princeton University Press, 1983).

Williams, Juan. "Reagan Tries to Convert Middle-Class Blacks to GOP," *Washington Post*, February 5, 1985, p. A3.

———. "White House Wooing Blacks," *Washington Post*, January 20, 1985, p. A17.

Wilson, William Julius. *When Work Disappears* (New York: Vintage Books, 1996).

Index

Abolition movement, 26–27
Affirmative action policies: defined, 100–101; legislative efforts to end or curb, 101–102; and Reagan administration policy, 96, 99
African American Advisory Committee, and GOP outreach efforts, 71
African American politics: dangers of deracializing, 22; defined, 22–23; historical overview of, 21–25; role of political context in, 24–25; stages of, 23–24; and two-party system, 15
African American Republican Leadership Council (AARLC), mission of, 79–80
African American women, incarceration of, 115
African Americans: codified second-class citizenship of, 33; and conservative ideology, 57–58; court decisions negatively impacting, 33; historical GOP linkage with, 1, 3, 25–26, 27–32; issues important to, 167; northern migration of, 23, 41, 44, 45; notion of linked fate among, 21–22; post-Reconstruction return to subservient roles, 32–33, 39–41; relations with political parties, 14–15; selected-issue conservatism of, 145–146; social conservatism of, 3
African emigration, Lincoln's support for, 40, 41
African National Congress (ANC), Reagan's charges against, 108, 109

American Anti-Slavery Society (AASS), 27
American Civil Rights Institute, 103
Ashcroft, John, 149
Atwater, Lee, 70, 130–131, 134

Barbour, Haley, 153, 154, 155
Barr, Bob, 153
Bell, Peter, 82, 83
Baum, Gordon Lee, 155
Bell Curve: Intelligence and Class Structure in American Life, The, 73–74
Berry, Mary Frances, 97, 98, 108
Bethune, Mary McLeod, 47
Black Alliance for Educational Options (BAEO), creation and financing of, 73
Black America's Political Action Committee (BAMPAC): goal and activities of, 80; national opinion poll of, 80–81
Black and tan Republican organization, establishment and development of, 43–44
Black capitalism initiative: criticism and failure of, 64–65; and minority procurement, 64; motivation for, 63–65
Black civil rights organizations, and South African apartheid, 108
Black codes, post-Reconstruction institution of, 33
Black economy: GOP policy proposals focused on, 62, 63–65; Great Depression's impacts on, 45

Black education, and GOP policy initiatives, 62. *See also* School choice initiatives

Black elected officials: party affiliations of, 4; and political context, 25; post-Reconstruction, 32*tab*; of Reconstruction era, 31–32; and Voting Rights Act, 104

Black employment: and black entrepreneurship, 63–65; and community impacts of unemployment, 67–68; and creation of black bureaucracy, 46; New Deal opportunities for, 46, 47

Black Politics: A Theoretical and Structural Approach, 22–23

Black professionals, and affirmative action policies, 101

Black Republican candidates, 6–7; "favored candidate" policy and, 77–78; GOP support for, 75–79; perceived viability and success of, 75–77

Black Republican Council of Texas (BRCT), 81–82

Black Republican Councils (BRCs), 88

Black Republican leaders, color-blind approach of, 166–167

Black Republican organizations, 62; black voter outreach of, 79–87, 88–91; conservative foundations' funding of, 71, 73; and conservative social policies, 80; financial support and problems of, 81, 89–90; lack of coordination among, 88–89; media coverage of, 90, 91*tab*; mission and importance of, 79; overview of specific groups, 79–87; Republican Party support for, 90–91; think tanks, 82–84; and white foundation grants, 79

Black voters: and appeals based on religion and morality, 22; conservative foundations' efforts to attract, 69–79; contemporary disenfranchisement of, 140–143; in Depression-era elections, 45–46; GOP's suppression and intimidation of, 140–144; 1948 shift in party identification of, 48; policy interests of, 3, 4–6; political and party activities targeting, 61–79, 87–88; and post-Reconstruction

Southern Strategy, 41–44; presidential vote and party identification of, 4, 5*tab*; and 2000 presidential election, 120–121

Black voting rights: and Fifteenth Amendment compliance, 103; government guarantee of, 48; Reconstruction-era establishment and elimination of, 16, 31–32, 118. *See also* Voting Rights Act

Blackwell, J. Kenneth, 6–7, 78

Bob Jones University (BJU): George W. Bush's campaign stop at, 138; tax-exempt status of, 147, 151

Bobach, Kris, 154

Bradley Foundation, 74, 75

Brotherhood of Sleeping Car Porters, 24

Bush, George H. W., 70–71, 82; Civil Rights Act veto of, 95, 110–111; Clarence Thomas nomination of, 146–147; racial liberalism of, 133; and Willie Horton campaign ploy, 134–135

Bush, George W.: and black Republican nominees, 77–78; black vote for, 1, 2, 4, 6; and civil rights enforcement, 100; and Confederate flag debate, 139; conservatives anger with, 8–9; Faith-Based Initiative of, 72; and GOP inclusion of black Americans, 6; school choice initiative of, 62; symbolic racial actions of, 138–139. *See also* 2000 presidential election

Buthelezi, Mangosuthu, 108

Cain, Herman, 77

Center for New Black Leadership (CNBL): internal struggle and failure of, 83–84; symbolic role of, 82

Center of the American Experiment (CAE), 82

Charles Martel Society (CMS), 153–154

Charter schools, and DC School Choice Initiative, 68–69

Chicago, Operation Double Check voter purge program in, 141

Christian Coalition: candidate support of, 20–21; and religious conservatives, 20

Christian fundamentalists, abolition movement role of, 26–27

Civil rights: conservative Republicans' views on, 19; Reagan's position and impact on, 96–100; Truman administration's efforts on, 48

Civil Rights Act of 1990: controversy over, 110–111; George H. W. Bush's veto of, 95, 111; and Republican emphasis on quotas, 111

Civil Rights Acts, 17; of 1866, 28; of 1964, 48, 51

Civil Rights Commission: Reagan's budget cuts and personnel changes in, 97–98, 99*tab;* and 2000 presidential election, 120–121

Clinton administration, and federal judiciary, 148–149

Coleman, William T., Jr., 147–148

Commitment '81, and black voter disenfranchisement, 142

Confederate flag debate, as metaphor for black relations with GOP, 139

Congress: Republican control of, 55–56; Republican partisanship and racial conservatism in, 50

Congressional Black Caucus (CBC), 25, 56, 152; and South African apartheid, 108

Connerly, Ward, 103

Conservative philanthropic foundations: anti-black research supported by, 73–74; black organizations created/funded by, 72–73, 75; black outreach efforts of, 74; conservative prominent black commentators/academics supported by, 73, 145; social funding of, 72; top-down outreach approach of, 72

Conservative Republicans: affirmative action opposition of, 101; "blaming the victim" position of, 24–25; color-blind approach of, 166–167; evolution of, 49; linked to racist and white supremacist organizations, 153, 156; movement away from black concerns, 17; paleoconservative vs. neoconservative views of, 18–19; Party takeover of, 95; political symbolism of, 127–129; and Reconstruction-era successes, 30–31. *See also* Racial conservatism; Southern Strategy

Conservative social policies, black organizations' advocacy of, 80, 82

Conservative think tanks, 82; funding of, 74–75; support for anti-black research of, 73–74

Conservative voters, GOP appeals to, 7–10

Constitutional framers, and political parties, 13

Council of Conservative Citizens (CCC), 151; racist and white supremacist beliefs in, 155–156

Davis, Jefferson, 151

Death penalty: as African Americans' disproportionately affected by, 167; Republicans' aggressive support for, 116–117

Democratic Party: African Americans' move toward, 45–48; and black interests, 6; and black voter loyalty, 7; coercion of black support for, 23; historical racial conservative domination of, 48; and post-Reconstruction southern "redemption," 43; shift on race, 53–54

Department of Justice, and racial discrimination in schools, 147

Dewey, Thomas, 57

District of Columbia, school choice initiatives in, 68

Dixiecrats, 150; states rights party of, 48; and Strom Thurmond's presidential bid, 48, 149–150

Dole, Bob, affirmative action legislation of, 102–103

Douglas, Stephen, 15–16

Douglass, Frederick, 31

D'Souza, Dinesh, 74–75, 166

Dubois, W. E. B., 31

Dukakis, Michael, 134

Duke, David, racial electoral strategy of, 135–136

Eisenhower administration, civil rights acts of, 17

Electoral politics, and third party choices and voter subgroups in, 15

Equal employment opportunity, government guarantee of, 48

Equal Employment Opportunity

Commission (EEOC), and civil rights enforcement, 97, 98–99
Evangelicals. *See* Christian fundamentalists

Fair Employment Practices Committee (FEPC), 46
Fair Housing Act of 1968, 97
Fair Labor Standards Act (FLSA), 111–112
Federal Communications Commission, and minority recruitment, 102
Felon disenfranchisement, 117–120; as beneficial to Republicans, 119–120; increased rates of, 117–118; political implications of, 118–119; public opposition to, 118; racial roots of, 118
Fiscal conservatives, and Republican government spending, 8
Flemming, Arthur, 97
Florio, Jim, 142
Fordice, Kirk, 155
Foreign policy, neoconservative views on, 18, 19
Fourteenth Amendment protections, black rights to, 33
Fourth Circuit Court of Appeals: case disposition criticism of, 148; Republican resistance to racial integration of, 148–149
Freedman's Bureau, 16, 26, 28; failure of, 41

Gantt, Harvey, 137–138
Gingrich, Newt, 145
Glenn, Dylan, 77–78
Goldsboro (North Carolina) Christian Schools, tax-exempt status of, 147–148
Goldwater, Barry, 17; black votes for, 4, 57; and Civil Rights Act of 1964, 51; and crime control policies, 113; racial conservative politics of, 50–51; Southern Strategy of, 129–130
Graham, Lindsay, 9
Gray, William, 102
Great Depression, and Roosevelt's New Deal policies, 46
Gregory, Roger, 149
Griffith, Lanny, 141

Harding, Warren G., 44
Harlem Republican Club (HRC), 84–85
Hate groups, post-Reconstruction formation of, 33
Hayes, Rutherford B., and Compromise of 1877, 41–43
Helms, Jesse: campaign use of racial code words, 111; King holiday opposed by, 106; racial electoral politics of, 136–138, 143, 149
Heritage Foundation, 73, 74
Hispanic voters, GOP's success with, 9
Hoover, Herbert, black support for, 45
Hoover Institution, 73, 74
Horton, William J., Jr., 134–135
Hurricane Katrina: failed federal response to, 85–86; and efforts to win black votes, 167

Ickes, Harold, 47
Immigration policies, 155; viewed as anti-immigrant, 11
Innis, Roy, 83
Institutional racism, in the United States, 50
Internal Revenue Service (IRS), and racially discriminating schools, 147–148
International Emergency Economic Powers Act (IEEPA), 109
International political education, and black Republican organizations, 81

Johnson, Andrew, 28
Johnson, Lyndon B., 130; and affirmative action, 65
Joint Center for Political and Economic Studies, 83

Kansas-Nebraska Act, 15
Kinon, Son, 143
Ku Klux Klan, 33; endorsement of Reagan, 132

Land reform, post-Reconstruction failure of, 28, 40–41
Liberal Radical Republicans, 16
Lily white movement, 43–44; and repudiation of liberal social policy, 164–165
Lincoln, Abraham, 27; racial views and

policies of, 27, 40–41; and two-party political system, 15

Lott, Trent: links to racist/white supremacist organizations, 153, 156; negative racial symbolism and overt racism of, 150–151

Loury, Glenn, 82, 83–84, 166

Majority-minority population, political implications on, 10

Marshall, Thurgood, 146

Martin Luther King Jr. holiday, Republican conservatives' opposition to, 105–106, 150

Martinez, Mel, 77

McCain, John, 138

Media: conservative black leaders' access to, 87, 90, 145; and Republican Party message, 165

Mehlman, Ken, 70, 71

Metropolitan areas, migration's political and demographic impacts on, 11, 41

Minimum wage increases: conservation Republican opposition to, 111–117; effects on job levels and employment, 112; liberal argument for, 112

Moral Majority: candidate support of, 21; and religious conservatives, 20

Morality, as GOP strategic tactic, 20–21

Multinational organizations, conservative Republican opposition to, 18

Murray, Charles, 166

National Association for the Advancement of Colored People (NAACP), 23–24, 46

National Black Republican Association (NBRA): and federal response to Hurricane Katrina, 85–86; mission and funding of, 85

National Black Republican Council (NBRC), 82; and African American outreach, 70–71

National Center for Public Policy Research, Project 21 of, 86–87

National conventions, African Americans' participation in, 4

Neoconservative movement, critics of, 18–19

New Deal era: black employment in, 46, 47; GOP recovery and reassessment during, 16–17; and Great Depression impacts, 46; and nondiscrimination in government programs, 46

Nixon, Richard: black capitalism initiative of, 63–65; black votes for, 57; and crime control policy, 113; and Philadelphia Plan, 65–66; Southern Strategy of, 51–52, 130–131

North Carolina, intimidation and harassment of black voters in, 143

Office of Management and Budget (OMB), 100

Office of Minority Business Enterprises (OMBE), 63–64

Olin Foundation, 73, 74, 82

Operation Eagle Eye (OFE), and black voter disenfranchisement, 142

Paperwork Reduction Act of 1980, 99–100

Party switching, 81, 135; contemporary facilitation of, 53; examples of, 54; and greater political power, 53; history of, 52; and ideological disagreement, 52–53; of 1990s, political impact of, 55; primary reasons for, 52–53

Philadelphia Plan: and federal affirmative action, 65; political significance of, 66; reasons for Nixon's support of, 65–66

Pinchback Society, 86

Political parties: African Americans' relationships with, 14–15; connective roles of, 13–14; and voter group targeting, 61

Political strategy, GOP's use of symbolism in, 144–153

Political symbolism, 127–157; and black GOP support, 127; categories of, 128–129; covert use of, 128; in electoral campaigns and public statements, 129–144; legislative and judicial implications of, 128; noncampaign use of, 144–153; "plausible deniability," 156; as political strategy, 128–129; racial language in, 127–128

Powell, Adam Clayton, 84

President's Committee on Civil Rights (CCR), guarantees of, 48

Private retirement investment accounts, pro-black marketing of, 62

Project 21, media coverage focus of, 86–87

Public housing, New Deal construction of, 47

Public school choice movement. *See* School choice initiatives

Public statements, GOP's use of symbolism in, 144–153

Public Works Administration (PWA), and black construction laborers, 47

Racial conservatism: and congressional partisanship, 50; defined, 49; as dominant ideology of American South, 50; GOP embrace of, 49–52, 54; symbolic language use in, 127–128. *See also* Conservative Republicans

Racial priming technique, 128

Racial symbolism, and social spending cuts, 152–153

Racist and white supremacist organizations, 153–156; David Duke's electoral strategy, 135; examples of, 153–156; prominent Republicans' links to, 151, 153. *See also* Charles Martel Society

Radical Republicans: and aid to newly freed slaves, 16; and expansion of federal authority, 28; legislative power of, 28–29, 30; liberal ideology and utopian vision of, 27–28; success of, 30

Reagan, Ronald: affirmative action position of, 96, 99; black votes for, 57; campaign kickoff in Philadelphia, Mississippi, 131–132; conservative Democratic support for, 132–133; and federal civil rights enforcement, 95, 96–100; and King holiday bill, 106; Ku Klux Klan endorsement of, 132; positions on race and social issues, 6; racial symbolism used by, 133; Religious Right's link with, 20, 21; social program beliefs and funding cuts of, 100, 151–152; and South African economic sanctions, 107–

110; Southern Strategy of, 131–133; symbolic racial language of, 127–128; and tax exemptions for racially discriminating schools, 147–148; and voting rights enforcement, 104–105; "welfare queen" symbolism of, 131, 152–153

Reconstruction: bigoted writing on, 30–31; and black political/social development, 30–32; black successes of, 31; election of black Republicans during, 31–32; GOP race record during, 29; GOP's opposition to, 103; legal dismantling of, 32, 42; southern Radical Republicans' support for, 26, 27–30

Reconstruction Act of 1867, 29

Regnery Publishing, 18; conservative Republicans published by, 154; and "radical right" causes, 153–154; white supremacy view of, 154

Religion, as GOP strategic tactic, 19–22

Religious conservatives (Religious Right): and contemporary Republican success, 19–21; Reagan's link with, 20, 21; and southern white vote, 20

Republican crime control policy: and death penalty use, 116–117; disproportionate effects on blacks, 114–115; and mandatory minimum sentences, 114–115; and post–civil rights political success, 113; and rehabilitation goal, 115; and sentencing disparities, 114; Supreme Court rulings on, 115; and three strikes policies, 115–116. *See also* Felon disenfranchisement

Republican electoral campaigns: covert and overt use of political symbolism in, 128, 129–144. *See also* Southern Strategy

Republican national chairs, and efforts to win black votes, 163–164

Republican National Committee (RNC): African American outreach role of, 70–72, 89; ballot security forces of, 142; and black candidates, 76–77

Republican National Lawyers Association (RNLA), and party purge and security programs, 143–144

Republican Party: abandonment of Reconstruction efforts by, 32–34; abolition movement and, 27; "alternative" black leaders developed by, 144–146; barriers to black support for, 2–6, 39–41, 165–166; and America's changing demographics, 9–11, 41; and closely-contested elections, 2, 6, 8; development and retention of black support for, 6–11, 16, 25–32, 61–91; early retreat from commitments to African Americans, 164; Eastern Establishment control of, 49; historical overview of, 15–21; ideology and policy shifts in, 17, 165; liberal-moderate ideology in, 15–16, 17; and minimum wage increases, 111–113; need for new sources of votes, 2; of New Deal era, 16–17; party/political activities to increase black support, 61–62, 69–79; probusiness platform of, 16, 17; Progressive-era fight for party control in, 16; progressive stance on race in, 25–26; racial conservatism in, 49–52; racial stereotyping by, 129; radical right emergence in, 18; religious conservatives' contribution to, 19–21; southern conservatives critical role in, 49; southern reconstruction program of, 25–26, 28–30; Southern Strategy of, 129–131; support base typology of, 9–10; support for black Republican candidates, 75–79; support for freed slaves, 25–26. See also Conservative Republicans; Radical Republicans; Republican public policies

Republican presidential nominees, comparative black votes for, 56*tab*, 56–57

Republican public policies: African American alienation from, 95–122; conservative takeover's impact on, 95; and equal educational opportunities, 62; on fiscal responsibility, 8; as impediment to black support, 95–122; initial, origins of, 15–16; and land reform failure, 40–41; post-Reconstruction policy shift toward blacks in, 39–41; and social conser-vative base, 122; on social issues, 17, 111–113, 151–153; targeting black concerns, 61, 62–69. See also specific policy area

Republican voter suppression, 140–144; background of, 140; and ballot security program tactics, 141–142; intimidation and harassment in, 143; and voter purge program initiatives, 140–141

Rise of Southern Republicans, The, 137

Robertson, Pat, 20

Roosevelt, Eleanor, 47

Roosevelt, Franklin D.: black support for, 45–46; racial record of, 46. See also New Deal era

School choice initiatives: black organizations' support for, 82–83; and black students' achievement/dropout levels, 66–67; critics of, 69; and education vouchers, 68; and failing schools' impact on black community, 67–68; GOP advocacy for, 68–69; pro-black marketing of, 62

Schools' tax exempt status, and discriminatory policies, 147–148

Segregation: and contemporary black politics, 23; lily white movement and, 43–44; race-driven de jure, 42

Sensenbrenner, James, 115

Slavery: and the abolition movement, 26–27; GOP policy on, 15–16

Social conservatives: dissatisfaction with George W. Bush administration, 8; social spending views of, 19, 74, 100

Social policies: and black Republican organizations, 80, 82; and concept of "undeserving poor," 152–153; conservative challenges to, 151–153; and lily white movement, 164–165; and minimum wage increases, 111–113; Reagan funding cuts in, 151–152

South African apartheid government, Reagan's opposition to sanctions against, 106–110

South Carolina, intimidation and harassment of black voters in, 143

South, the: GOP appeals to white voters

in, 9–10, 20; GOP conservative dominance in, 50; post-Reconstruction return of white power to, 32. *See also* Reconstruction

Southern conservatives: critical GOP role of, 49; and Democratic Party's shift on race, 53–54

Southern migration, and political party appeals, 41, 44

Southern racial conservatives, 48; and Democratic Party's shift on race, 53–54; power broker role of, 49; shift to GOP, 54

Southern Strategy: defined, 129; evolution of, 130–131; and evolution of Republican Right, 49–50; of Goldwater's campaign, 129–130; and Hayes-Tilden Compromise of 1977, 41–42; lily white movement in, 43–44; Nixon's implementation of, 51–52; Nixon's use of, 130–131; and partisan realignment of the South, 51; post-Reconstruction use of, 129; of Reagan, 131–133; use of code words in, 130

Sowell, Thomas, 73

States' rights: GOP's embrace of, 4; Reagan's advocacy of, 96; and white supremacy concept, 131–132

States' Rights Democratic Party, 48

Steele, Michael, 7, 78–79, 81

Stevens, Thaddeus, 28, 29

Sumner, Charles, 28

Swann, Lynn, 7, 78

Tancredo, Tom, 153, 154

Thomas, Clarence, 82; as head of EEOC, 99; Supreme Court nomination of, 146–147

Thurmond, J. Strom: as Dixecrats' presidential nominee, 48, 149–150; party switch of, 53

Tilden, Samuel, 41

Trading with the Enemy Act, 109

Truman, Harry: appeal to African Americans, 57; and civil rights, 48, 57; landmark legislation of, 48; and military desegregation, 57; racial policies of, 48

2000 presidential election: and felon disenfranchisement, 119; voting irregularities affecting black voters in, 121–122

US Agency for International Development (USAID), Gray Amendment and, 102

US Constitution, on factionalism and political parties, 13

Voting rights. *See* Black voting rights

Voting Rights Act (VRA) of 1965: development of, 103; Reagan's attempt to weaken, 104–105; success of, 104

White supremacist organizations: conservative Republicans' ties with, 153, 156; and immigration issues, 155

White Brotherhood, 33

White Citizens' Council, 155

White racial conservatives, and black political behavior, 22

White voters: and GOP's electoral success, 7, 9–10; GOP's religious ideology and, 20; southern, GOP appeals to, 9–10, 20

White, Ronnie, 149

Williams, Walter, 73

Witherspoon, Buddy, 156

Wolfe, Kris, 141

Women's rights, conservative opposition to, 96

Woodson, Robert, 166

Work Projects Administration (WPA), 46

Wynn, James A., Jr., 149

About the Book

THE REPUBLICAN PARTY ONCE ENJOYED NEARLY UNANIMOUS support among African American voters; today, it can hardly maintain a foothold in the black community. Exploring how and why this shift occurred—as well as recent efforts to reverse it—Michael Fauntroy meticulously navigates the policy choices and political strategies that have driven a wedge between the GOP and its formerly stalwart constituents.

Michael K. Fauntroy is assistant professor of public policy at George Mason University. His publications include *Home Rule or House Rule? Congress and the Erosion of Local Governance in the District of Columbia.*